*Julia Pizzuto-Pomaco's meticulous study provides two important new directions for New Testament studies. Her study fills a gap in New Testament scholarship as she follows new directions in anthropology by treating woman as agents rather than just passive members in communities of men. Her groundbreaking work not only introduces a new framework for understanding the dynamics of women in the early church but also provides a more robust methodological approach for using anthropological models in New Testament studies. Rather than using an anthropological model as a lens by which to view the text, she uses anthropological methodology to construct her model. In her study, anthropology dialogues with the text providing a transparency in the development of her model that is refreshing.*

*To develop her model she intentionally chooses modern anthropological studies that explore the agency of women in the Mediterranean. Using the concepts of women's honor, place, power and relationships found in these studies, she continues the dialectic between data and anthropology as she examines primary sources on women in Greek, Roman and Jewish cultures refining her model. The result is that she provides the reader with a specific and multidimensional view of women's agency in each context.*

*Her nuanced application to the greetings in Roman 16 provides an example of the insights her model can bring to Paul's writing on women and how context affected women's participation in the early church.*

Dr. Sue Russell
Professor of Missions and Contextual Studies
Asbury Theological Seminary

*Julia Pizzuto-Pomaco brings to the fields of biblical and women's studies a much needed reliable and nuanced social scientific model. Based on primary sources from anthropological studies, Pizzuto-Pomaco considers women's roles in the social values of shame and honor, power, public and private settings, kinship, and religion in the ancient Mediterranean Greek, Jewish and Roman cultural contexts.*

*As a test case, she applies her model to Romans Chapter 16 in the New Testament, and from her findings raises the suggestions that in a society where woman rarely received honor from men, the fact that Paul did not distinguish among the genders when he honors Christians for their service to the Lord and specifically gives women honor is very significant.*

*She also notes the difference between the public and private settings in these cultures may more realistically be considered simply the difference between the world of men and the world of women. Because women had more power in their domestic settings (their world), the early Christian house churches naturally gave women the opportunity to have more power. It is possible that when the Christian church became institutionalized and moved away from the house churches, women began to lose some of that power.*

*She also notes that although different in each of these cultures women had more power than previously thought and used it in varying creative ways. Pizzuto-Pomaco's model is well worth applying and updating to see what more cultural nuances can be gleaned from the biblical text and more specifically, the women in those texts.*

    Dr. Deborah Winters
    Associate Professor of Old Testament
    Palmer Theological Seminary of Eastern University.


*The apostle Paul exhorted the Galatians that "there is neither Jew nor Greek, neither slave nor free, there is neither male nor female; for you are all one in Christ Jesus." In her groundbreaking study, Julia Pizzuto-Pomaco demonstrates that Paul's declaration was neither an isolated slogan, nor utopian speculation, but a startling reality. Pizzuto-Pomaco respectfully utilizes the insights of modern anthropology, feminism, and the social-sciences, to develop a nuanced model by which to examine the realities of women's lives in the ancient world. Treating in depth subjects such as "public-private" identity, definitions of "honor and shame," and perceptions of "power," she discovers that while women often operated under male-imposed boundaries, they were also able to maneuver within them, exercising creative (although real) authority over households, among kinship groups, and cultic bodies.*

*    Against the backdrop of Hellenistic, Jewish, and Roman societies, Pizzuto-Pomaco successfully argues that a text such as Roman 16 suggests that inasmuch as Christian women (and Paul) reflected broader cultural standards, in many ways, within the innovative "family" model of the Christian community, women transcended them, acquiring equality, status, and honor, that was revolutionary in antiquity.*

*    Pizzuto-Pomaco's work is a text-book example of how careful attention to cultural context combined with a close-reading of biblical texts, work together to illuminate our understanding of the early church. Her methodology and conclusions will provide scholars with an excellent foundation for further exploration of women in the New Testament, even as her insights have much to say to students, clergy, and lay-people about unity, diversity, and equality in contemporary Christianity.*

    Dr. Scott Morschauser
    Associate Professor at Rowan University in Ancient History

# From Shame to Honor

## *Mediterranean Women in Romans 16*

### Julia Pizzuto-Pomaco

EMETH PRESS
www.emethpress.com

*From Shame to Honor: Mediterranean Women in Romans 16*

Copyright © 2017 Julia Pizzuto-Pomaco

Printed in the United States of America on acid-free paper.

All rights reserved. No part of this book may be reproduced, or stored in a retrieval system or transmitted in any form or by any means, electronic, mechanical, photocopying, recording, scanning or otherwise, except as permitted by the 1976 United States Copyright Act, or with the prior written permission of Emeth Press. Requests for permission should be addressed to: Emeth Press, P. O. Box 23961, Lexington, KY 40523-396. http://www.emethpress.com.

Library of Congress Cataloging-in-Publication Data

Names: Pizzuto-Pomaco, Julia, author.
Title: From shame to honor : Mediterranean women in Romans 16 / Julia Pizzuto-Pomaco.
Description: Lexington : Emeth Press, 2017. | Includes bibliographical references.
Identifiers: LCCN 2017036791 | ISBN 9781609471163 (alk. paper)
Subjects: LCSH: Bible. Romans, XVI--Criticism, interpretation, etc. | Women--Biblical teaching. | Women in Christianity.
Classification: LCC BS2665.6.W65 P59 2017 | DDC 227/.1067--dc23
LC record available at https://lccn.loc.gov/2017036791

Front Cover Photo
Catacombs of Priscilla, "The Cubiculum of the Veiled Woman"
used with permission from the Pontifical Commission for Sacred Archeology

To my family (Joe, Anna, John and Joshua), who are my most gracious gifts from God. I am blessed beyond measure.

"Every good and perfect gift is from above…" James 1:17 (NIV)

# Contents

Foreword ..................................................................................................... ix

Preface ........................................................................................................ xi

1. Introduction ........................................................................................... 13

2. Mediterranean Women: Forming a Cultural Context Model of Interpretation ......................................................................................... 19

3. An Introduction to Nuancing the Model and a Brief Look at Ancient Greek Women Through Common Mediterranean Values .......................................... 49

4. Jewish Women in Ancient Mediterranean Culture ............................................ 61

5. Women of Ancient Rome: Understanding Their Values and Behaviors ........ 97

6. Romans 16: A List of Greetings or Evidence of Women Leaders? .............. 125

7. Romans 16: Cultural Context and Interaction with the Mediterranean Model ..................................................................................................... 143

8. Concluding Thoughts ............................................................................. 165

Bibliography ............................................................................................. 171

# Foreword

Julia was my esteemed colleague when, until six years ago, we taught at Palmer Theological Seminary in Pennsylvania. When Julia finished her PhD, she kindly shared with me her dissertation, which I have since cited (in its unpublished form) in several of my books, including in *Spirit Hermeneutics*, my Romans commentary, my forthcoming academic Galatians commentary, and eleven times in my Acts commentary.

I knew much of the existing literature regarding women in the New Testament, but barely any works from a sound anthropological perspective. Further, most of the anthropological work on the New Testament that I had read worked from general anthropological models or from generalizations about Mediterranean culture, rather than exploring more detailed anthropological fieldwork of the Mediterranean world.

Julia's work fills an important lacuna. Rather than simply extrapolating from generalizations, her work offers more thick description based on ethnographic data. It thus offered the most sophisticated anthropological approach to traditional Mediterranean gender roles that I knew of in New Testament studies.

Recognizing this, I began urging her to publish her dissertation. It was work that genuinely needed to be done, but should not have to be redone in the future if this research achieved only Julia's degree. It needed to become more widely available in research libraries and to scholars and students working on the broad subject of women in the New Testament, and particularly on women in Paul.

The author of a work is sometimes the most aware of its limitations and thus most humble about its contribution, but Julia has finally brought this work to the stage of publication. Although the intervening years have undoubtedly created some lacunae in her bibliography, they have not reduced the value of her contribution. Beyond the level of generalization, few New Testament scholars take into account hard data on gender roles in Mediterranean culture. Because of its distinctive contribution, this book thus remains one of the "must-read" works engaging gender questions in the New Testament.

Dr. Craig Keener, June 2017

# Preface

*From Shame to Honor: Mediterranean Women in Romans 16* was first written as a doctoral thesis for the fulfilment of a PhD at the University in St. Andrews, Scotland, received May 2003. Over 14 years have passed since its writing and editing. Much has happened in the world of scholarship and in the author's own professional work in the ensuing years. Having not published it at the time it was finished was regretful and yet I felt too much time had elapsed. Despite the dating of the sources, I was contacted by a valued colleague who wished to see it published. Dr. Craig Keener went as far as to contact a publishing press on his own and set up a contract for me on the basis that I could publish this work exactly as it was written in 2003 (he did so knowing I would likely refuse otherwise, due to family obligations if I had to completely revise it). It would be an unusual choice to make, but given the challenges that unfolded in my personal life over the years, it made sense. Therefore, this work does read without any major edits and does not make the claim to be updated with scholarship that is available in 2017.

Since social context is such an important part of this work let me take some author privilege and share that in 2002 as I was completing my doctoral work (some portion of which I spent in the hospital on bedrest), three beautiful babies were born into our family. Joshua, John and Anna are now healthy 15-year-olds and are the greatest gift God has ever allowed my husband and me to have a hand in shaping. As we will see in the research that follows women have always been involved in the care of children and family. It is not simply a sociological construct that women have long prevailed in the area of childrearing but began surely as a matter of biology. In my current household we have an egalitarian style of parenting, marriage and vocation. Yet, the important sacrifices women (and men) make to raise their children and care for their elderly parents (my mother Juele Pizzuto passed from this life into the next in our care in 2014) cannot be overlooked.

I would like to offer up thanks to those who worked with me at the University of St. Andrews all those years ago and surely influenced my questions and analysis that formed the completed work. Dr. Philip Esler was my supervisor in the first part of this work and enabled me to pick up the tools of social scientific criticism, anthropology and ethnography. My second supervisor, Dr. James Davila, empowered me to find my voice and apply biblical feminist critique to the larger questions I had as I tweaked social scientific models. I am thankful for their input as well as that of colleagues and friends during my time of study at the University of St. Andrews in the fall of 1997 through spring 2003. It should also be noted that some portions of chapters six and seven of this book were adapted or excerpted from my previously published chapter, "Unity in the Midst of Diversity: The Early Church at Rome as Reflected in Romans 16" in *Who Killed Goliath? Reading the Bible with Heart and Mind*, Robert F. Shedinger and Deborah J. Spink, editors (Judson Press, 2001), used by permission of the publisher. Finally, to my dear husband Joseph who was willing to serve as an editor, encourager and all-around research assistant, I am indebted.

Though I have been influenced by the help and support of other scholars and assistants, I am completely responsible for the final work and any mistakes here within. I would ask however in your critical analysis that you remember that though the publication date is 2017, the last major update was in 2003. Perhaps someday the time will come for a full revision, but until then I am grateful to Emeth Press and publisher Larry Wood for helping to bring this work to birth after 20 long years of laboring. It's been a joy to watch it moving from when it was just an inkling in a young scholar's heart into a world so different from the twentieth century in which it began. The model from 2003 continues to provide applicable tools for grappling with ancient texts through eyes of wonder and layers of cultural baggage.

# 1
# Introduction

*From Shame to Honor: Mediterranean Women in Romans 16* explores the cultural context of women in Romans 16 and seeks to shed new light on the discussion of the role of women in the early church. A social-scientific model of cultural values is constructed based on the findings of anthropological studies in the Mediterranean. The model is nuanced to reflect the insights gained from the study of women in ancient Greek, Jewish and Roman cultures. Anthropological studies are one lens through which these insights are viewed to seek to understand the values and behaviors of women in the Mediterranean. Hence, the nuanced model ultimately sheds light on the study of women in Romans 16 who were a part of the Mediterranean culture. Such a model is also useful as a guide to understanding women in New Testament texts as they relate to the understanding of women in their ancient context.

This study of Romans 16 employs the above outlined social-scientific method as well as a biblical feminist critique and the skills of traditional historical-critical method. One might wonder what profit could be gained from the study of a list of greetings. It is the proposition of this thesis that a deeper exploration of Romans 16 is needed. Numerous studies have already explored Romans 16 in the original languages, in the social-historical mode and with a feminist analysis,[1] yet Romans 16 has not been a centerpiece of any extensive work. It has, rather, been an aside, an additional chapter, an article, a paragraph or an addendum often found within the discussion of women's roles in the New Testament. However, this work seeks to make it the center of the study and a test case for the use of this nuanced model for the study of women in the New Testament.

This work argues we often miss cultural clues that would help us to understand the world of women in the first century C.E. Women did indeed have a vital role in the early church. This understanding leads the scholar to begin to comprehend how women were systematically minimized in their ministry roles as the church became institutionalized. As the emerging church progressed from the private, or domestic sphere, to the public, or institutional sphere, it moved from the domain of women to the world of men. Thus, the institutionalized church became less accessible for women as it became more established in the world of men. This work is one step in the trajectory that seeks to establish what happened to such women. This book raises pertinent questions, but given the scope such a study would require, it is focused on the more limited question of how we understand the women of Romans 16 when viewed through a cultural context model.

Why is such a study necessary? Much has already been written on social-scientific criticism and the New Testament by scholars such as Malina, Esler, Moxnes, Neyrey and Elliot.[2] The focus of such works has mainly been issues related to the cultural context of men in the Mediterranean world. The model Malina developed in his 1993 revised edition of *The New Testament World* lacks specific attention to the world of women. Often male anthropologists are not able to access the world of Mediterranean women, and thus their data and research become skewed through the eyes of men. Female anthropologists such as Dubisch and Fernea[3] have been able to penetrate such worlds. The results of their research form the basis for the nuanced model developed in this work.

Social-scientific criticism provides us with new prisms through which to view raw data. It helps us bridge the two thousand years between our world and New Testament times. It also allows us to look beyond Western cultural views and discover how the Mediterranean social script differs from our own. While such perspectives have added to our understanding of New Testament texts they continue to need nuancing in relation to their discussion of women in the text. This work is distinct from others that have used social-scientific criticism in that it emerges from women anthropologists' studies and a broad base of traditional works. It also differs from the work of feminist scholars such as Osiek and Torjesen.[4] Both women use concepts from social-scientific criticism, but neither develops a model nuanced specifically to understand ancient Mediterranean women. Both scholars have contributed tremendously to the debate over women's roles in the early church. Osiek develops the concept of the house church and Torjesen accentuates the public/private divide that both helped and hindered women in the first few centuries of the church. This work develops the issues they have raised, taking them further and leaving us with a model that can be used with other New Testament material.

As we begin, let us first consider why we need a model and how one might describe it. Carney asserts that using models is not a matter of choice. He suggests that we use models all the time to inform the way in which we view events, interactions and the world around us. We, however, do not always use them consciously. When we employ them unconsciously they operate without our control and can color our view of the situation or data (Carney 1975, 5). According to Carney, models are not easy to define, yet he comes close to providing a clear picture of what occurs when a model is formulated: "A model...acts as a link between theories and observations. A model will employ one or more theories to provide a simplified (or an experimental or a generalized or an explanatory) framework which can be brought to bear on some pertinent data. Models are thus the stepping stones upon which theories are built" (Carney 1975, 8).

Models can also give us a different perspective on the material we are considering. They free us from being locked into one way of thinking which is often based on our limited world view. Models give us a more expansive view of the situation. Rather than focusing on only one aspect of the data, greater clarity is gained by considering all angles (Carney 1975, 9). Using this approach in biblical studies can help us to avoid allowing our preconceptions to guide our interpretation of the text. Models can help us to be aware of some of the twenty-first-century Western (in the case of this writer's culture) baggage we bring with us to the task.

Esler agrees with Carney's view that models are operating all the time and are either conscious or unconscious. He acknowledges that through the process of using a model, interpreters must bring their own perspectives into the open and in doing so are made more aware of their blind spots. Esler strongly emphasizes the nature of models as comparative and their use as a heuristic tool. Such comparisons allow new questions to rise to the surface but do not supply any answers. He asserts that the texts we study are the source of any answers we might seek. Esler suggests that what makes a model important is its usefulness to raise new questions and insights, helping us to see beyond the traditional and obvious. He also notes that a model cannot be proven right or wrong, true or false (Esler 1994, 12, 13). It seems imprudent however to accept a model on the basis of a high degree of compatibility but without a solid grounding in raw material. Social-scientific criticism has been criticized by more traditional scholars for this very reason,[5] therefore, the model developed in this work will be different. Although a model cannot be proven, more extensive work can be done to compare the primary sources of the ancient world with the anthropological studies of the Mediterranean world. We can develop a level of compatibility between the two worlds which supports the validity of the questions the model helps to raise.

Malina defines a model as "patterns of abstract thought" or "patterns of relationships among abstractions" (1993, 19). He also considers them generalizations, abstract reflections of life experiences that are simple and approximate. He, like Esler, speaks of models that can be validated but not be proven by following traditional scientific inquiry. He suggests the purpose of models is to bring about greater understanding of an event, situation, culture or people (Malina 1993, 19, 20). The process of studying a complex society and patterns in society can be broken down into simpler abstractions which form the basis for models (Malina 1993, 26).

The model this work constructs addresses cultural patterns and values of the ancient Mediterranean. We need to consider how various perceptions of societal structures, cultures, values and norms are understood. Malina offers us a few options. He highlights the social systems theories that most cultural anthropologists use to construct their models of culture. The first is structural functionalism, the second is conflict theory and the last is the symbolic model (Malina 1993, 22-24). Structural functionalism suggests that everything in society exists in social systems that are related to one another. There are institutions such as government, education, religion and family that relate to one another and are made up of subsystems. Society shares values, norms and culture. When something happens to one of these systems all others related to it are affected. Systems attempt to achieve homeostasis or equilibrium.

Alternatively, conflict theory suggests society is in a constant state of flux. It proceeds on the idea that social systems place constraints on one another, exist in conflict and do not seek the consensus that the structural functionalism model aims to achieve. Finally, the symbolic method suggests that people hold onto symbols which in turn keep groups of people cohesive. People interact symbolically through sets of roles, expectations, patterns of behavior, status and shared norms. Malina draws on anthropology that approaches society from these various perspectives (1993, 21-24).

This work will use some of the frameworks these models employ. To accept the cohesiveness of shared cultural values and norms one must acknowledge the social systems model. People function in relation to one another in systems and subsystems. They are affected by what happens in any part of their social system. They also relate to one another symbolically in social roles such as mother, father, teacher, son, daughter, sister, brother, friend, enemy, etc. These ways of looking at society undergird the view that we can study societies systematically and that cultural values models can help us to raise questions that perhaps have been overlooked.

Esler in *Modelling Early Christianity* suggests the modelling found in social-scientific criticism offers insight, not necessarily truth (1995, 7). This book will look for patterns in Greek, Roman and Jewish societies that also are evident in anthropological studies of the Mediterranean. Such nuancing of the model suggests a higher degree of reliability in the insights and questions it highlights. It also suggests that patterns of behavior, norms and culture that are deeply ingrained in a society might be found through the centuries. Every society in some way relates to this model, in that the issues addressed are basic considerations fundamental to human ways of relating. However, each society responds differently to these constructions. For example, the issue of kinship is a very different concept in modern American society than it is in ancient Mediterranean culture. Kinship in America refers mostly to the nuclear family and might include both paternal and maternal relatives who may or may not be in the locality. Kinship in ancient Mediterranean society would include an extended family, usually local, often on the paternal side and would be an extremely influential component of society.

Chapter two of this thesis explores these values further and lays out the model this work develops. This Mediterranean cultural model is based upon the careful study of the works of Malina and a multitude of cultural anthropologists. The values which have risen to the surface form the basis for this construction. Such values appear different when they are focused on a study of women rather than a general study of the ancient Mediterranean. Some values prominent in the male world do not arise in the world of women. For example, challenge and response and patronage[6] do not seem to be prominent in the writing of cultural anthropologists who are studying Mediterranean women. Chapter two guides our exploration of Greek, Jewish and Roman women. It also forms the basis for the discussion of Romans 16 and provides a useful tool in studying other New Testament texts that address women.

In chapters three through five the model is used to ask questions of the primary material found in the Greek, Jewish and Roman worlds during and surrounding the first century C.E. In this study the model is nuanced so that it not only represents values found in anthropological studies of modern times, but it also builds a bridge to the ancient world. Only the values that appear prominent in each of these time periods are addressed. Therefore, all three chapters are not entirely uniform in structure but have their own individual formats based on the material found in the primary sources of that culture. As the study unfolds it becomes evident that although these three cultures are often intertwined in the discussion of women in the ancient world, much more could be gained if they were studied separately. Greek women appear to have been more secluded than their Roman and Jewish sisters. Roman women had the most freedom and were less bound than the others by gender restrictions. These nuances in turn inform the study of Romans 16. For example, the freedom and activity found among Roman women is reflected in the active participation of the women of Romans 16 in their faith communities.

Out of these studies a cultural context model of the Mediterranean has arisen which includes the values of honor and shame, women and power, public and private, women and relationships, and women and religion. Each of these values helps to inform our understanding of Romans 16. The people mentioned in Romans 16 come from the Greco-Roman world. Some of them were Jews, others were Romans and perhaps some were even Greeks. Thus, the model looks at all three of these cultures and considers whether the values raised by anthropological studies are found in ancient times.

Chapters six and seven focus on a deeper exploration of Romans 16. Included in these chapters are grammatical, literary and contextual studies. The cultural values that arise in the Mediterranean model are used to ask questions of Romans 16. As the model sheds light on Romans 16, the conclusion in chapter eight points out the ways in which our understanding of Romans 16, and ultimately women in the early church, has been expanded from this study. It also highlights some implications of this study for the Christian church today.

As we will see, the use of modern anthropological data to shed light on the values of the ancient world has considerably added to our study of the biblical text. Understanding the private nature of women's lives contrasted with the public world of men helps us to understand why women appear secluded at times in New Testament texts. Recognizing the importance of women's shame helps to explain why modesty was such an issue in Pauline passages. The model also highlights women's early involvement in house churches, which, while they were public (people interacted with others outside of their own kin), were also private because such involvement took place within the domestic sphere. This nuanced model expands models such as Malina's which discuss many of the values of the ancient world but do not consider their impact on women. Thus, when Malina's model or another similar approach is used, the role of women is slightly skewed and therefore not accurately portrayed. This study helps us to see Romans 16 more clearly, view women in the early church more easily, and gives us a model for future use in New

Testament texts concerning women. Ultimately, when we understand better some of the cultural restrictions placed on women, and appreciate the freedom they were given in the early church in the first century, our exegesis will be more nuanced and reliable.

# Notes

1. Bernadette Brooten, "Junia...Outstanding among the Apostles," in *Women Priests, A Catholic Commentary on the Vatican Declaration*, ed. Leonard Swidler and Arlene Swidler (New York: Paulist Press, 1977), 141-144; Elisabeth Schüssler Fiorenza, "Missionaries, Apostles, Coworkers: Romans 16 and the Reconstruction of Women's Early Christian History," *Word & World* 6/4 (1986): 420-433; and Robert Jewett, "Romans as an Ambassadorial Letter," *Interpretation* 36/1 (1982): 5-20.

2. Bruce J. Malina, *The New Testament World: Insights from Cultural Anthropology*, rev. ed. (Louisville: Westminster/John Knox, 1993); Bruce J. Malina, *The Social World of Jesus and the Gospels* (London: Routledge, 1996); Philip Esler, *The First Christians in their Social Worlds: Social-scientific Approaches to New Testament Interpretation* (London: Routledge, 1994); Halvor Moxnes, ed., *Constructing Early Christian Families: Family as Social Reality and Metaphor* (London: Routledge, 1997); Jerome Neyrey, *Paul, in Other Words: A Cultural Reading of His Letters* (Louisville: Westminster/John Knox, 1990); John Elliott, *What is Social-Scientific Criticism?* (Minneapolis: Fortress Press, 1993).

3. Jill Dubisch, "Culture Enters Through the Kitchen: Women, Food, and Social Boundaries in Rural Greece," in *Gender and Power in Rural Greece*, ed. Jill Dubisch (Princeton: Princeton University Press, 1986); Jill Dubisch, "Gender, Kinship and Religion: 'Reconstructing' the Anthropology of Greece," in *Contested Identities: Gender and Sexuality in Modern Greece*, ed. Peter Loizos and Evthmios Papataxiarchis (Princeton: Princeton University Press, 1991); Elizabeth Warnock Fernea, *Guests of the Sheik: An Ethnography of an Iraqi Village* (New York: Anchor Books, 1969).

4. Carolyn Osiek, *What are they Saying About the Social Setting of the New Testament?*, rev. ed. (New York: Paulist Press, 1992); Carolyn Osiek and David L. Balch, *Families in the New Testament World: Households and House Churches* (Louisville: Westminster/John Knox, 1997); Karen Torjesen, "In Praise of Nobel Women: Gender and Honor in Ascetic Texts," in *Discursive Formations, Ascetic Piety and the Interpretation of Early Christian Literature, Part I*, ed. Vincent Wimbush. (Atlanta: Scholars Press, 1992); Karen Torjesen, *When Women Were Priests: Women's Leadership in the Early Church and the Scandal of their Subordination in the Rise of Christianity* (San Francisco: Harper, 1993).

5. Bengt Holmberg, *Sociology in the New Testament: An Appraisal* (Minneapolis: Fortress, 1990).

6. For a further explanation of challenge and response, see Bruce J. Malina, *The New Testament World: Insights from Cultural Anthropology*, rev. ed. (Louisville: Westminster/John Knox, 19930029, 34-37; and for patronage see Malina, *New Testament World*, 101-102.

# 2

# Mediterranean Women: Forming a Cultural Context Model of Interpretation

## Introduction to the Model

Why is it necessary to have one more biblical interpretation method, one more level of exegesis? This thesis suggests a more thorough method needs to be developed, thus it takes an existing model and expands as well as redefines it. Bruce Malina's anthropological model of the cultural script of the Mediterranean world found in his 1993 book *The New Testament World: Insights from Cultural Anthropology* has clearly informed this research. In his work he draws a picture of ancient Mediterranean society which encompasses the values of honor and shame, limited good, kinship and the public/private divide. This research goes beyond such constructions and is immersed in the cultural anthropological studies of the twentieth-century Mediterranean world. The search to understand women of the Mediterranean is the goal, out of which a nuancing of Malina's model emerges. Clearly a debt is owed to his research of first connecting such cultural values to the New Testament text.

This research stands independent and its focus is different from Malina on two counts. Malina's work is geared toward college students and has been simplified so as to be accessible to his audience. Thus, he explains the concepts in a way that seems to accept the cultural construct without seriously asking whether the model is sufficiently supported by ancient evidence. An examination of his notes and bibliography reveals an inadequate number of ancient sources and anthropological research. In a survey of similar literature, it appears that other such texts by different authors have often been geared for college level (e.g. *Palestine in the Time of Jesus*, *The Handbook of Biblical Social Values*, *What is Social-Scientific Criticism?* and *The Social Sciences and New Testament Interpretation*).[1] Horrell, in his discussion of social-scientific approaches, also levels such a criticism at Malina. He suggests that there is perhaps an "over-dependence" on the model. He also asserts that more extra-biblical ancient sources are needed to show the model's connection to the ancient world (Horrell 1999, 14). Osiek, in her summary and critique of Malina, echoes the same concern over the lack of first-century non-biblical sources (1992, 35). The model nuanced in this work addresses some of these concerns.

## Interdisciplinary Interactions

As is evident in the above discussion and the introduction, this work attempts to marry two methods of biblical interpretation. In recent years both the fields of social-scientific criticism and biblical feminist critique have added to our traditional historical-critical insights. While the two do not often meet, in this model they are melded together. The two specializations have much to learn from one another and have nothing to fear; one need not compromise the other. The more holistic a method of interpretation the closer it should bring us to our ultimate goal of understanding the biblical text in its original context. Therefore, it is the intention of this work to develop a social-scientific model of interpretation that will integrate and be complementary to a biblical feminist critique. We must first explore a foundation for each of these methods before we might hope to bring them together.

Social-scientific criticism is a subdiscipline of biblical exegesis (Elliott 1993, 7). It works in tandem with other methods of interpretation. Elliott suggests that social-scientific criticism considers the text both as a product of and a response to the social and cultural context in which it was written. It studies both the author's and intended audience's cultural and social systems. It combines an understanding of the interactions between the social sciences, and anthropological, historical and archaeological research and constructions (Elliott 1993, 8). This approach in relation to the New Testament is concerned with the study of the Mediterranean in a modern context as it might shed light or raise new questions regarding the context of the New Testament.

It is important in studies of women not to constrict one's understanding of them via past androcentric views or within an established, predetermined framework. Women have often only been seen through the lens of the usually male researcher who has limited access to their world. As a result, women's lives often do not fit with their idealized role. Thus, it is the goal of this work to use a model that includes studies of women by women, as well as the more traditional male-centered studies.

Biblical feminist critique is a method drawn from a variety of different feminist authors including Schüssler Fiorenza and Trible.[2] Trible calls our attention to texts that are often overlooked, such as those found in Judges including the story of Jephthah's virgin daughter and the unnamed concubine who is cut into pieces and distributed throughout Israel. She encourages exegetes not to ignore such hard texts but to ask instead what might be learned from them. Sometimes what is said is just as important as what is not stated. Fiorenza sharpens our focus on reconstruction and the history of women in the biblical text. She challenges exegetes to go beyond traditional male-centered interpretations and to ask questions about gender and the role of women. While in no way does this thesis attempt to analyze the work of either of these two scholars or biblical feminist critique as a whole, it does nuance the study of Romans 16 through the consideration of questions which have been influenced by such methods.

The two diverse perspectives will hold each other in balance. The development of the social-scientific model will be primary. However, it will be shaped within the context of raising questions concerning gender and within a framework of seeking to focus on the history of women in the ancient world. The model will be nuanced and informed by this biblical feminist critique. It is a critique uniquely biblical because it does not arise from post-Christian thinking but is rather worked out through a dialogue between faith and the pursuit of intellectual rigor. It engages with the biblical text directly and does not entertain ideas that are found outside of the text and imposed upon it through one's own preconceptions. Rather it seeks to be exegetical and to avoid eisegesis, studying the biblical text within its original context. It is deemed "feminist" because it seeks to look at the text from a woman-centered context, asking questions that may have been missed in prior explorations done by men or without an intentionality to pursue the story of women.

## The Model as Shaped by this Study

A model is a tool used to shed light on the text by intentionally framing one's perspective rather than operating out of one's ethnocentric presuppositions. This model will be constructed by "principles" that are gleaned from anthropological studies intended to illuminate the Mediterranean context. Those of us involved in this field can only begin to see a clearer picture when we challenge our own assumptions before we research, interact or read a text for biblical interpretation. The focus will be on allowing the anthropological findings to set the agenda. Therefore, the model developed has arisen from anthropologists' raw material. It is surely shaped by work that has already been done, but some new areas of focus have been developed such as that of women and power and women and relationships. The model will periodically dialogue with existing literature where distinctions need to be made.

This study will begin with a look at the concepts of honor and shame. The work will also examine the power, or lack thereof, that women have within Mediterranean society. It will go on to distinguish between the public and private role of women, seeking to reframe these terms. This research will then explore relationships, as Mediterranean women's lives are heavily involved in relationships with their kin and with other women. It will finish by considering women's participation in the cycle of life from birth through marriage, parenthood and death. Women have unique roles to play in each of these areas. As already acknowledged in chapter one, all cultures have some elements of honor and shame, public and private, relationships, etc., yet this thesis will explore the unique importance and meaning these concepts hold within the Mediterranean world and, in particular, for Mediterranean women. They are core Mediterranean societal values.

In the exploration of such values it is the hope that we will begin to build some cultural bridges between our twenty-first-century world and the ancient world of the Mediterranean. Ultimately such bridge-building will enable us to interpret better the cultural elements of New Testament texts. As we begin to understand a world different from our own we will be less likely to misinterpret, misunderstand and miss the point of key texts concerning the role of women in the New Testament.

There are not many New Testament scholars who have taken the time to explore more deeply these anthropological concepts. Malina has formed his model and several others from the Context Group[3] including Esler, Elliott, Oakman and Hanson draw from his work. We now turn our attention to the nuancing of the model.

## Honor and Shame

It is important to consider what work already exists on the topic of honor and shame as it relates to Mediterranean women. One of Malina's main contributions of key interest to this thesis is in the area of honor and shame.

Malina suggests that honor is the pivotal Mediterranean value (1993, 34). While one would be hard pressed to disagree with him, it is the way in which he defines honor that is troublesome. He suggests honor might be described as attitudes and behavior that are deemed socially acceptable which intersect with the boundaries of power, religion and gender (Malina 1993, 31). While he recognizes the importance of these three areas, he does not address female honor or its relationship to male honor until well into his discussion. Rather, he begins by defining challenge and response as the interactions people—"invariably males"—engage in by which they ascribe honor (Malina 1993, 35).

Malina does note that women can be the catalyst for a game of challenge and response (1993, 35). Thus, we might infer women, in turn, do influence the honor men receive, although Malina does not characterize their power in such a way. He distinguishes female honor as a sense of modesty, self-control and purity, and acknowledges that a woman's dishonor reflects on her male kin. He describes the honorable woman as one who has a concern to maintain her positive shame (Malina 1993, 49, 50).

Malina is somewhat contradictory when he discusses honor which is connected to the family. He notes that anyone outside of a blood relative is considered a potential enemy, and a stranger is a certain enemy. He notes that the genders do not mix, but males interact with other males and females converse only with females. He goes on to say that interactions that take place are considered not a social gesture but rather as activities of opposition and suspicion (Malina 1993, 38). In such interactions would not women be responsible to protect the honor of their family by guarding their actions? As we will see in our nuancing of the model, Malina takes his generalizations too far. He would benefit from exploring the possibility that women were not as powerless and secluded as he seems to suggest.

Malina discusses collective honor where the head of the group takes on the responsibility of protecting the honor of the entire group. He suggests male honor is symbolized by the protection and authority he exerts over his family in addition to the defense of his and the family's reputation (1993, 45).

Malina appears unaware of the gender bias male researchers bring to the text. Yet Norwegian scholar Halvor Moxnes reminds us of the need to be gender sensitive in these studies. Moxnes, in Richard Rohrbaugh's primer *The Social Sciences and New Testament Interpretation*, is aware of gender bias. He acknowledges that until recently the predominant view of honor was developed from a male perspective heavily shaped by the work of Julian Pitt-Rivers (Moxnes 1996, 21). Most discussion of honor centered around public or male space. He notes that females were compelled to maintain their sense of shame,[4] but he does not explore in what other areas women might experience a sense of honor, or recognition in the eyes of others (Moxnes 1996, 21).

Moxnes goes on to cite the work of female biblical scholars and the different priorities and methods they have brought to the discussion. He reminds the reader that most ancient literature was exclusively written from a male perspective. Moxnes writes that anthropologists find it difficult to access the world of women and thus their findings are skewed. He cites the work of Lila Abu-Lughod, a female anthropologist who spent considerable time among the Bedouin in Egypt, as important to the understanding of female modesty codes (Moxnes 1996, 31-33). Her work, like that of Warnock Fernea and Dubisch, is first-hand and focuses on women. Abu-Lughod describes the need for veiling which has arisen out of the close proximity of non-kin. When unrelated males are present, women must remain veiled and out of sight as much as possible (Abu-Lughod 1986, 73). While Moxnes includes the work of Abu-Lughod, he does not acknowledge that the problem of gender bias is lessening due to the research of many up-and-coming female anthropologists, which this work will highlight. We now turn our attention to the traditional and the nuanced understanding of the values of honor and shame, from the anthropological study of Mediterranean cultures. We will go on to look at a "nuanced" model and rely on feminist anthropologists to supply us with the data.

## The Traditional Understanding

Honor and shame are two related and yet opposed concepts in the Mediterranean society. According to Pitt-Rivers, honor is the "value of a person in his own eyes, but also in the eyes of his society" (1966, 21). To be honorable one needs a sense of shame. A person who is dishonorable has no shame. Women's shame comes from their sense of sexual purity. Each gender employs different codes of behavior (Peristiany 1966, 42). Moxnes makes it clear that honor and shame exist as social values in nearly all cultures. However, in Mediterranean societies these values play a dominant role (Moxnes 1996, 19).

According to Campbell's study of the Greek shepherding community of Sarakatsani, the *ideal* woman was revolted by sexual impulse and activity. Women dressed modestly, which can be a means of disguising the physical difference of their female sexuality. Women who were not married must remain virgins. Even married women must have purity of thoughts and actions. A woman's honor ultimately depended upon her community's view of her. Men were meant to protect her honor from the outside world (Campbell 1964, 146).

Some examples of such honor codes can be found in the experiences of Warnock Fernea in Iraq and her eventual compliance with the wearing of the *abayah*, or veil covering (1989, 6).[5] When she first arrived, her husband Bob told her that the people believed "an uncovered woman is an immoral woman"

(Warnock Fernea 1989, 6). When women walked down the street they could quickly cover their faces with the abayah if they saw a man they did not know. The abayah gave them protection from the outside world and from the advances of strange men (Warnock Fernea 1989, 25).

It was believed that women might lose their modesty and become shameful if they were spoken about by men in public. A woman was said to show herself only to two people—the midwife and her husband. A woman who was deemed "skinless" has lost her sense of shame (Peristiany 1966, 182). An unmarried woman's virtue reflected directly on her parents and her brothers, who were responsible for protecting and avenging her honor (Peristiany 1966, 182). Thus, when one speaks of feminine honor it is often in reference to sexual modestly and propriety (Peristiany 1966, 183).[6] Wikan (1982, 148) notes that a man's honor was inextricably tied to his female kin's behavior. She goes on to point out that women move in a different world than men. Therefore, female modesty, which is so valued in the man's world, is not as much a priority in the woman's sense of honor. Hospitality and other qualities rank higher (Wikan 1982, 160).

A need for physical covering also translates into a need for impulse control. According to Dubisch, in Tinos, Greece it is believed women are weaker than men and are, therefore, more prone to sin. Women maintain the family honor by not acting on their impulses but by hiding their inner selves and practicing restraint (Dubisch 1995, 197, 198). Women, particularly virgins and young brides, are potentially a danger to the family's honor. Their behavior can affect the status of all the men to whom they are related. These men shared in the protection of their virtue. They also shared in the consequences of the woman's behavior (Winkler 1990, 74).[7]

In Edremit it is believed that women are weak and ten times more passionate than men. They are compared to gunpowder, and it is said that the presence of a male could ignite them (Fallers and Fallers 1976, 258). Women are seen as in need of protection from themselves and from others. Peristiany found that women are judged unable to defend their own honor, thus they need men to represent them (1966, 28). Men in protection of their female kin are jealous when their wives, mothers or sisters are approached by an unrelated male (Fallers and Fallers 1976, 258). As a result, men experience dishonor when their female kin are threatened.[8] When a woman's honor is questioned, consequences can affect the offending male and others. Warnock Fernea tells of a time when she inadvertently caused trouble for a woman in the village by encouraging her to accompany her on a car ride with another woman and a male friend. Her friend's life had been at risk because permission had not been sought from her family, and her reputation in the eyes of the village was now in question (Warnock Fernea 1989, 257-261). According to Warnock Fernea (1989, 39), women were not discussed by men in public, thus what had happened was a severe breach of cultural standards. Due to the honor/shame code women and men rarely become friends outside of their kin groups. A friendship might imply a questionable and perhaps adulterous relationship (Loizos and Papataxiarchis 1991, 18).

Living under these constraints, women pose a constant threat to the honor of their male kin (Campbell 1964, 57). Women do not often go to the community well alone because men are known to sit by it and watch the women. If a woman goes to the well on her own too frequently her reputation will be sullied regardless of the behavior she exhibits (Campbell 1964, 86). In El Nahra a woman who loses her honor is also in danger of losing her life at her own family's hands (Campbell 1964, 100). Other threats to the honor of a family include broken engagements and adulterous relationships (Campbell 1964, 128, 152).[9] If a woman's honor is lost she is likely to marry a widower if she is not killed and if she marries at all. She will often be taken as a second wife to help care for the first man's wife and her children (Campbell 1964, 303).

Moxnes writes that honor and shame are related to separation of males and females. He suggests that these values "reflect the power structures of ancient Mediterranean society" (Moxnes 1996, 21). Pitt-Rivers defines shame as the "feminine counterpart" to the honor and manliness of the male. It is a quality that is morally connected with concepts of right and wrong. Once lost it is considered as never having been truly attained and is not likely to be recovered (Pitt-Rivers 1961, 110). Some of the most serious insults a man can receive refer not to his own personhood but to that of his female kin. The behavior of the females reflects on the whole family positively or negatively. The combination of women's shame and men's "manliness" forms the family's moral unit from which the children receive their sense of shame (Pitt-Rivers 1961, 115). Inversely, a mother's honor is tied to the honor of her children (Campbell 1964, 169). Mediterranean family members are clearly intertwined in relationships governed by the values of honor and shame.

Traditionally, women maintain their shame and in so doing uphold the honor of their family. They maintain their shame through their physical appearance and their lack of visibility. They are meant to be sexually pure and disciplined. Any breach of their shame by an outsider will likely bring about violent repercussions as their honor and their family's honor is protected by their male kin. As we have seen, honor and shame are not only values but play dominant roles in Mediterranean society (Moxnes 1996, 19).

## Nuancing the Traditional

In the past section we reviewed data that suggested women naturally maintain their shame, which is considered part of their womanhood. In this section we will go one step further to consider whether a woman can receive honor if she maintains her sense of shame (Delaney 1987, 40). There are few dialogue partners in this section as the only scholars that discuss this nuancing of honor are the female anthropologists whose work we rely on as primary material. It is, therefore, with them that we will seek to learn how such a study might shed light on ancient Mediterranean women. It appears that women received honor from helping men in their lives maintain honor, by being active participants in their own honor, by maintaining their shame, and through their interactions with other women.

It seems clear that women's chasteness, or lack thereof, directly affects their male kin's self-esteem (Friedl 1986, 51). Sarakatsani women are expected to help men control themselves. Women in that society are responsible for helping men stay honorable, for if men are accused of dishonor the blame is said to fall on the women because they did not shame the men into the correct path (Campbell 1964, 289). Goddard (1987, 173) suggests that women are not simply passive with regards to honor because they do wield power over men as they are a "source of danger" for them. Dubisch found that the actions of any one individual reflects on the honor of the whole family. Women are to be modest and chaste and men are to provide for and defend their families (Dubisch 1986, 208). Each one within their gender role contributes to the maintenance of honor within the family.

Blok states that honor is only meaningful in relation to shame (1981, 431). Thus, one might want to go further and say that men need women to perpetuate their sense of honor. Furthermore, it is clear that women are important and active participants in the code of behavior. Women not only represent the honor of their husbands but also that of their natal families (Mason 1975, 650). Wikan argues that women have a passive honor. Their honor is not received directly but through the codes of behavior that they maintain. Women may be passive in the world of men but can receive honor in their own world (Wikan 1982, 72, 73).

According to Goddard, men relate to honor actively while women are passive. The honor of women is often viewed within the context of its reflection upon men. It is viewed as a resource which men controlled. It is important to question how women view this code and view their own honor (Goddard 1987, 168).

In El Nahra, Warnock Fernea observes women's attachment to gold jewelry. They display it constantly and make a point of saying it is their own. It represents a sense of security in a shifting world between the natal family and the transition to their husbands' families. The community may even take vengeance on men who attempted to seize the gold of women from their tribe (Warnock Fernea 1989, 33). Could this display of finery be a possible source of honor for the women? Having gold and lots of it, seems to give them prestige among the other women and in some ways among the people of the community.

Dubisch also learned that women could attain honor as it is given by other women. In her study at Tinos she found that honor is defined as a human quality that involved morality, hospitality and keeping social expectations. Shame in this context means not doing the right thing. Her conversations with villagers did not reveal any distinction based on gender. She believes honor and shame can be applied to both men and women (Dubisch 1986, 202).[10]

Honor and shame are clearly core values that impact women's lives and roles in Mediterranean society. Given the abundance of evidence in different communities it is likely that this is an established social pattern, perhaps one that has been perpetuated for centuries. This code of behavior seems to be linked to sexuality. Women appear to be passive, yet looking closer one can see they are in control of man's greatest possession—honor. To believe that women were not aware of this power or did not know how to use it for their advantage would be naive. This causes us to ask questions about women's relationship to their own honor and shame as well as that of their male kin. One way to better understand such women will be to explore their ways of expressing and obtaining power.

## Women's Power and its Interpretation

This section of the model has not been developed further in the writings of social-scientific scholars. It comes from a reading of the anthropological data and specifically the work of female anthropologists. It is necessary to understand this construct in order to ask more pertinent questions about women's power in the New Testament. Women's power, or lack thereof, will impact their relationships with others in their community, particularly those in positions of authority. Traditionally this topic has lacked depth both in biblical studies and anthropology.

In traditional anthropological studies women have not been viewed as the actors. It is necessary to challenge this perspective and ask questions about their lives and interactions from their point of view. We need to ask how women achieve power in a society where they are viewed by men—and often even their own gender—as powerless. How do they achieve their goals even if ultimately they accomplish them in a roundabout way? It would be naive to think that women are just pawns within their social system. They find creative ways of obtaining power that male researchers unfortunately tend to overlook in their studies. The culture in which they move and breathe is not fixed and static but rather has room for flexibility. It is also far different than our own and requires a constant checking of one's assumptions. The element of gender is clearly impacted by the paradigm of power and powerlessness (Dubisch 1986, 27).

We first need to ask, "what is power"? Additionally, when we study this concept what are we studying and how does this "power" display itself in a Mediterranean woman's world? To first look at the broader concept we turn to social anthropologists and how they have defined power. According to Wrong power is associated with skill, mastery and one's ability to perform. Taking the definition a bit further he suggests that power is evidenced in the social relationships between groups or individuals (1979, 1, 2). He goes on to recognize that power also involves the ability to have influence over others and might be considered "a capacity to control" (1979, 6). He also highlights the fact that power is not necessarily hierarchical but indeed someone may hold power in one sphere over a person who holds power over them in another sphere (1979, 11). This type of power would reflect the picture of Mediterranean women who clearly are not outside the realm of male authority yet they may have some influence of their own.

Power can also be understood in relation to the resistance one's actions might create (Wrong 1979, 21). Thus, Wrong identifies persuasion, manipulation and force as forms of power (1979, 23). These forms of power are also possibly displayed in the Mediterranean woman's world. Even though Wrong acknowledges that these forms of power are not necessarily effective means of power they are an attempt for a person to impact on another's behavior (1979, 32). Russell distinguishes between "traditional" and "naked" power. Traditional power persists over time and is sanctioned by the community. Naked power is not based on tradition or mutual agreement but rather stands on its own such as in military conquest (1986, 21). He also notes there is "power behind the scenes" which is found in unexpected places and gained by personal means (Russell 1986, 27).

What does the concept "power" mean in a Mediterranean woman's world? Dubisch gives us some ideas based on her experience in rural Greece. She believes women are not necessarily seeking "power" as it might be understood in the Western sense as an individualistic and aggressive linear progression towards possession of one's goals. Rather the goals both of males and females in the Mediterranean are not based on individual gain but rather are social in nature (Dubisch 1986, 27). Women do not necessarily embody direct power, rather they have a measure of influence that enables them to get their way through others. Such a structure could be viewed as different "spheres of power" (Dubisch 1986, 18).

Power can be obtained through both economic and social means. Women in the Greek village of Vasilika gain economic power through their ability to bring land into the family. The land usually comes as part of a woman's dowry which is maintained in her control through her natal family. The other household goods and her trousseau that she brings can add to her status within her new household (Friedl 1986, 49). Women get the best and the largest portion of land from their natal families along with household goods and money to make up a dowry. Therefore, women provide the land which they work along with their husbands, and they contribute to the household budget (Iossifides 1991, 141).

Friedl emphasizes the fact that women have informal power within their households, and as a result have power over economic decisions and the production of goods in that realm. They also have a role in the economic and marital decisions that affect their daughters and sons. The family makes up the most significant social and economic unit within Greek society. The power that is wielded within this framework is indeed significant (Friedl 1986, 51).[11]

Women also gain power through the tongue, defending and advancing themselves through the only available means—their ability to communicate. Skills that involve language such as gossip, manipulation and arguing can give them some measure of indirect power (Harding 1975, 295). Women may not ask direct questions but ask rather for a piece of what they want. Women are not likely to ask for exactly what they want for fear they might not receive it and see an advantage in at least receiving a partial concession (Harding 1975, 292).

As Dubisch entered her field work in Greece she expected to find shy, retiring figures, mere shadows of humanity, based on what she had read in Greek studies that mention women in the 1960's and earlier. However, she found women to be far greater and more complex than she realized. They were the ones who often organized her social contacts. Women were open and friendly toward her, inviting her and her husband into their homes. They always offered hospitality and would then seek to learn about the researchers. Many of the women were strong and active, confident in their role within their household and as wives. They even scolded and nagged their husbands (Dubisch 1991, 36). She believes that other anthropologists in Greece and throughout the Mediterranean area have encountered similar discrepancies. The women they encountered are not suppressed or passive but instead strong and self-assured. Dubisch says, "The dissonance that I experienced between the anthropological ideology of 'honor and shame' and my experiences 'in the field' was analogous to the dissonance experienced by many women in my own society between ideologies of gender and their own experience as women" (1995, 199).

Thus, Dubisch seems to pinpoint the problem of the power imbalance between the genders. Even in Western society women are often in a struggle with men over power issues. Either side can easily portray the other as having less power than they actually do, just by virtue of not understanding how the other gender obtains power. Women in the Mediterranean need to be studied from their own vantage point, from within their shoes, and not through the researchers' particular understandings of power.[12]

Rogers argues that the distribution of power between male and female in peasant societies starts with the assumption that males are dominant. The model which develops from this perspective does not take into consideration the empirical evidence which shows women wielding power. She believes male dominance is in operation as a myth, that women form a balance between the informal power they hold and the overt power men exert. The myth is perpetuated because both need it to maintain their realm of power. The peasants overall feel a lack of power within their society, and, thus for men there is a desire to be perceived as having more power in the home than perhaps they actually wield (Rogers 1975, 752). Dubisch suggests, based on Friedl's study of the appearance of prestige, that men's display of public activity is not an indication of their power. It is more likely a reaction to their lack of power in the central point of society—the domestic realm (Dubisch 1991, 44). In her experience in Iraq, Warnock Fernea (1989, 56) also realized just how much women influenced the men in their lives. They had an impact on their husbands and particularly on their sons. They were "silent" examples and helped to determine the outcome of events via their indirect influence which some might call manipulation.

Dubisch (1986, 5) suggests that looking at society with woman in the foreground gives us not only a different picture of women but also a different view of society. Thus, when we take the time to assess power—both overt and covert as it relates to gender—we are given a more complex picture of the Mediterranean world. It does not fit as easily with our past notions of women in that part of the world. We are challenged to rethink our understanding of gender roles and the outworking of power. To get a better understanding of the concept of power we will begin to define the worlds within which men and women moved.

## Redefining Public and Private Spaces

There might be good reason to reconsider the language we use to speak about public and private spheres. What does public mean? Is it really referring to the world of men, and does private refer to the world of women? What makes something public? Is it a public event if men are the only people present? If so, then why do we not consider women's segregated activities also public if they are done in the presence of other women? Why is the space of the home considered private, separate or even inferior? There seems to be good reason to suggest that the terms "public" and "private" may not be altogether accurate when looking at the world from women's eyes.

Malina suggests men and women live most of their existence apart from each other. He suggests the Mediterranean world is defined by gender which affects the way one relates to others and to society (Malina 1993, 49-50).

*The Traditional Understanding*

Regardless of the definition of space there can be no doubt that women and men are segregated along gender lines. Within Friedl's study of Vasilika, the *agora*, or market, is an example of the most obvious public space of segregation. Women may pass through the agora on their way to other places, but no women over the age of fourteen will go to the agora without a compelling reason. The agora is a socially constructed area for men. The women will not enter coffee houses except on festivals such as Easter or Christmas when they are accompanied by their husbands or male relatives (Friedl 1986, 42-43).[13]

Traditionally public spaces are those places outside of the home such as the cafés, village squares and markets which are a part of men's domains. The private spaces have been defined as homes and neighborhoods. Women will tend to use the residential streets which are not often travelled by men. In a village in the south of France, Reiter discovered that women entered public space only when they went to church. However, it seems that men did not often congregate in that particular public space. Men reportedly said that "the church is for the women, but we have our own chapel on Sunday mornings—the café" (Reiter 1975, 256).

Warnock Fernea tells a story that describes the public and private distinction women felt in El Nahra. There was an old bridge that used to allow the women a side entrance to the bazaar and a way over the canal without being noticed. They could slip away to visit friends, pray in the mosque, and purchase small items in the bazaar without being noticed by men outside their kin group. A new bridge was built at what the designers felt would be a better location joining the busy coffee shops with the bazaar, but the builders did not realize that they were interfering with an established social network. Women thus no longer used the bridge except when necessary, because it had now become "too public" (Warnock Fernea 1989, 49-50). While we cannot take specific examples and turn them into fact, we are beginning to see a pattern here. Women and men in the Mediterranean go to great lengths to operate in different spheres.

We must take this discussion one step further and consider whether women were secluded within the home or merely restrained from entering men's worlds. Once when Warnock Fernea and her husband had American visitors, women from the tribe came to stay with Warnock Fernea, or "Beeja" as they called her, to keep her company. It was a great honor because the women had begun to consider her like one of them. They thought she would have to serve the men during their visit and be secluded from them (although this was not the case). Warnock Fernea decided to play the role the women expected of her and as a result she did not get to visit with her husband's friends, but did learn the valuable experience of what it felt like to be in seclusion with the women (1989, 274-279). Seddon found similar divisions in a rural village in Morocco where women were rarely seen outside of the home. They often stayed indoors for days at a time and only saw their husbands and children (Seddon 1976, 190).[14]

The way men and women talk to each other in the different spheres is also telling. Campbell describes how in public a man will address his wife in harsh tones making requests in a stern voice. Campbell says it is important for other men to see his role as head of the house. In public a wife is expected to be silent and submissive. She does not laugh or smile with her husband in the company of outsiders (Campbell 1964, 151-152). Campbell found that women are not expected to show their emotions in public, except when in mourning when such behavior is acceptable. A husband will not be affectionate towards his wife in public. Women do not shout to each other or their husbands in public (Campbell 1964, 289). In public a man and woman walk separately, with the man in front and the woman behind him. When visitors are in her home a woman never eats with her husband and the guests. In the extended family women serve men, who eat first, and women eat what's left over (Campbell 1964, 151-152). As we can see through a diversity of locations and situations the boundaries between public and private, and what behaviors are acceptable in each, are clearly drawn.

Rogers reports that women are not very interested in men's concerns. They will often not allow men access into their own world as they will stop talking and change the conversation when men approach (Rogers 1975, 741). According to Pitt-Rivers, "The role of women, as in all societies, centers upon the home" (1961, 85).[15] Such women's work involves caring for children, home and family needs along with caring for some smaller farm animals. Ideally, women do not work in the field, but those of poor families do work the land. Women do not go into cafés, but stay within the boundaries of the home and visit one another (Pitt-Rivers 1961, 85-87). Women say that the activities that take place in cafés "are boring and incomprehensible", and men say the same of women who meet together in homes (Reiter 1975, 268).

According to Dimen women are always assigned along with children to the private or domestic domain. Women are involved in the tasks of procreation and socialization. Men have a role in this domestic process as well but mostly in the role of social dominance. They are more involved in the arenas of social control and politics (Dimen 1986, 58). Dimen argues that in the private sphere of the home there is to be found a sense of pride, security and self-esteem for the husband and the wife. In the household the man finds solace from the hostile public world (Dimen 1986, 62).

In Eressos, Greece, women are also found within the domestic realm. They tend to resist public space and would rather send children on errands to the market than go themselves. They will attend public events such as weddings and other festivals. The house and the area immediately surrounding it is seen as the women's domain. Women do think it is important to go to church, and they at times must work in the fields. The rest of their time is spent in their neighbors' homes (Pavilides and Hesser 1986, 68, 69).

Women believe it is their destiny to be married and that marriage will be a full-time job (Reiter 1975, 268, 269). According to Harding, in the Spanish village of Oroel a woman "knows" her house and family and a man "knows" his fields and trees. Women keep the household running, people fed and clothed. Their primary work is in the home, "the place where lives are made" (Reiter 1975, 286).

Traditionally men and women were seen as moving within two very distinct worlds that may at times overlap but always kept their boundaries. Women were not necessarily in seclusion but were restricted in their interactions with unrelated kin, particularly with men. Men also were restricted in their contact with women. Neither sex was able to interact freely without some repercussions to the honor of their family. Yet we would be remiss if we did not explore these realms further. There are almost always exceptions to the rules and, therefore, to say women never leave their world for the world of men may be an overstatement. We need to be attentive to the context where the rules do not apply, for later we will be studying women of the New Testament who broke these rules and did enter into the world of men. By identifying these exceptions we will gain some insight into the women of the first-century C.E. world.

*Nuancing the Traditional*

The traditional understanding of public and private spaces needs to be reexamined. There is much discussion of this topic in the field today which this section will explore. Men and women use and move in space differently and at separate times (Reiter 1975, 256-57). In Colpied women are considered guardians of the private sphere, demeaning the public sphere of men and claiming it does not have as much importance as their own. Reiter suggests women are secure in their role and do not consider themselves inferior (1975, 272).

Women serve and reproduce the family and ultimately the "kinship network" within the private sphere while the men participate in that which is outside the domestic (Reiter 1975, 273). Women ultimately are involved in the most important resource in all societies—the producing, sustaining and nurturing of people (Reiter 1975, 281). This involvement in the lifeblood of society gives them an area from which they can leave their imprint on the community.

In Edremit women are often secluded but seem to fill their environment with social interaction and exchange with other women. Fallers was invited to the home of a dressmaker who had five apprentices working for her. She was able to see how women worked and socialized at the same time. The shop was in the dressmaker's home which subsequently also became a place for the community of women to gather (Fallers and Fallers 1976, 253).

Fallers observed women hairdressers who worked from home and did women's hair for weddings and parties. Women worked as nurses, midwives, fortune tellers and also functioned as healers. The world of women had a framework and structure of its own. When women gathered with other women they brought their own leaders and specialists. They organized their own social frameworks. Women worked, socialized and performed ceremonial acts in their own separate sphere. This separateness allowed women to experience more freedom in their activities (Fallers and Fallers 1976, 253).[16]

Dubisch says that one could argue all roles in some way are public in that they are "defined and evaluated by a larger community". In this way women and men can both be seen as actors (Dubisch 1995, 207). Women cook publicly at festivals and celebrations. Hospitality is associated with their role in the home. When they offer such hospitality they maintain the honor of the family and are somehow venturing out into a public role as such activities will reflect on their status in the community (Dubisch 1995, 210).

Du Boulay (1986, 141) speaks about the phrases that relate a woman to her house. A woman is often described as being "in the house." She is also said to hold the house together, for it is said that the house cannot exist without the woman. The meaning of the Greek word for house is a combination of house plus offspring. Thus, the house really refers to the household which includes the people in it. The family is the main social group not just economically but also religiously and symbolically. The life of the family fills the house. The physical, social and even psychological elements of their lives take place within the house. It is also a place of spirituality and religion. There are icons within its dwelling and religious celebrations take place within its walls. Since the house falls in the domestic realm women are "functionally" associated with it (Dubisch 1986, 197).

Du Boulay found on the island of Euboea that the private domain of the house has a somewhat sacred quality to it. It is considered a refuge from the outside world. Men frequently refer to the "woman in the house." When saying he has to ask his wife about something a man may instead say, "I must ask the house" (Du Boulay 1986, 146, 147). Women as agents, as the main operators in the domestic realm, are sitting "on the threshold of public and private" (Dimen 1986, 57). According to Dimen (1986, 56) they are both overtly resentful about their confinement to private space and yet are also proud of their independent ability to keep their households in running order.

Dubisch goes on to point out that in Western society the domestic side of life is often devalued and dissociated from the "'real' social world" (1991, 40). The domestic life is seen as straightforward and without problems, and it is often taken for granted. Thus, when women are studied by Western ethnographers they are often not a focal point and their work is not highly valued (Dubisch 1991, 40). Western-minded people often miss out on the importance of domestic life in Greece and the focal point women are within it (Dubisch 1986, 18).

Dubisch also examines the religious roles of women in Tinos, particularly in regard to pilgrimage. They have a very public and overt display of emotion and pain as they make their way up the steps of a sacred church. People make way for the pilgrim, particularly one who was inching up the steps on her stomach with a paralyzed child on her back (Dubisch 1995, 218). Dubisch seems to want us to question why these actions are not considered public displays on the part of women.

Some anthropologists are questioning the terms public and private themselves and are no longer seeking to differentiate them. Women's roles have long been defined as private because they are not involved in the world of men and men's activities have been defined as public and exclusive of women. Dubisch suggests that we allow for the possibility that women do function in some public ways as men also function within the private sector. She argues that many ethnographers focus on the importance of marriage for women but do not consider the importance of marriage for men. A Greek man is not a full member of society until he is married. It is only via his relationship with a woman, his bride, that he is made complete in the eyes of his community, and the same has been said of women. The two realms—public and private—are joined together in this union (Dubisch 1991, 44, 45).

Women who maintain the private realm are perhaps symbolic of the greater cultural tradition. Tentori suggests that women are keepers of the domestic life. While the men are away shepherding, the women maintain the sense of family and home (Tentori 1976, 277-278). The mother is the symbol and center of family life as the hearth and its fire are in the center of the home. Physical warmth and protection are provided by both (Campbell 1964, 151). At the center of any home is usually the kitchen and the hearth or fireplace. It is within this place that the most important functions of the household take place. Women gather to cook, members gather to meet, eat, and to sleep occasionally. Children in past times were born here. The hearth came to represent the centrality, the staple and the perpetuation of the household. It is women who most often fulfil functions related to the hearth and home (Iossifides 1991, 141). As a woman matures she becomes the moral center and physical focal point that keeps the extended family unified. The father decreases in importance as he gets older (Campbell 1964, 66). It is said by the Sarakatsani that "the mother is the heart of the family" (Campbell 1964, 168).

The private and public divisions between men's world and women's world are quite interrelated and yet distinct. It is also clear that within both worlds there is legitimate scope to see both public and private elements when these terms become more inclusive. When we define the public and private division as more than just outside the home and inside the home, we find that there is a depth that we did not see before. We might perhaps redefine the divide as between activities done inside and those done outside of one's immediate kin group. In this type of comparison we could define the spaces as men's world and women's world and still end up with a distinction compatible with the public and private divide. However, it would be a broader framework because women's world would thus be on par with men's as they are both equally valuable in the endeavor of human life. It seems in some cases a matter of semantics but one that helps to clarify what we actually mean when we say public and private spaces. Thus,—as the opening remarks of this topic alluded—more work needs to be done in this area to nuance the concepts of public and private making them more inclusive for both males and females. We have learned that women are seen more often in religious festivals, special occasions and among kin. What we know of the participants in the early church suggests they functioned as fictive kin in religious activities. These distinctions may have made it more accessible for women to play prominent roles in leadership and in what would seem to our "Western eyes" as public space.

*Women and Relationships*

There is a pattern among Mediterranean women of building and maintaining relationships. Society in the Mediterranean is considered to be dyadic in that the social group is of higher importance than the individual. Women are embedded in the male kin of their family and receive their identity from these relationships (Osiek 1998, 176, 177). However, women are not as one-dimensional and housebound as they have often been portrayed. It is important to highlight this aspect of their lives because it forms the basis for the informal power they wield, the day-to-day activities they engage in, and it helps us to understand that their world operates outside of the bounds of the public or male space. Private or female space, as we have already ascertained, does not necessarily translate into seclusion. Their worlds are just as intricate as those of the men in their families. Just because there is a difference in how women function does not mean there are no interactions with others outside of the family living in their household.

On the contrary, they share strong relationship ties with both their kin and other women in the community. Women's relationships are not necessarily visible in public. They might stop and speak to each other when they pass in the street, but they are more likely to visit in their homes. They identify (as do men when relating to men) with women of the same age range and class. Kin relationships are the most important. A strong bond exists between mother and daughter, and sisters are also close and visit often. Women visit their cousins, their aunts and nieces (Reiter 1975, 200).

Neighbors also visit one another. The neighborhood grouping gives women a sense of community and identity. Widows usually become the center for such visiting. Women come by in the widow's early days of mourning to bring her comfort. They visit more than once and sometimes regularly. There is no male to break up the visiting pattern, thus, visits can continue without interruption. This time of later years in a woman's life has been likened to the man as he retires from his labors and spends his days in the café. The older widow no longer has a husband or children to care for (Reiter 1975, 260, 261). Women tend to be more intimate with local kinship groups while men have associations with kin who are farther away in actual distance (Reiter 1975, 274).

Women maintain kinship ties and pass down kinship tales. From a woman's youth she has heard about her relations through kinship stories. The world of women revolves around people and their cares and concerns (Harding 1975, 287). Women bake bread together and make clothes in sewing circles. In Oroel they gather only to wash their clothes in a village wash basin. Much dirty laundry in the figurative sense is aired here, and gossip tends to be plentiful (Harding 1975, 300). According to Harding, "Gossip, then, is the collection, circulation, and analysis of certain portions of village script" (1975, 301).

Women's relationships with other women and with kin form the building blocks of the social system. They form central relationships that if one does not participate in they are "socially displaced" (Dubisch 1991, 40). Women are the organizers and central ingredients to the social system of the family. One of the most important familial relationships is between a woman and her mother. Dubisch learned this concept when she was pitied by some of the people of Tinos because her mother was far away (1991, 40). The same was true for Warnock Fernea. The women were sad for her because she had no children, and her mother was not nearby. One wise woman among them said to her, "when you have children, you will not feel so alone without your mother" (Warnock Fernea 1989, 35, 36). Ties between mother and daughter and other kinswomen are strong throughout the Mediterranean. Patrilocal marriage can distance them physically, but research suggests women maintain a strong bond with their natal family even after marriage.

The common relationships we often hear about from the ethnographers are usually kin related. Women frequently are introduced to a new set of kin through their marriage. There are often conflicts between a mother-in-law and a new bride. In Anatolian society these tales are well-known and are the subject of many folk songs, anecdotes and jokes. The bride is considered outside of the family and is often painfully aware of her separateness (Kiray 1976, 264). The disputes between mothers-in-law and wives are often over the issue of authority in the household (Abu-Zahra 1976, 164).[17]

Brothers' wives that live together are known to have frequent clashes. This can often quicken the splitting up of family groups. Women may be jealous of one another particularly if they perceive that another brother's family has more material wealth than their own. They may not like sharing the authority of the household with other women (Abu-Zahra 1976, 164). The community of brothers are often closely tied to one another and to the rest of their natal family, thus their wives would also be affected by these ties (Abu-Zahra 1976, 166). The wives of the brothers often get together to make special food for women who are in childbirth or to celebrate occasions such as birth. When food has to be prepared to entertain guests they will come together (Abu-Zahra 1976, 167).

A woman's incorporation into her new family is very slow. At the start of the marriage there are various ceremonies in Tunisia that involve gift-giving between the families which are intended to strengthen the relationships. A woman who births her first baby has crossed a milestone, however, the last rites of passage into the "new" family do not occur until her sons are grown. Until the point of her "full" incorporation into her husband's family she is still connected with her natal brothers who are responsible for her in times of crisis, and also her burial if she dies. One's maternal kin is very important. A married sister may continue to receive material support from her brothers if they are wealthier and her husband is in need. She will often then be responsible for helping her brother's wives with their household work. If a woman is divorced or her husband dies her father or brothers are responsible for her well-being and maintenance (Abu-Zahra 1976, 165).

When Whitaker studied the Ghegs of northern Albania he learned that women continue close ties with their natal family into their married lives (1976, 198). Just studied the people of three villages on the island of Meganisi. The most important element he saw that held their lives together was kinship. It seemed to interact with every aspect of the village life (Just 199, 115). Rogers found in her study of a peasant village in France that women formed informal groups that were made up of kin and neighborhood ties. They kept in close contact with each other through the domestic duties of washing their clothes, buying their bread and buying milk. Houses were built close to the street, and women could, therefore, see each other through the kitchen in the front of the house (Rogers 1975, 738-739).

Women share social connections mostly through the practice of visiting one another. When Warnock Fernea visited the women in El Nahra they always treated her to hospitality. It was important for them to offer her the very best coffee and sweets even though it was a hardship on their finances. The guest would initially protest the trouble they will cause, but the host will always insist. They would go through this ritual each time, and in some way the host was meant to feel appreciated. It was a ritual Warnock Fernea learned to perfect (1989, 44). Wikan also noted the importance of visiting among the Sohari women. She claims it is the highlight of women's day-to-day life. Food and hospitality are a part of that ritual (Wikan 1982, 109). Women visit others who live in close proximity only during the times when their male kin would not be home (Wikan 1982, 114).

Women also support one another at times of crisis. When the sheikh's son was extremely ill his wife was surrounded and supported by her female friends as she watched vigilantly at her son's bedside, waiting for him to improve (Warnock Fernea 1989, 177). When Warnock Fernea herself was sick the women from the village came to sit by her bedside and sympathize with her even though she did not particularly desire their company. The women seemed to feel it was their duty to be present during sickness or crisis when their woman friend might need them (1989, 274).

Women also spend time with other women in the context of celebrations and festivals. When Margaret Fallers went to an engagement party in Edremit the men and women were clearly segregated. Women attended a party that was made up only of women who celebrated with the bride. Again during a three-day celebration of marriage women ate and had fellowship separately. Men danced with other men and women danced with other women (Fallers and Fallers 1976, 248). The separate spheres of men and women seem in these cases to enhance and strengthen the relationships between people of the same gender.

Some studies done by women anthropologists who can access the world of women shed light on what women do when they are together. Women gather in Oroel to tell stories which they keep anonymous but are usually based on truth (Harding 1975, 296, 297). In past times women worked together on the creation of young girls' dowries by making handicrafts. Women had dowry showings which many of the women in the community attended. It drew them together in a strong bond and gave them satisfaction to show their finished products within the dowry (Salamone and Stanton 1986, 112).

Women are socialized by the other females in their home and trained to become an acceptable member of women's society. They learn to joke or be good listeners. Perhaps they learn to give advice or sing or dance. Women gather in these groups also to work together in the afternoon and evening accomplishing their handiwork and being sociable. Wealthier women have a more formal style of visiting. Each member of the group entertains the others in her home once a month (Fallers and Fallers 1976, 252). Visits between women regardless of their social class seem to be a major component of the Mediterranean woman's life.[18]

In the village of Hatzi in western Crete, Kennedy studied the friendships that have developed among unrelated women. These relationships are significant because they are outside of the kin group and they unite the women in a common solidarity as most married women have moved outside of their natal home (Loizos and Papataxiarchis 1991, 20). These same-gender relationships garner support for the effort it takes to complete the demands of domesticity within kinship (Loizos and Papataxiarchis 1991, 21).

Women often keep their childhood friends. Childhood is remembered by some as the highlighted time of their lives. When women marry and leave their village friendships become more difficult. Friendships, according to Kennedy, are rare when women become adults. They visit within the confines of their home while men are in the fields or when they are at the spring washing their clothes. Women have no specific place or time for relaxation like the men do when they go to the café. Even if they do meet up with other women they usually only visit while they are doing hand work such as sewing (Kennedy 1986, 128, 129).[19]

Relationships by women with unrelated women and kin are a part of women's survival networks from which they gain advice, support and the enthusiasm to care for their husbands, families and home. The skills of relationship building seem to be components of a woman's socialization process. They learn early on that they will lead lives separate from the men in their family and that they will want to build meaningful relationships with other women. They also seem to be prepared to have strong kinship ties with both their natal family and in-laws. The consideration of women's relationships, what they mean to women, what they say about women and how they function in society as a whole, is an area of study that needs expansion. It is also an area that might point to why women seemed so connected in the greetings of Romans 16. Women know how to network and know how to make their contacts count. Phoebe could perhaps open doors for Paul through her relationships that would help him to advance his work of the gospel in Rome even though he had not yet physically been there himself. We must first see whether this paradigm of women's relationships played out in the Greek, Roman or Jewish world. If such a framework proves consistent then we might understand the women mentioned in Romans 16 on a deeper level.

## Women and Religion

Women also have a clear role in the religion and morality of their society, functioning as transmitters of cultural values. They pass on to their children the meaning of institutions and hierarchy and how to work along with them. In doing so they also teach their children self-respect and the ability to challenge the structure of society. They help other adults (men) to remain in the public domain while still being connected to the private sense of integrity (Dimen 1986, 58).

In Middle Eastern societies women are considered carriers of tradition (Kiray 1976, 261). Women are seen as bearers of a group identity. They are opposed to any outside variants. Their centrality is based on the importance of kinship. Women maintain a deep identity and strong values that create an "us versus them" dichotomy (Goddard 1987, 184-185). Goddard suggests that women represent the values of self-sacrifice, commitment, generosity and a mutual reciprocity. They are the focus of the group's identity and they perpetuate that identity (Goddard 1987, 185). One detriment might be that women who carry traditions might then be excluded from various activities (public sphere) on the basis of the control of their sexuality which is so important to the family. Because they play the roles of "boundary makers" and "carriers of group identity", it is critical that women protect their honor (Goddard 1987, 190).

The women connected to the house are also connected to the life cycle of their families from birth to death, from the mundane to the sacred. Women are associated with salvation, spiritual protection and hospitality. The house and their work in it serves as a mediator between the sacred and the everyday (Du Boulay 1986, 143). Women are the mediators between the spiritual and material worlds. They pray for their families, attend church, keep religious ritual and celebrations, and care for the graves of their kin (Iossifides 1991, 141).

During the Islamic holy month of Ramadan, Warnock Fernea experienced the religious intensity of the women in El Nahra. During daily *krayas* religious readings were given by mullahs who were male and female religious teachers. The sexes were divided for the religious teaching taught by someone of their own gender (Warnock Fernea 1989, 105). Gradually, Warnock Fernea noticed women beginning to beat their breasts and nod their heads in rhythm to the song. Sobs began to spread around the room, and by the end of the storytelling the women were weeping and chanting. They covered their heads with the abayahs and cried loudly. This gathering held a great social and religious importance to the families represented (Warnock Fernea 1989, 110, 113).

In Edremit women gather for the religious recitation of the poem describing the life of Mohammed. Women go to mosques only occasionally, as they are not even required to be there on religious occasions. Within the inner society of women, services are conducted by other women who are trained in the knowledge of some Arabic for the Koran reading and who can orally lead recitation and worship (Fallers and Fallers 1976, 252).

Religion has been said to offer women a place in public space. There are symbols contained within religion that support and sanction power in the domestic realm (Loizos and Papataxiarchis 1991, 14). Women attend church more frequently than men. They are considered the guardians of the family's spiritual well-being, which is also associated with their physical condition (Dubisch 1995, 210). A woman will light an oil lamp or candle in front of the icons in her home before a holy day or when the family needs divine intercession. Women often make religious vows and complete pilgrimages for the people of their family who are ill or attempt to ward off pollution or the evil eye for those who are well (Dubisch 1995, 211).

According to Pitt-Rivers, segregation is still observed during religious festivals in Alcalá. Women and men walk separately (Pitt-Rivers 1961, 87). Women are yet said to symbolize the inside or that which is hidden (Dubisch 1986, 36). In the church in Greece the hierarchy is male but most of the participants are female. They spend much of the focus on emulating Mary perhaps because for women she contains both the embodiment of virginity/purity and motherhood (Dubisch 1991, 42).

There is clearly an interest in the Mother of God as the gateway through which God entered the world and saved it. Women are symbolized in their activity in the home: "from woman sin was born and from woman salvation was born" (Dubisch 1986, 165). They are perceived in Tinos as sinners through Eve and somehow made honorable by the Mother of God (Dubisch 1986, 165).

Women, by symbolically representing family, culture and religion, intrinsically have a permanent role and fixture in the perpetuation of Mediterranean society.

Their involvement with religion is a strongly held value embedded in their identity. As we shall see, women in first-century culture also found an outlet for expression and public participation within the institution of religion.

## Women Through the Cycle of Life and Their Roles in the Family

Women participate in the process of life from birth to death. They have significant roles in life's transitions such as at marriages and funerals. It is important to understand Mediterranean women within the roles they play. They are present and play roles within rites of passage that are experienced not only by women but also by men. The very fact that women are significantly involved at these important life events causes one to further question the central role they play within their society.

Malina asserts that these transitions are related to kinship. He defines kinship as the norms that maintain human relationships "which are directly based upon the experiences of birth and the birth cycle, from the womb, through developmental stages, to death" (Malina 1993, 117). Women are a part of this process as they are embedded in their kin. In subsequent nuancing of this model in the Greek, Jewish and Roman worlds, the categories may appear slightly different, for each culture emphasized women's involvement to different degrees in these stages. Yet there is to be evidence that women's role in the life cycle is not simply a modern construct.

Hanson suggests the household is the most basic form of kinship (1996, 66). As we will see this perspective coincides with the idea that the early Christians formed a family unit together in household churches. If Christians are considered to be fictive kin by way of such groupings then we must also consider how this cycle impacted the life of the church. McVann suggests that the Christian movement intended to replace the family at the center with the church, making it central to life, as a new family (1998, 78).

Hanson and Oakman suggest that in the first-century Mediterranean world kinship was primarily contained within the social domain. Therefore, all social institutions interfaced with and impacted the family (Hanson and Oakman 1998, 20). They go on to suggest that a society's concept of gender shapes its understanding of kinship (Hanson and Oakman 1998, 23).

*Marriage*

Hanson and Oakman suggest that marriage did not just impact individuals but rather had communal and social implications (1998, 31). One of the first rites of passage a person, particularly a woman, passes through is the marriage ceremony where she moves from daughter to bride. On a bride's wedding day, according to Warnock Fernea, she is not meant to notice anything. All day long the bride, along with women friends and relatives, sits a vigil waiting for the bridegroom to arrive. They paint the bride's hands and feet with henna.[20] She wears all the jewelry she owns. She is allowed to eat breakfast but nothing else until after the wedding when she will share her first meal with her husband (Warnock Fernea 1989, 137-139). Women at special times such as these share in grooming rituals and fellowship with one another.

Another woman was observed called Azzie who moved away from her family to a local town. She did not know her husband before they were married. She had not had any children yet but had been married for three to four years and was still called the "bride" by her husband's family with whom she lived. She only occasionally went to visit her natal family. Her mother infrequently came to visit her (Fallers and Fallers 1976, 249). She suffered from not having a child and from separation from her own mother.

In Edremit women are not usually forced to marry but their husband is often chosen for them (Fallers and Fallers 1976, 253). Women do not expect companionship from their husbands, but expect men to indulge themselves in their free time. Marriage is a rite of passage in a woman's life. At the three-day-long wedding ceremony, the emphasis is not on the couple but on the uniting of the two family groups. Women participate in the wedding when the mother presents gifts to her daughter, the bride. The bride, once married, is only then considered a full adult (Fallers and Fallers 1976, 253). She will no longer be under her family's supervision but will be transferred to her husband's household.

The woman's family may have mixed emotions when her marriage is arranged. They will be pleased that they guarded her honor and protected her reputation, but they will also experience grief over the fact that they will be losing a daughter. They might feel anxiety over what her life will be like with "strangers" (Campbell 1964, 132). In El Nahra when a bride leaves her home there is screaming and crying out with pain on the part of family members. One mother Warnock Fernea observed was grief-stricken as her daughter left home for the last time (1989, 139). As part of the parting ritual among the Sarakatsani, the family walks the girl to the groom's party. They sing a song to express their grief as they walk (Campbell 1964, 60). In Libya a bride experiences a similar time of transition and is also treated as a stranger in her in-laws' home (Mason 1975, 650). Women sympathize with the bride, knowing she will have to leave home and remain with a strange man (Campbell 1964, 276). Sisters marry according to seniority, the oldest marrying first. Campbell suggests there is no competition between them (1964, 178).

In Turkey marriage is women's number one goal. They are prepared all their early lives for it. They are also prepared to adapt to their husband's family who are likely to be hostile to her (Kiray 1976, 268). Women are subservient to their husbands and to their relatives. Only after many years does her status rise when she became a central figure in the family (Kiray 1976, 270).

Women sometimes are initiators in their sons' marriages. A woman will listen to what others say about a girl through informal discussion. The girl must be a virgin. Her family usually offers more for her dowry than they can afford (Tentori 1976, 279, 280). The two to be married do not usually meet until the day of the engagement.

Campbell's research finds that the marriage takes place in two parts beginning with the betrothal which is considered a half wedding. The marriage ceremony is only complete when the bride is taken to the home of the groom (Campbell 1964, 52). The bride remains in seclusion for much of the celebrations (Campbell 1964, 62). Once the bride and groom consummate their marriage they have to prove the bride's virginity (Campbell 1964, 63). Sohari women also have a bride price that is returned in half to the groom should she turn out not to be a virgin (Wikan 1982, 206). A bride who bleeds is considered honorable; one who does not is disgraced (Wikan 1982, 224).

*Role of Women as Wives*

Wives are to be devoted and hard-working, good housekeepers, cooks and mothers. The ideal wife is quiet and submissive to her husband's wishes (Warnock Fernea 1989, 56). A "model" wife is one that stays close to home, stays out of the view of strangers, cares for the children and house, and prepares good food for her husband and his guests (Warnock Fernea 1989, 50). Women care for infants and children. They also cook, sew, weave, mend, embroider and prepare trousseaus for their daughters (Friedl 1986, 47). In addition to caring for people women are expected to care for chickens, new lambs and kids. They raise vegetable gardens and are also responsible for the outside condition of their house (Dubisch 1986, 48).

Women often work by themselves. Their work is heavy and can be monotonous. Women make repairs to the house and chop wood. They garden, collect wood for the fire, bake bread and wash clothes. They keep their houses clean. Women also share in their labors together. They borrow things from one another and share in the tasks of using the neighbor's oven and washing their houses. They will exchange wool and food with one another. They also collect water together at the end of the day (Dimen 1986, 60-61). The role of a wife is certainly multi-faceted. Women must be versatile and hard working. Their lives center on the private sphere of the home, yet they are often found not in seclusion but in the company of other women.

*Parenthood*

The Sarakatsani believe children inherit traits from both parents (Campbell 1964, 45). Blood is believed to be equally transmitted by both parents to the children (Iossifides 1991, 138). Sons receive their father's "manliness" and daughters their mother's sense of "sexual shame" (Campbell 1964, 45). Sons bring honor, daughters do not. There is a saying that states a man wants sons "so that his name will be heard" (Campbell 1964, 56). Abu-Lughod also found that sons were preferred and daughters were considered worthless, in her studies of a Bedouin community of Egypt (1986, 119). Wikan notes in the Sohari culture both men and women prefer sons (1982, 75). Kiray also found in Turkey that women do not gain recognition until they give birth to a son. Women will then begin to be more accepted by their husband and his family (Kiray 1976, 266). Iossifides in Epirus, Greece found that women did not become legitimate members of their new household until they bore children, particularly males (1991, 140). Women are then associated with their husbands' families through their children (Kiray 1976, 140).

When a woman gives birth she is said to have fulfilled her "true" nature. The Garrese stress the proverb, "a woman without children is like a tree without fruit" (Giovaninni 1981, 413). Women have a highly valued role in the family as that of mother. When they are identified with the Mother of God it is believed they can be redeemed from their sinful natures (Dubisch 1995, 198). Women are the parent who is most responsible for the care of the children (Rogers 1975, 741).

Another role women play in relationships is that of mediator. Women are mediators in kin relationships between their husbands and sons, working toward the resolution of problems between family members. Many believe a woman's most important relationship is with her son (Kiray 1976, 264-266). It is understandable then that she would want him to have a smooth relationship with his father.

*Death*

Women mourn and lament for the dead. They also tend the family graves and prepare ritual food offered at memorial services on All Souls' Days (Dubisch 1995, 211). Warnock Fernea observed the women of El Nahra wailing in a funeral procession. They also paid a condolence visit to a woman who was mourning. All the women sat together crying in silence, rocking back and forth on their heels. Warnock Fernea was impressed by the integrity of their emotion (1989, 289, 291). Abu-Lughod also experienced this communal activity of wailing and crying with the deceased's women kin. She notes it awakened in her feelings of unresolved grief in her own life (Abu-Lughod 1986, 21). She describes it as a ritualized crying that had deep roots in the loss of one's own family members (Abu-Lughod 1986, 67).

When a person dies their female kin begin to wail along with other women (Abu-Zahra 1976, 168). The prestige of the dead is made known by the number of women wailing in public. When the dead person is prepared for burial it is the mother and sister that perform the preparation (Abu-Zahra 1976, 168). Du Boulay also found in her study that the task of preparing and washing the body is performed by women. Women perform the acts of ritual purification. Women also have to prepare food and coffee for all who will come to visit the next day (Du Boulay 1991, 66).

The wife or mother is the chief mourner at the death of a husband or child. For twenty-four hours after the death, before the body is buried, the woman does not leave the body. She sings dirges and expresses her grief through screams of lamentations. She leads other women as they beat their breasts and tear their hair and cheeks (Campbell 1964, 168).

The women are responsible for the memorial service. They sing and lament and observe the task of mourning. Men carry the body, make the coffin and take it in procession from the church to the graveyard. Women wear black, pull their black head scarves over their faces, and do not entertain any kind of celebration (Du Boulay 1991, 66-68). Women who have recently been bereaved do not leave the house except for what is absolutely necessary. They do not even go to church for at least 40 days because of the joy that is celebrated there. Women continue to lament for months and years to come (Du Boulay 1991, 69).

Women are very public in their displays of dramatic laments (Dubisch 1995, 205). Women may be considered as performing or acting publicly provided they have an audience even though they often gather in "private" places for the lament performances. These laments can take on the form of stories about themselves or others (Dubisch 1995, 212). Women express their sense of identity in the form of emotional statements and actions (Dubisch 1995, 213). Laments are recited as poetry and are sung. They involve a heightened level of emotion but usually take place in someone's home or the fields. They are also performed at a ritual such as a burial or funeral service. There are social elements that go along with the lament which benefit the women. They help to create strong bonds among women who share a deep and intense grief together (Caraveli 1986, 177). Women thus have a history and ritual associated with death, grief and burial. At this time of community expression, the bounds of public and private divisions do not restrict their involvement. It is not surprising then as we consider the role of Mediterranean women in the ritual of death that in the Gospels we see women going to the tomb with spices to prepare Jesus' body.[21]

## Conclusion

In the construction of this model women have been observed in their environments on their own terms. Mediterranean women have a strong sense of their role in the family and in society as it relates to the family. Their role within the home seems to be valued by both men and women alike. They are socialized all their lives to be wives and mothers. These are their two most important life roles.

Yet they are also raised to be in relationship with others, particularly other women. They have their own social sphere in which they live, work and play. They often are not afforded direct power by the men in their lives, but they are wise at knowing how to indirectly achieve their goals.

They are people of character, substance, complexity and even diversity. There are general principles that run across their lives and their societies that can be studied and understood, but the women themselves cannot be studied by making generalizations. They are unique and yet a part of their social group. They hold in tension the "ideal" role men expect them to play and the actual reality they live out every day.

How then can this model of women in the Mediterranean in a fairly modern context inform our understanding of women in the New Testament, and particularly in the Pauline epistles? The answers are not as straightforward as one might hope. These two concepts of womanhood being studied are separated by two thousand years, and there are bound to be some gaps that are too wide to bridge. Yet it is possible to glean principles from the modern context that may stir questions about the past.

From what has been studied in this work one could explore what honor and shame meant in ancient times. It might be useful to further explore whether women could feel a sense of honor as well as shame. One could go on to ask how women gained power in New Testament times. Was it directly or indirectly, and what were the avenues open to them? There is also clearly room to question the concepts of the definitions of private and public realms. Such distinctions most surely existed in the early church. What did these distinctions look like in ancient times, and how did women function in them? How did the concept of the house church impact women's ability to take leadership responsibilities in the early church?

The idea of different spheres of women's worlds and men's worlds raises the question of whether women in ancient times had similarly close-knit ties with other women or whether they were more secluded than today. Were women in New Testament times more associated with religion than men, and how would this impact their role within the Christian community? It is important to consider what role women played in the life cycle. It would seem likely that family and marriage would be just as, if not more, essential in a peasant society than a modernized industrial society. Finally, one also would want to understand whether women had played significant roles in death and the birthing process as well as celebrations such as marriage in ancient times. While all these questions will not necessarily be answered in this work, the model does highlight different questions and ways of understanding the New Testament world. This will be helpful in our look at Romans 16.

The patterns and questions that have emerged from this study connect women of antiquity and the women who have been studied in modern times. A map is forming that can guide us through the very tricky maze of understanding a culture two thousand years removed from one's own and many miles away. Hopefully, as the model is probed and changed in the course of its development, it will shed new light on women in the Mediterranean context and those insights will add to the understanding of women in the New Testament.

In chapter three we will consider general questions about how the model is nuanced by these cultures, and we will also briefly examine Greek women. Yet Greek women are not as integral to the discussion of Romans 16. We focus more heavily on Jewish and Roman women. The model at this stage has considered anthropological material. We are now taking it one step further than other works in this field. A detailed and thorough look at the primary material in the ancient Greek, Jewish and Roman worlds has yet to be done. Our intent at looking into these cultures is to affirm, critique and nuance the current anthropological model. The broad values that are discussed in the model and in the primary material are not meant to reconstruct historical reality. Instead, the model provides clues to the culture of women who lived in the ancient Mediterranean world and is general in nature. The model helps us to raise more nuanced questions about the interpretation of biblical texts. More discussion on how the model relates to the primary sources will follow in chapter three.

It is essential that these three cultures be considered since the text and the New Testament existed within the milieu of the Hellenistic world in which all of these cultures intermingled. The Greek culture overlays the Hellenistic world as its thinking was imposed upon the known world during the reign of Alexander the Great and then radiated throughout the first-century world. Greek continued to be the prevalent language spoken, and the norms, cultures and values of such a society are surely essential to this study. Following on the heels of this discussion will be a focus on Jewish culture. Certainly much New Testament thinking was born within the Jewish world and even impacted Christians in places as far away as Rome. The nuances of the Jewish culture must be understood because we are focusing on

Rome, with its known Jewish population and the many Jews who were a part of the church in that city. Ultimately, however, we spend a great deal of time exploring the Roman culture as indeed the letter to the Romans including the text of Romans 16[22] was centered in Roman culture. We need to understand the nuances of women within such a culture in order to glean the most from the text at hand. The next three chapters will therefore focus on nuancing the model in light of these three cultures. The insights and questions raised from such a careful study will deepen our understanding of Romans 16 and its meaning for the church today

# Notes

1. K.C. Hanson and Douglas E. Oakman, *Palestine in the Time of Jesus: Social Structures and Social Conflicts* (Minneapolis: Fortress, 1998); John J. Pilch and Bruce Malina, eds., *The Handbook of Biblical Social Values* (Peabody, Mass.: Hendrickson, 1998); John Elliott, *What is Social-Scientific Criticism?* (Minneapolis: Fortress, 1993); and Richard Rohrbaugh, *The Social Sciences and New Testament Interpretation* (Peabody, Mass.: Hendrickson, 1996).

2. Elizabeth Schüssler Fiorenza, *In Memory of Her: A Feminist Theological Reconstruction of Christian Origins* (New York: Crossroad, 1983), and *Searching the Scriptures: A Feminist Commentary* (New York: Crossroad, 1993); Phyllis Trible, *Texts of Terror: Literary-Feminist Readings of Biblical Narratives* (Philadelphia: Fortress, 1984).

3. This group consists of scholars interested in the field of social-scientific criticism and the Biblical text. They critique one another's work and continually collaborate in the area of social-scientific interpretation of the Bible. Information about their studies can be found at http://www.contextgroup.org.

4. Shame in the ancient Mediterranean culture conveyed a sense of modesty and propriety. Its secondary meanings contain the negative connotation of embarrassment over one's actions. The first definition listed is the one most used in this thesis. Yet the two concepts are clearly linked.

5. The Sarakatsani also donned the black veil (Campbell 1964, 276).

6. The honor code was similar in Edremit. Young girls were trained in modest behavior and were cautioned not to attract the attention of men outside their kin group (Fallers and Fallers 1976, 252).

7. Additionally, Whitaker, who studied the Ghegs, sheep herders in northern Albania, suggested that virginity was essential to marriage and chastity was a necessity in forming the "ideal of family honor." The family would look for proof of the fact after the wedding night (Whitaker 1976, 199).

8. For example, in Edremit husbands and brothers violently defended their female kin (Fallers and Fallers 1976, 259). Kenna also found that men on the Greek island of Nisos were dependent upon the chasteness of the females in their family to maintain their honor (1976, 348).

9. Tentori found similar codes of behavior in a southern Italian village. If a young woman aroused a youth's attention by behaving improperly it could destroy her reputation and imperil future offers of marriage (1976, 278). Pitt-Rivers in his book *The People of the Sierra* agrees that women who have their first engagement broken are faced with great difficulty and may find it hard to secure another engagement (1961, 96).

10. Delaney (1987, 35) and Giovaninni (1987, 61) both suggest that an honor code cannot be applied universally and is not precise.

11. Another example is Abu-Lughod's description of the Haj's mother as a key person in the camp and, in fact, the "ultimate moral authority." It was only after the Haj's mother approved of her that Abu-Lughod found acceptance in the community (1986, 21).

12. Reiter also argues that men who are researchers often present a "group's reality" rather than admitting that they can only discern part of the picture. As a result women are often glossed over and ignored. She makes the assertion that whether male or female, all researchers are products of their own cultures and inevitability will see even the culture they are studying through those lenses (Reiter 1975, 12-13). In exploring past works on kinship such as Campbell's 1965 study, Dubisch (1991, 33) finds that most of them have dealt with women only in reference to their relationship to men. Women surely exist outside of their relationships to men even in a society as restrictive as the Mediterranean.

13. Churches are public places in which women are found, however, gender segregation exists there too. Women are not allowed to go beyond certain points by the altar. They also usually stand at the back of the church while men stand at the front, yet on occasions of weddings and baptisms such distinctions are not as pronounced (Friedl 1986, 44).

14. Other examples of the seclusion of women exist in the work of Wikan in her observation of Sohari women. She notes that the inside of homes is the women's sphere (Wikan 1982, 36). Women avoid the markets and streets except for perhaps widows who are not attached to male kin (Wikan 1982, 51). Even at weddings and other public ceremonies rules of segregation are observed. She suggests the entire Sohari culture is divided into public and private realms (Wikan 1982, 51). Women seem to function in a myriad of interrelationships that sustain them even though they appear to be separate from men's space.

15. This seems to be a broad statement that cannot be substantiated by his work in Spain alone. It is this type of generalization that is not helpful to the study of women.

16. Within a Turkish village, Kiray (1976: 261) also found a clear distinction between male and female worlds.

17. For more information on women's relationships with their mothers-in-law see Carmelo Lisón-Tolosana, "The Ethics of Inheritance," in *Mediterranean Family Structures* (ed. J.G Peristiany; Cambridge, Cambridge University Press, 1976): 307 and Loring M. Danforth, "The Resolution of Conflict through Song in Greek Ritual Therapy," in *Contested Identities: Gender and Sexuality in Modern Greece* (eds. Peter Loizos and Evthymios Papataxiarchis; Princeton: Princeton University Press, 1991): 103.

18. Warnock Fernea experienced the inner network of women slowly as they allowed her to enter their space. A turning point came when they visited her once and insulted her cooking. They told her the rice she cooked was bad, and instead of continuing to mock her they showed her how to cook rice their way. After this event she was much freer in visiting the women, and women also came to visit her (Warnock Fernea 1989, 78).

19. Women in Naples also maintain networks of neighbors and kin. They exchange goods and favors with one another (Goddard 1987, 185).

20. In Edremit when a woman known as Emine was getting married her friends also painted her hands and feet with henna (Fallers and Fallers 1976, 249).

21. Mark 16:1||Luke 24:1.

22. See discussion in chapter six on the authenticity of Romans 16's connection to the rest of the letter.

3

# An Introduction to Nuancing the Model and a Brief Look at Ancient Greek Women Through Common Mediterranean Values

## Nuancing the Model with Ancient Sources

This chapter serves as an introduction to our look at the primary sources applicable to the Greek, Jewish and Roman worlds of the first century C.E. Because of a paucity of sources addressing women in the first-century Greek world, and since our text directly relates mainly to Roman and Jewish women, chapters four and five will focus on women from those societies. Greek women will be explored briefly at the end of this chapter. It is also important for the integrity of the model to include at least a cursory look at Greek sources, since the farther-reaching implication of this model is that it can be applied to other New Testament texts beyond Romans 16. As already stated, the Greek world certainly had an impact on the Jewish and Roman cultures mainly due to Alexander the Great's influence. Hellenization was an overlay to the first-century Mediterranean world. The New Testament, written in *koine* Greek, testifies to the sweeping influence of Hellenization.

It is critical to make clear how the model will be nuanced by the primary sources. The anthropological studies give us one view, a modern perspective that hopes to connect to the ancient world. The ancient sources, however, are steeped in the values and customs common in the first-century world. Thus, consulting the ancient texts corrects or confirms the assumptions and hypothesis developed in the anthropological model. Ultimately, we have a model that is nuanced by primary sources from the first century.

This approach has several limitations. This work is intentionally trying to avoid the retelling of history. The cultural-context model developed here is concerned with values, norms and patterns in behaviors. It is not concerned with what women did or did not do in ancient cultures. It must be acknowledged that the difference between studying history and social patterns is not automatically visible. Clearly the two disciplines overlap, interact and relate to one another. Nevertheless, it is a distinction that this thesis attempts to recognize. In an effort to highlight the differences between history and social context, this study is not focused on the specifics but rather on the general. We make generalizations about our values, culture and norms all the time, for when analysing these trends we speak of what is most common, most universal in the society, not the details of what occurred in chronological order. Dialoguing with such a model will generally illuminate our text. The goal is to look at a biblical text (in this case Romans 16) from a fresh perspective. One has to be careful not to take these generalizations concerning, for example, honor and shame and public and private and turn them into fact. We can only examine hypotheticals and only consider what the culture might have been like.

We bring our own perspectives to our studies, and, as objective as we try to be, we still cannot be certain that our interpretation of primary sources is correct. Two thousand years is a long time to have elapsed, and it erodes our ability to accurately reconstruct history. Thus, this work has chosen to focus on the reconstruction of values, norms and social patterns and trends that will help to fill out our overall understanding of the ancient world.

Another limitation that arises from this distinction between history and social values is that the dialogue partners are more limited. This research has reviewed the secondary literature on Greek, Roman and Jewish women but has presented this material as a discussion point rather than a critique. It would appear inconsistent to evaluate work that was concerned with a different objective. It is only reasonable to assume that diverse conclusions may arise when using different methodologies for divergent purposes. Thus, what has been done in this work cannot be rightly compared to a historical study of women in the ancient world. However, there are places highlighted where distinctions can be made and where this research can benefit from historical studies and the results they have found. Thus, much of the interaction with secondary sources may not seem well-defined or as interactive as one might see in a typical scholarly work. Yet this thesis is anything but standard. First of all, it is interdisciplinary, meaning time and space limit the study of each area (each area of Roman, Greek and Jewish women could be a dissertation in itself). We are receiving a mere taste of each subject and considering only material relevant to the model. Therefore, it is unreasonable to compare and critique elements of this thesis with works that set out to do something entirely different. Ultimately, much of the secondary discussion appears as an overview to make one aware of the various perspectives and studies available on each topic. As already mentioned, places of commonality are noted and when appropriate scholarly material is critiqued.

Another limitation arises when we consider the methodology used to collect and consider the primary sources of each culture. The primary sources were chosen because they are standard texts of the first-century C.E. world. There certainly were choices made as to sources that would be included and those that would be left out. There simply is not enough space to include all the possibilities. Each chapter has its own explanation of which sources were consulted. This work tried to stay as close to the first-century world as possible, however, in some cases it did dip a little further on either end, either earlier or later sources that were particularly relevant.

Once sources were selected the material was not read to reconstruct history but rather to find social patterns and values. Social patterns are not built on specifics but instead are visible in recurrent themes. The sources were looked at for points of connection with the model whether to nuance or affirm it. Other material found in these sources related to women, although it may have been interesting, was not included if it did not enhance our understanding of social values and patterns.

A final limitation of this work is the intentional study of general values and cultural patterns, which subsequently means that making distinctions in race, class and locale were often not possible. A further nuanced analysis of each of these cultures could consider whether these values differed among the social classes. For example, material on women in one part of the Roman world or another could be separated and implications could be considered. Yet it is not feasible to make these distinctions in the generalist approach this work takes. Where distinctions can be made they will be, but drawing such distinctions is not the intent of this study.

In the following pages a brief discussion of Greek women is highlighted. The next two chapters on Jewish women and Roman women, respectively, will examine the social patterns in each of those societies in a deeper way.

## Greek-speaking Hellenistic Women in Egyptian Sources

The term *Greek women* is hard to define, for they were not limited to one time or place. Greek-speaking women were found all over Alexander's empire and the influence of the Greek culture continued into the first century C.E. Thus, we will consider two plentiful sources that highlight only one area of the Greek-speaking world: Egypt. The choice of Egypt is not based on locale but rather on resources that come in the form of Plutarch from Alexandria and Egyptian papyri. Plutarch is an excellent source offering a wealth of material related to Alexandrian views on women. There is an abundance of papyri in Egypt to be studied. Thus, the decision was made to focus on the single geographic area of Egypt due to the sources available and because of space constraints. There was not room for an expansive study of Greek women in other locations. Egyptian papyri inform us about women's interactions in marriage, divorce and, among other possibilities, the sale of property. Again, we are only sampling Greek culture and are only seeking to create a general picture that will tell us a bit about the Hellenistic world and will help us to nuance the anthropological model. We will rely more heavily on the sources that focus on Jewish women and Roman women in chapters four and five.

Each chapter that considers ancient women in relation to the anthropological model will follow the same pattern as that in chapter two in relation to the core values of the Mediterranean by looking at the categories of honor and shame, women and power, public and private, women and kinship and religion. Where the material does not say anything to the particular section of the model, it will not be discussed.

Thus, in this discussion of Greek-speaking Hellenistic women in Egypt, we will examine only the patterns of honor and shame, public and private, women and power, women and relationships, women and kin, parenthood, death and religion.

## Honor and Shame

We find a wealth of information in the early historian Plutarch. Plutarch often writes from second-hand knowledge but yet draws our attention to some insightful laws and cultural norms that he sees as important in the first century, even if the event occurred centuries before. According to the ancient lawmaker Solon, an adulterer caught in the act was killed, but a man who raped an unmarried woman was only fined a small fee (Plutarch *Sol.* 23.2). Thus, the laws concerning the regulation of women's sexuality were conflicting. Women were to be protected if they were married, but if they were not, they were considered almost fair game. Alternatively, the law also protected women who were virgins, as virginity was a prized commodity. Plutarch says of Solon's Laws that "...no man is allowed to sell a daughter or sister, unless he find that she is no longer a virgin" (Plutarch *Sol.* 23.2, Perrin). Thus, it can be inferred that women may have been seen as being unable to take care of themselves and needed their honor protected. Yet if a woman has been defiled she loses all value, except to be sold as a slave.

Plutarch himself shares in the image of a silent and dependent woman as ideal. In talking about a virtuous woman (σώφρονα γυναῖκα), Plutarch in his *Advice to the Bride and Groom* writes that a bride should be visible when in her husband's presence but should conceal herself in the house when he is not present (Plutarch *Mor.* 139.9). Again, he uses the image of a virtuous woman saying, "τοὐναντίον γὰρ ἡ σώφρων ἀντενδύεται τὴν αἰδῶ," that such a kind of virtuous woman puts on modesty (Plutarch *Mor.* 139.9). This modesty is exemplified for Plutarch by male dominance as he writes that the husband's leadership is evident in a virtuous household (Plutarch *Mor.* 139.11).

Plutarch also wrote of the virtuous woman saying, she should be concealed physically and in her speech, which out of modesty are not for public display. She needs to be guarded in her speech, particularly in the presence of outsiders, "since it is an exposure of herself" (Plutarch *Mor.* 142.31, Babbitt). A woman purposefully did not want to draw attention to herself. Specifically, her appearance, including clothes and makeup, should not draw attention to her person. If she did too much to make herself look nice she was shameless. The ancient Greek woman was truly at the mercy of her community's opinions. We see this picture of modesty clearly in the New Testament church as women are called upon in 1 Corinthians 11:5ff to wear head coverings.

In an Egyptian marriage contract dating from 92 B.C.E., Apollonia is charged not to dishonor her marital home or to "cause Philiscus to be shamed by any act that brings shame upon a husband" (*Select Papyri* No. 2, lines 28-30, Hunt and Edgar). A woman had the capacity to bring dishonor or honor to her home.

It seems evident from this brief glimpse of the primary material that women in ancient Greek society were constrained by the perception of their shame amongst their kin and society. They were considered possessions of their male kin and they did not have much freedom to determine their own destinies. These examples are affirmations of the cultural context model that the anthropological material has already laid out. Yet if we consider the model there is also the suggestion that women did receive honor at certain times and places. Is this picture of shame all encompassing, or were there exceptions to the norms?

*Nuancing Honor and Shame*

During the end of the Hellenistic era however, we come upon Cleopatra, an Egyptian woman who was clearly honored by her contemporaries as ruler and as a woman. Her people honored her in death as in life according to Plutarch. He said in relation to Antony, "...the shamefulness of the honors conferred upon Cleopatra gave most offence (to Antony)" (Plutarch *Ant*. 36.3, Perrin). When she visited Athens with Antony the people were said to have honored her and greeted her at her house (Plutarch *Ant*. 57.1). Plutarch tells us that her body was to be buried with Antony's both in "splendid and regal fashion." In regard to the women who were her faithful companions, it was said they "also received honorable internment" (Plutarch *Ant*. 86.4). We must carefully consider that the evidence in this section is referring to a woman of royalty, wealth and notoriety. Surely we cannot generalize these findings to other ancient women. However, we do at least learn that there is limited evidence for some women receiving honor. We go on next to consider whether such women held any power and whether there was a clear division of the sexes over public and private spheres. We need to explore how much each gender stayed in its own sphere and to understand how this cultural construction interfaced with honor in the ancient world. We need to understand whether Greek women were able to wield any power at all, whether it be overtly or through manipulation and covert tactics.

*Women and Power*

Women and power is another consideration of our model. Did ancient Mediterranean women wield power, and, if so, what did it encompass? Cantarella notes that women such as Olympias and Cleopatra were movers in the political realm. Such women usually achieved power by succession or through their male kin and were certainly not the rule, but rather the exception (Cantarella 1987, 92-93). She also discusses women's exclusion from the political scene of the Greek city (Cantarella 1987, 40). She concludes that although women in the Hellenistic era had more freedoms and were more expressive, they continued to be rated as second-class citizens in literature, thought and the culture in general (Cantarella 1987, 97).

Women had some control over men via their dowries, which seem to have been very powerful tools to achieve their own desires. Plutarch warns women against the reliance they had on their dowries by saying, "...a wife, then, ought not to rely on her dowry or birth or beauty, but on things in which she gains the greatest hold on her husband, namely conversation, character and comradeship" (Plutarch *Mor*. 141.22, Babbitt).

Blundell points out that women also held some power even though they were dependent on the men in their lives for their very existence. Although this may seem a clearly passive state of existence, women did, however, have some power to wield. The state was dependent upon the economic stability of the *oikos* ("family") for its vitality and well-being, and this meant that children had to be produced and reared. Women in their traditional role as mothers were then necessary to the state and their continued co-operation was required. For the bearing of children was another key role that women played in Greek society, and one that provided them some limited power (Blundell 1995, 76).

Women thus may have held indirect power. In Plutarch's *Advice to the Bride and Groom* he speaks of women who use magic spells upon their husbands to gain mastery over them through the manipulation of men's desires (Plutarch *Mor.* 139.5). There is also a backlash to this kind of indirect power seen in Plutarch as he goes on to say, that women who prefer these weak-willed men to those who are more sensible are being guided by the blind rather than one's who possess knowledge and truth (Plutarch *Mor.* 139.6). He also suggests that a woman's wealth should influence how she is treated. Plutarch comments on this by saying that as a man is aware of the stature of his horse he should also be cognisant of his wife's status (Plutarch *Mor.* 139.8). Women thus seemed to gain power through their wealth, their role in procreation, and through indirect means such as their dowries and their relationship with their husbands.

Cleopatra was the exception, for she was a woman who wielded direct power in the ancient world as ruler of Egypt in Hellenistic times. Cleopatra was said to have a presence of persuasiveness, eloquent discourse and fluency in different languages (Plutarch *Ant.* 28.2). Thus, not only could she "persuade" to get what she wanted, but she was also known to be intelligent. As queen over many, Cleopatra, when she appeared in public, often wore the sacred robe of Isis and was called the "new Isis" (Plutarch *Ant.* 54.6). Plutarch said of her, "it was not easy to see how Cleopatra was inferior in intelligence to any one of the princes who took part in the expedition, she who for a long time had governed so large a kingdom by herself, and by long association with Antony had learned to manage large affairs" (Plutarch *Ant.* 56.3, Perrin). After her death, her statues remained standing after even though those of Antony were torn down (Plutarch *Ant.* 86.5). Cleopatra made her mark on history not as a shrinking violet but in boldness and with power.

Many Hellenistic women continued to have male guardians to represent their interests in the law. In 55 C.E. Demetria appointed her guardian to represent her in court due to her "womanly weakness" (*Select Papyri* No. 60, line 13, Hunt and Edgar). Apollonia's guardian in a marriage contract dating from 92 B.C.E. was her brother Apollonius who received her dowry for her (*Select Papyri* No. 2, lines. 5-7).

Hellenistic women were not known for the power they wielded, yet they do not seem to be entirely submissive in all matters and at all times. One such exception among Hellenistic women was Cleopatra. Moreover, Greek women were not as one-dimensional as has often been portrayed. They walked a fine line between leading their households and families while at the same time being led by their husbands in matters outside the oikos. We need to now determine how secluded or free they were in their movements between public and private spheres.

*Public and Private*

Is an attitude of seclusion evident in the first century C.E.? In Pomeroy's discussion of the Hellenistic time period she focuses on "royal" women such as Olympias, mother of Alexander the Great and Cleopatra, Queen of Egypt (Pomeroy 1975, 124-125). She notes that these women are exceptions and that the "common" women did not experience as much freedoms as they did. When we turn to Plutarch we see some evidence of the values of public and private continuing, but perhaps the enforcement of such a seclusion is less prominent.

Plutarch in his *Advice to the Bride and Groom* says that typically women are kept at home and are silent. Women should only speak to her husband or through him as her representative (Plutarch *Mor.* 142.32). He does not assert these ideals as hard and fast rules but rather as the likely practice. The values have continued but perhaps the reality is not as easy to enforce as women move into the Hellenistic era and beyond.

As we consider Greek papyri we will see a slightly different date range from 200 B.C.E. to the 200's C.E. We first consider women and their inheritance. Valeria Tertia (173 C.E.), although called a minor, was named heir of her father's property (*Select Papyri* No. 260, lines 4-5). Tamystra (164 or 196 C.E.), a daughter of Kenthnouphis, appeals to the authorities to help her retain the inheritance her father left her. Her father's brother and her cousin sought to have the land taken away from her on the basis that the cultivation of state land is a burden for women. She says that they claim because she is a woman and childless she is unable to provide even for herself much less keep up state lands (*Select Papyri* No. 284, lines 1-16). Marcus Aurelius Saras (237 C.E.), an ex-gymnasiarch and senator, wrote on behalf of his two daughters to accept the inheritance left to them by their mother (*Select Papyri* No. 326, lines 9-12). It seems unusual that women were able to inherit, but it is important to note a male guardian often represented them. We find evidence of women using guardians also in business dealings.

We read of an olive carrier, Thenekouis, (99 C.E.) whose terms of her contract are spelled out. She had one of her male kin as a guardian who represented her legally in the contract (*Select Papyri* No. 17, lines 7-8). Dionysia (5 C.E.) leased a papyrus marsh that belonged to her and her son (*Select Papyri* No. 41). Endeomonis and Soeris (135 C.E.) were both represented by their husbands who were their guardians. They agreed to divide the property in which they leased and each irrigated (*Select Papyri* No. 52, lines 1-6). Thommous (67 C.E.) had her guardian sign over her inheritance to her brother Sambas (*Select Papyri* No. 54, lines 34-40). Demetria (55 C.E.), through her guardian, acknowledged that she is unable to attend court by reason of "womanly weakness." Therefore, she designated her grandson to be her representative in court (*Select Papyri* No. 60, lines 13-15).

We also read of women who loaned money and were paid for services rendered. Jamystha (141 C.E.) borrowed 3,500 drachmae of silver and she needed to repay it within one year with interest (*Select Papyri* No. 70, lines 8-11). Heradous (112 C.E.) borrowed 1,612 silver drachmae from Jascarion through the bank of Harpoanation (*Select Papyri* No. 74, lines 9-11). We read of Sarapias (187 C.E.), a slave, who nursed a baby girl for her master and was paid for her services (*Select Papyri* No. 79, lines 11-16).

Thus, from the above survey it seems as though traditional space separations into public and private were not an easy task, particularly for poor women. There does seem to be a custom among the wealthy to have separate rooms and for "modest" women to remain at home, yet it does not appear to always work so clearly in actual practice. Most women also were not active in legal or business dealings without a male guardian. We also want to look at the evidence for women who were not so secluded and who did venture out from behind the traditional restrictions.

## Nuancing Public and Private

The Greek public and private spheres did not continually stay separate. As changes began to occur in the world around them and as progress moved forward so were these spaces increasingly affected. During the Hellenistic period, the divide between public and private spaces began to lessen. Women began to move out of mainland Greece and into the expanding world of Egypt and Asia with their husbands or even independently. Public and private spheres began to blur, but not disappear (Blundell 1995, 200).

Women, although they suffered severe disadvantages in ancient times, were also able to achieve things that may seem impossible given their circumstances. We will begin to see the ways in which their lives began to move from domesticity to the more "public" world of men.

Although there are some examples of powerful women such as Cleopatra, there does not seem to be enough evidence to suggest that women as a whole experienced the ability to move around the public sector as the exceptions did. Women as a whole in the Greek world appear to be more secluded than their Roman sisters, whom we will look at in a later section. Yet in Hellenistic times under Roman rule they do seem to have gradually been given more freedom than they had ever experienced.

## Women and Relationships

Women also had relationships with their mothers-in-law, as they often lived in their homes. Plutarch speaks of a custom in Leptis, Africa of a bride on the day after her wedding who asked her mother-in-law for a pot, and the mother-in-law says she does not have one. The bride is expected to recognize the mother-in-law's hostility. Plutarch writes she should "try to cure the cause of it, which is the mother's jealousy of the bride as the object of her son's affection." Plutarch suggests the bride needs to develop the groom's affection for her while ensuring his affection for his mother is not reduced (Plutarch *Mor*.143.35). He encourages the woman to be more inclined to show deference to her husband's parents then her own (Plutarch *Mor.* 143.36).

He also notes the importance of recognizing the friction that can develop in marriage through relationships between women. Plutarch quotes Hermione in Euripides' *Andromache* as saying, "Bad women's visits brought about my fall" (Plutarch *Mor.* 143.40, Babbitt). He then goes on to suggest gossip and jealousy between women can create marital discord. He suggests a woman who is sensible will be on her guard against gossip and will not listen (Plutarch *Mor.* 143.40). He also shows that jealousy created between admiring one's wife and another woman does not give one harmony (Plutarch *Mor.* 144.43). Thus, relationships between women were portrayed as both essential and possessing the potential for problems.

Women clearly lived and moved in a world different and distinct from men. This does not, however, make one world of a higher rank than the other. Perhaps the private world to which women were traditionally relegated had more to it than seclusion and separation. Perhaps women interacted in a separate sphere that cannot fairly be deemed private, as they were seen interacting with people (particularly women) outside of their kin. If males socialized mostly with men and females with women, what made the world of men public and the world of women private? Who defines and constructs these terms for us?

However we resolve the issue of public and private, it seems evident that women did move beyond the home to engage other women. Recalling the model developed from current anthropology, we remember the work of Warnock Fernea among the sheikh's women in Iraq.[1] Such women formed complex networks of relationships with one another that sustained their daily lives. In the New Testament we see how the women in Romans 16 functioned as a part of a network of people that Paul can rely on when he comes to Rome and when he sends Phoebe on ahead of him. Women were embedded in the lives of their kin and in some ways eked out their existence in and through relationships. This connection with other women is significant to the understanding of their lives and also can be applied to their later role in the formation, growth and development of Christianity.

## Women and Kin

*Marriage*

A woman's life was tied inextricably with her husband's. Plutarch writes that wives should have no feelings that are their own (*Mor.* 140.14). He also says wives should not have their own friends but share only in their husbands' friendships (Plutarch *Mor.* 140.19). It seems Plutarch is advocating that women be a mere extension of their husbands and not be entitled to a life of their own.

Yet in some first-century marriage pacts there is evidence that women were given at least some protections. In a marriage agreement from 92 B.C.E. Apollonia is able to share property in common with her husband and is protected from her husband marrying another woman (*Select Papyri* No. 2, line 12). Another marriage contract from 13 B.C.E. notes that the wife cannot be ill-treated or removed from the home, or suffer another wife or the husband will be fined the dowry plus one-half. She is also not to defile or bring dishonor to their home or she will forfeit the dowry and be charged a fine (*Select Papyri* No. 3, lines 12-31).

As we have seen, marriage changed the lives of women, it could even be said to be a necessity in the ancient world. Women were concerned with this rite of passage throughout their early years and then had to live within its bounds in their remaining time. Their rights were minimal, their feelings minimized and their lives diminished in many cases by the control exerted over them in this rite of passage.

*Parenthood*

Parenthood in the Hellenistic era was no less complicated. Women could be contracted out for their mothering skills. In 13 B.C.E. a certain Didyma became a wet nurse for an orphan child and was paid monthly in silver and oil (*Select Papyri*, No. 16, lines 7-11). Wealthy women did not have to mother their own children, only to supervise the process. Others also made choices about the keeping of children. That male children were of prime importance is illustrated in a letter from Hilarion to his wife Alis (1 B.C.E.). In it the husband commands that when she gives birth she should keep a male child but cast out a female (*Select Papyri* No. 105, lines 5-6). A mother was expected to reject a female child and leave it for dead if that was her husband's will.

Yet the raising of children was also a source of pride for women in the first century as Plutarch acknowledges in his consolation to his wife after the death of their daughter. He reminds her that in partnership they have raised their children and that they have found great fulfilment in this activity (Plutarch *Cons.* 608C).

We see a clear acknowledgement that women were a necessity in the procreation process. As much as men tried to deny women's contribution the facts were inescapable. Thus, parenthood became an outlet for self-expression for women in some ways that men could not completely control. It was an important role in every woman's life, and if she was lacking a child it became even more sought after.

*Women and Religion and Death*

Two other important and also related issues are women and religion and women and death. In 1995, a work entitled *Women in Antiquity: New Assessments*, edited by Richard Hawley and Barbara Levick, dealt with both of these topics. Nixon (1995, 89) considers Greek religion, in particular the cults of Demeter and Kore, noting that while there are both male and female deities in this polytheistic milieu, the males still have ultimate control. She points out that in the story of Demeter and Kore this power structure is overturned. She goes on to assert that in these two cults women have a degree of control over fertility rites (Nixon 1995, 92). Pomeroy (1995, 113) takes a deeper look at families, funerals and identity roles in the ancient world. Clark, in *Women in the Ancient World*, discusses women in religion. She asserts that women had long exercised a sense of religious freedom (Clark 1989, 33). For it was within religion that they were able at times to step outside of the bounds of family.

## Conclusion

We see that Hellenistic women in the Greek-speaking world, specifically Egypt, were closely connected to women of the Mediterranean today. They were guided by values of honor and shame and had little overt or legal power over their relationships. There were a few exceptions of wealthy or powerful women but they should not be completely discounted. We will soon see Greek women were the most secluded and least active women of the three we will study. Yet our look at the primary material has found that the Hellenistic era clearly signaled changes and such women began to receive more freedoms. To nuance our model more fully we will need to explore first Jewish women and then Roman women.

## Notes

1. See E. Warnock Fernea, *Guests of the Sheik: An Ethnography of an Iraqi Village* (New York: Anchor Books, 1969, 1989).

# 4

# Jewish Women in Ancient Mediterranean Culture

## Overview of Sources Used and Consulted

The sources used for the study of ancient Jewish women are diverse, and their limitations need to be recognized at the outset. Josephus, a first-century C.E. historian with a Palestinian background, is a primary source heavily relied on in this chapter. Philo of Alexandria gives us a Graeco-Egyptian perspective from the first century C.E. The Apocrypha, considered intertestamental literature dated between 200 B.C.E. and 100 C.E., will be discussed as well. Babatha's archive originates in Roman Arabia, but she is a woman of Jewish origin. Josephus gives us his view of historical events, and both he and Philo give us their interpretations of women found in the Hebrew Scriptures. Neither writer intends to focus on women and certainly this skews their writing on women. Women are usually mentioned as incidentals or appendages. Thus, within Josephus and Philo one finds some historical narrative but also a great deal of theological narrative and interpretation. Babatha's archive, however, offers us a look at an affluent Jewish woman's legal documents in the early second century. These documents reflect issues such as marriage, guardianship of a child, property disputes, loans and widowhood. Thus, these four sources give us a diversity of geographic regions and literary genres from which to study the values accorded to first-century Jewish women. We could attempt to separate out each reference into theological narrative, interpretative history and legal document, but this process would prove time consuming and ultimately unnecessary. As already stated, this work does not attempt to present a historical picture of the first-century Jewish woman, for other scholarly works have already accomplished this task.[1] This thesis suggests there is a pattern of social values in the Mediterranean world that can help us understand the writings of the New Testament in a new light. Thus, we are looking for a broader and different depiction than a historical account.

The material comes from a variety of sources, both Palestinian and from Jews in the Diaspora. It is important to note that a separation of these two categories would be helpful, but that is not a feature of this study. Because this work focuses on general values and patterns of Jewish women, the specific study of individual locations would prove inconclusive. In looking at the source, examples were chosen that best interacted with the model either to affirm or correct it. Therefore, the goal in considering these sources is to nuance the model and consider values and patterns. Thus, not all the illustrations of women in the text are referred to in this thesis. Because of limited space, and due to the fact this work presents an overview of values rather than a historical account, the selection of resources was narrowed.

As mentioned above, this thesis will discuss the works of the first-century historian Josephus. Although Josephus was by no means directly concerned with women in his narrative, from time to time pieces of their history appear in his writings. There are cultural elements of the first century in Josephus' interpretations of Hebrew Scriptures in his *Jewish Antiquities*. Along a common thread the works of Philo, another first-century C.E. Jewish writer who focused on the interpretation of Hebrew Scriptures, will be explored. A Hellenized philosopher from Alexandria, Philo had his own slant on Hebrew Bible material. While it is acknowledged that both historians wrote from their own perspective, they also represent to some degree the world view of their culture. As already noted, the archives of Babatha and Salome found in the Cave of Letters in Nahal Hever near En-Gedi will also be considered. Since we are looking at documents attributed to just a few women, the evidence is limited. However, we are given a peek into how they experienced their culture. Evidence found in their archives suggests these women were wealthy and, therefore, were in a minority in their culture (Lewis 1989, 24). Yet they offer us a privileged look at their personal dealings with husbands, fathers, sons and the other women in their lives.

One first-century corpus not specifically addressed by this work is the New Testament. It is not used as a resource because it is the subject for which the model is constructed. To employ it as a source might compromise the model's integrity.

In general, the Hebrew Bible is not used as a primary source in this study, although it is referred to when commentary about it appears in other first-century writings.[2] However, the book of Leviticus is cited in the section on clean and unclean issues. Overall, it was decided that the complexity of dating and vast time span in the Old and New Testaments would only lessen the clarity of data. It is, however, important to note that many of the values displayed in the model can be found in both the Old and New Testaments.

The Dead Sea Scrolls are not used as a primary source. Even though some of the scrolls are considered to be from the first century C.E., the references to women are too scant and the dating of other scrolls too uncertain for them to be a reliable tool in this study of Jewish women.[3] The Pseudepigrapha is also not used as a primary source because the cultural values and patterns found in it are similar to the material in Josephus and Philo and there is not space for all of it. Nevertheless, some of the most relevant material, found in Pseudo-Philo, is briefly referenced in the discussion on honor and shame because it does have a nuance to bring to the model. Several secondary authors including C.A. Brown, Bauckham and Halpern-

Amaru do suggest the significance of Pseudo-Philo in the discussion of Jewish women in the ancient world.[4] The intent of this thesis is to look at primary sources in light of the cultural context model and determine if they affirm, critique or nuance the model. There was not time nor space to include all the available primary sources. It is necessary in such a broad, multidisciplined thesis to make choices about what material will be studied.

These resources compose the foundation of this chapter. They are used to understand the model within ancient Jewish culture, and they are analysed differently from any other work found on Jewish women in ancient culture. Yet in order to distinguish how this research is unique, it is necessary to first review what has come before. Thus, we begin by discussing the secondary works that are concerned with Jewish women of antiquity. Most studies on women in antiquity approach the subject with the intent of writing a history of women. This research, however, is seeking to grasp the roles and values of women in such a society. Roles and values differ in that they are embedded in the heart of the culture, they are not simply a description of historical events and details. They appear more consistent over time. The purpose of this study is to understand how values, not specific historical events, influence the biblical text. Therefore, our dialogue partners will be limited.

Another limitation of this study is that many of the available secondary sources on Jewish women focus on the first temple period or earlier and are not clear in their time delineations. It also must be noted at this juncture that no other author has captured the interdisciplinary combination of anthropology, primary material and social-scientific criticism that is found in this work. There are similar ideas outlined in some of the secondary works as will be highlighted below. They were, however, not arrived at in the same manner nor pursued to such a degree as they are here. Various aspects of the model form the basis for our discussion of these secondary works. The literature review is found at the start of each discussion, where such resources are available and applicable.

## Honor and Shame

Some secondary works highlight the important values of honor and shame for ancient Jewish women while others do not acknowledge them, or only briefly touch on them. Swidler addresses the issue of modesty, and thus shame, in his discussion of head coverings. He asserts that Jewish women wore head coverings in public and that if they were without one they were viewed as shameful and a divorce could follow (Swidler 1976, 121). Archer (1990, 212) views the veil as a sign of woman's subordination to her husband. While in society's eyes her husband did rule over her, one must question whether the veil primarily symbolized this domination. The practice of honor and shame had a far more powerful influence than Archer seems to recognize and veiling would indicate an expression of such values. Archer (1990, 246) does address women's public modesty and says women were expected to avert their eyes from men and to always display an appropriate demeanor.

In Archer's work, however, there are additional points where a discussion of honor and shame would be useful. She addresses the status of the barren woman but does not mention the dishonor this condition brought her and her family (Archer

1990, 18). Archer is at least aware that these values existed but does not often bring them to bear upon the material (1990, 21). Women in such a culture, as we have already seen, clearly faced disgrace when they were not able to produce heirs. While Archer is not fully aware of the issues surrounding honor and shame, she does, however, acknowledge the disgrace that accompanied a breach of a woman's modesty. She (Archer 1990, 25, 27) addresses the dishonor that a defiled virgin brings upon her father and family.

Ilan touches on the values of shame by discussing women's hair. She cites Luke 7:38 and John 12:3 and the example of the woman who washes Jesus' feet with her hair, suggesting that the negative reactions of the people towards this woman could be because of the immodesty her unbound hair signifies (Ilan 1995, 130). Ilan could have expanded her discussion of a woman's shame when talking about marriage and about a young girl's early life. While her work addresses these areas which are related to honor and shame issues, Ilan does not discuss these cultural values to any significant degree.

Most authors of Jewish women's ancient history do not give sufficient time to the values of honor and shame. Yet as their purposes differ from those of this work it is necessary to keep their context in mind before judging the extensiveness of their research. The following discussion of the primary material will highlight these values and show evidence for the existence of such ideas in the ancient Jewish world. This work stands apart in such an in-depth discussion of these cultural values and their relationship to the primary material.

# A Look at the Primary Material

Honor and shame are two values which our model has revealed to be pervasive within Mediterranean society. If we recall, honor is a state traditionally afforded to males by other males. Honor as we saw it nuanced in the model suggests that women may perhaps experience a sense of vying for honor amongst other women, but usually will not obtain honor in the eyes of men. Alternatively, shame was quite clear in the model and consisted of a sense of modesty, virtue and chastity. Often women's shame was related to the protection of her sexual purity. We will remember that the honor of a family could be threatened by a women's violation or her lack of shame. In this section we will pay careful attention to the way honor and shame were exhibited in ancient Jewish society.

## Honor and Shame According to Philo and Josephus

Honor and shame are values so embedded in Jewish society that they are visible as far back as the Hebrew Bible writings. Honor and shame can be traced back to Hebrew Bible narratives, a source of religious and cultural narrative for the Jewish community. Although some of these texts were written a thousand or more years before the first century C.E., they nevertheless suggest that over time these values have been incorporated into Jewish culture. We learn of their importance when we look to Jewish writers such as Philo and Josephus and see how Hebrew Bible texts and their values continued to be discussed in the first-century world.

Josephus calls our attention to the first narrative of the Hebrew Bible, the interaction of Adam and Eve and the serpent in Genesis chapter two. In his interpretation, Adam blamed the woman for her deception, and the implication is that God punished Adam for yielding to the woman (Josephus *Ant.* 1.48-49). Shame seems to be, in Josephus' eyes, a consequence of the fall. Eve has long been viewed as bringing dishonor upon both Adam and herself. In Jewish tradition Eve was seen as both evil and the mother of all the living, both blamed for original sin and excused for being weak.[5]

There are elements of honor and shame in Josephus' account of Abraham and Sarah as they journeyed through Egypt (Josephus *Ant.* 1.161-168, Gen 12). Abraham told Sarah to lie and say she was his sister. As a result, Scripture says God sent plagues because of Sarah, but Josephus offers a fuller account that stresses the outrage of this action even more. He says before Sarah could be defiled "God thwarted his criminal passion by an outbreak of disease and political disturbance" (Josephus *Ant.* 1.163, Thackeray). These actions were credited to "the wrath of God, because he had wished to outrage the stranger's wife" (Josephus *Ant.* 1.164, Thackeray). After talking to Sarah and learning the truth the king made it clear that "We had wished to contract a marriage alliance and not to outrage her in a transport of passion" (Josephus *Ant.* 1.165, Thackeray).[6] The elements of these cultural values are more prominent in Josephus' account than in Genesis, as the former emphasizes a woman maintaining her sexual shame and modesty.

In Jewish tradition Sarah has often been equated with virtue, chastity and modesty, so revered as to be above other women (Gen 18:11; Philo *Flight* 128, *Drunkenness* 56-61). She is said to be delighted in one husband and in watching her home (Philo *Flight* 154). Philo calls Sarah a woman of "paramount virtue" (τὴν ἄρχουσαν ἀρετήν) (*Alleg. Interp.* 3.244, Colson and Whitaker). In describing Sarah's death Philo writes of Abraham, "he lost the wife who was the darling of his heart and gifted with every excellence" (Philo *Abraham* 245-246, Colson). She had proven her commitment, left her own kin and followed him. Thus, the continual discussion of Sarah's modesty and chastity exemplifies the importance of such values in ancient Jewish society. Sarah was being held up as an ideal for all Jewish women to emulate.

Philo describes Hagar as also being motivated by shame, saying that is why she departed from the home of Abraham. She was prompted by her shame and humiliation to act, which Philo calls "the outward expression of inward modesty" (ἕνεκα τοῦ σωφροσύνης ἀπεικονίσματος, αἰδοῦς) (Philo *Flight* 5, Colson and Whitaker). Modesty and shame are thus portrayed as outward activities that reflect a woman's inner being.

There are other respectable women in Hebrew Bible tradition found within these first-century writings. Of Rebecca, Philo says she "...was a virgin and a very beautiful virgin, because virtue is essentially free from alloy and false semblance and defilement, and alone among created things both beautiful and good" (Philo *Posterity* 39.133, Colson and Whitaker). Again, this is an expansion from Scripture, for in Genesis 24 we only read that Rebecca was a virgin which no man had "known.' When Rebecca saw Isaac for the first time she asked who he was. When she was told that it was Isaac "...she took her veil and covered herself" (Gen 24: 65).[7] As we have already seen in the development of the model, the veil appears to be a sign of shame and modesty that virtuous women maintain.

Josephus' recounts that Rebecca calls her brother the guardian of her maidenhood: "I am called Rebecca, and my father was Bathuel, but he is now dead, and our brother Laban directs the whole household, with my mother, and is guardian of my maidenhood" (Josephus *Ant.* 1.248-249, Thackeray). Because Rebecca's father had died it was her brother's responsibility to protect her shame. Josephus expands on Scripture making clear that Bathuel was dead and Laban her brother was now the next of kin that would guard Rebecca's shame. Thus, men guard women's shame and protect their honor.

In *Questions and Answers on Genesis*, Philo describes the veil covering that Rebecca wore as a "visible symbol of clear-shining virtue" (Book 4.143, Marcus). In describing a wife charged with adultery the priest is to remove her "kerchief" because in this way she is stripped of her "symbol of modesty." Women who are innocent keep their heads covered (Philo *Spec. Laws* 3.56). Once again, we see that the covered woman suggests one who is modest and morally excellent.

We read of another woman's experience of shamefulness and her brother's revenge in the story of Tamar, the daughter of David. Josephus tells us she "was still a virgin and of such striking beauty..." (*Ant.* 7.162, Thackeray and Marcus). "Because of her virginity" and "because she was closely guarded" we are told that Amnon her half-brother lusted after her (Josephus *Ant.* 7.162-166, Thackeray and Marcus). He asked her to "lie" with him, to which she responded, "No, my brother, do not force me; for such a thing is not done in Israel; do not do anything so vile! As for me, where could I carry my shame? And as for you, you would be as one of the scoundrels in Israel..." (2 Sam 13:12,13). The element of shame is apparent when Tamar adds, "Oh no, do not force me to this nor be so impious, my brother, as to transgress the law and bring upon yourself dreadful shame" (Josephus *Ant.* 7.168, Thackeray and Marcus). She begged him to ask the king for her in marriage, but he refused. After he violated her he sent her away, and Tamar says that "...this wrong in sending me away is greater than the other that you did to me" (2 Sam 13:16). Josephus spotlights her shame by telling us Amnon sent her away in broad daylight (*Ant.* 7.170) so that everyone might see her disgrace.

## Honor and Shame in the Apocrypha

In the intertestamental literature such as the Apocrypha there are also examples of honor and shame in the Jewish culture. In Tobit we read of the misfortunes of Sarah. Sarah, the daughter of Raguel, had been married to seven husbands all of whom died. Due to her misfortune, Sarah decided to hang herself but then was concerned about the shame it would bring her father. She prayed for God's help saying, "...I am my father's only child; he has no other child to be his heir; and he has no close relative or other kindred for whom I should keep myself as wife...hear me in my disgrace" (Tob 3:15). Sarah did not want to bring shame upon her father and she also did not want to continue in her own shame. A woman who was unmarried was surely in disgrace, particularly one whose groom dies before the wedding night was over, which was assumed to be caused by demonic infection.

We further read of Susanna, a woman who protected her shame. Susanna, wife of Joakim, was called a beautiful woman and "one who feared the Lord" (Sus 1:2). We read that "Her parents were righteous, and had trained their daughter according to the law of Moses" (Sus 1:3). Many judges and important people met with Susanna's husband. One pair of judges saw Susanna and plotted how they might violate her (Sus 1:7-14).

They came upon her while she was bathing and threatened her, saying if she did not consent to be with them, they would say she had sent her maid away because a man was with her. Susanna would not agree and cried out loudly. When she was accused "...the servants felt very much ashamed, for nothing like this has ever been said about Susanna" (Sus 1:27).

The next day Susanna was summoned to appear before the leaders of the city, to face possible death. She came with "her parents, her children and all her relatives" (Sus 1:30). She came veiled, but they unveiled her perhaps as a way to gain even more power over her. The judges told their story and because they were well respected and had much power due to their positions, the assembly believed them and condemned her to death (Sus 1:41). Yet God heard Susanna's cry and rose up Daniel who would not support such an outrage (Sus 1:46). After Susanna was vindicated we read "Hilkiah and his wife praised God for their daughter Susanna, and so did her husband Joakim and all her relatives, because she was found innocent of a shameful deed" (Sus 1:63). Brooke suggests that Susanna's decision could be paralleled with Eve's decision in the garden (1992, 102). Yet Susanna makes the right choice, she does not sin and she is faithful to her husband. Brooke claims Susanna is a figure of Eve and suggests that paradise can be regained when evil men are triumphed by a faithful woman (1992, 109, 111).

This story of Susanna is an example of the importance of women's sexual shame being protected and kept pure. A woman's reputation among the people was extremely important and could bring her praise or condemnation. Even a woman who was merely accused of indecency could easily become an outcast. We see the importance of the story of Susanna and her testimony of honor in the early church. Paintings of this account can be found in one of the oldest catacombs in Rome, the catacomb of Priscilla (Carletti 1982, 26).

The book of Sirach[8] offers various opinions about women as well, and most are not complimentary. We read about a woman's wrath, wickedness and great iniquity in Chapter 25 (15, 17, 19). Ben Sira warns men not to be enticed by a woman's wealth or beauty (25:21). He also comments on Eve, saying, "From a woman sin had its beginning and because of her we all die" (Sirach 25:24).

Women are presented as evil and dangerous (26:22). We read of the importance of protecting one's modesty in 26:24: "...a shameless woman constantly acts disgracefully but a modest daughter will even be embarrassed before her husband" (26:24). Sirach suggests a wife who honors her husband appears wise, but the one who "dishonors him in her pride" (26:26) will be considered ungodly. In chapter 42 we read of the worries a father had over his daughter (verses 9-14). In verse ten he fears her modesty might be lost, and in verse 14 we are told that a woman brings shame and disgrace. Even though Sirach takes such a negative view of women, we can see that the values of honor and shame are significant in his writing. Camp discusses honor and shame in Ben Sira noting how these values are linked with economic and sexual issues. Wealth and women are symbols of male power and honor. Women and their behaviour have the ability to control men's honor (Camp 1991, 38, 39). Trenchard rightly points out that a noteworthy feature of Sirach is the amount of space the text devotes to women. He claims that seven percent of the material addresses women and two-thirds of this seven percent is to be found in pericopes of five verses or more (Trenchard 1982, 1). Surely Sirach is a valuable source for this study despite the negative lenses through which Ben Sira views women.

Throughout Jewish tradition, the values of honor and shame are clearly at work. Women represented the family, and it was important to men's honor that the chastity of their women kin be protected. Women's shame was represented in their need to protect their sexual purity.

The interaction of honor and shame in the ancient world surely impacted Jewish women as can be seen from these examples and many others including some in the Hebrew Bible. Such values were intertwined in the understanding of what it meant to be male and female and were a continual concern for a Jewish woman throughout her life. Through a variety of sources we have seen that women in the ancient Mediterranean were bound by a strict honor code. The protection of their modesty and chastity was an essential component of their everyday existence. We now need to ask the question, did ancient Jewish women also receive honor?

## Nuancing Honor and Shame

It is important to acknowledge at this point a small first-century C.E. work that has much to say about women. Pseudo-Philo is a first-century Palestinian document, a retelling of the biblical narrative from Genesis to I Samuel. It was initially thought to be written by Philo, but because of vocabulary, style and content its connection with Philo has been disproved (C.A. Brown 1992, 11). The main importance of Pseudo-Philo to this thesis is the emphasis it places upon women. There are several women mentioned and their stories are expanded on from Scripture. Noteworthy women include Jael, Deborah, Jephthah's daughter and Hannah. Of Jael and Deborah we read of their courageous acts on Israel's behalf (chs. 21-22). Deborah's story is one of conquering hero, rallying and just judge and a much-loved matriarch. The song of Deborah, recorded in Scripture, is expanded in Pseudo-Philo (ch. 22) highlighting the importance of her role in Israel's history. In Deborah's song Sisera's mother is called Themech. She is perceived in this passage not as meek and mild but as bold and confident (Halpern-Amaru 1991, 98).

What is even more noteworthy is the speech Deborah gives as she is about to die. She calls herself a woman of God (33.1) and tells the people to obey her as their mother. She beseeches them to let the law guide their paths (33.3). We are told the people mourned and lamented for her for seventy days. The book of Judges does not tell us about her death or the people's response to it.

Another significant woman according to Pseudo-Philo is Jephthah's daughter. She is unnamed in Judges but Pseudo-Philo calls her Seila. A great deal of space is taken up telling us about her reaction to Jephthah's vow and her resignation to her death. We do not read her lament in Judges, but in Biblical Antiquities we are invited into her private thoughts and losses.

The fact that Pseudo-Philo[9] highlights these biblical women brings them honor. These women were obviously important enough to the community from which this work originated to fill out the gaps Scripture leaves us with and reconstruct the possibilities of who they were. Halpern-Amaru discusses Pseudo-Philo's emphasis on motherhood. He suggests Pseudo-Philo exalts the role of mother and focuses on women who were mothers. Pseudo-Philo names the mothers of Sisera (31:8), Samson (42:1) and Micah (44:2) who are unidentified in the Bible (Halpern-Amaru 1991, 94). When women are not associated with the maternal role, Halpern-Amaru suggests Pseudo-Philo fails to highlight their positions and develop their stories in his narrative. Women in Pseudo-Philo are viewed as leaders, parents and even villains (Halpern-Amaru 1991, 106).

We do not have the space and time to delve into other Pseudepigrapha texts, but we can at least mention Joseph and Aseneth which also highlights women. Aseneth converts to Judaism prior to her marriage. The positive change in her is evident. Aseneth is displayed in this narrative as an independent, powerful and resourceful woman. She achieves her worldly goals by finding out it is more important to become a child of God (Pervo 1991, 154). Pervo suggests that romantic Greek novels focus on what women should want. However, Jewish narrative focuses perhaps on what women really did want (Pervo 1991, 160).

In Josephus and Philo we read some of the same stories found in Pseudo-Philo, but the emphasis on women is not present. In Josephus we read of several powerful women who surely received honor—Herod's sister Salome, his wife Mariamme, Queen Helena, Queen Alexandra and Queen Shelamzion. We will explore some examples of their power and explore in the section on women and power.

Surely the fact that women were honored in expanded stories of Scripture and the fact that royal women were given significant space in historical documents speaks of a society that in some way honored its women. Most of these women were upper class and powerful, but we cannot overlook their existence. We will find out more about these Jewish women as we consider their relationship to power.

## Women and Power

Did Jewish women hold direct or indirect power, and how did it look different than that of Roman and Greek women? The model causes us to ask these questions, and as we find out about Jewish women and power we will further nuance the model.

*Discovering Eve* appeared in 1988, and in it Meyers is attentive to the context surrounding the ancient Israelite women. She situates the women within the culture and social environment of ancient Israel (Meyers 1988, 22-23). She begins her work with a discussion of patriarchy and power. From this foundation she develops the geographic and social setting of ancient Israel, an agrarian society (Meyers

1988, 47). Although she goes beyond the scope of this paper by referring to a time period much earlier in Israel's history, she does use an approach to the material similar to that which is found in this thesis. This necessitates the acknowledgement of her work.

She discusses the kinship ties and household composition of a Jewish family as well as the role of women and their distinction from men. Her work is significant in that it combines an understanding of anthropology, sociology, and history. It does not approach the material from a social-scientific perspective but with an awareness of it. She instead employs a social-historical methodology. We are both clearly concerned with accurately hearing the voice of women in the text. We study different texts, though, with Meyers focusing on Genesis and this work on Romans 16. The methodology and intent to discover values and culture are, however, similar.

Meyers addresses the topic of women and power in two different sections of her book. She begins by discussing patriarchy and power. She distinguishes between power and authority based on Max Weber's work *The Theory of Social and Economic Organization*, noting that authority is sanctioned by the hierarchy but power is instead influential in social interactions but not sanctioned by the community (Meyers 1988, 41). She discusses the work of anthropologist S.C. Rogers in France where it was found that men held authority while women possessed power and both genders participated in a system where this balance/imbalance was maintained (Meyers 1988, 42-43). She argues that although men had authority in ancient Israel, women held tremendous power. Women were still considered as having lesser value than men, yet they were not dominated by them (Meyers 1988, 44-45). Women at the same time were powerful shapers of their society and also bound by the limitations of their culture and restricted to certain roles.

In chapter eight Meyers specifically addresses "Female Power." She highlights the importance of the household in pre-state Israel, when the society was agrarian. She argues that large groups of the family did not diminish women's capacity to control. They only had more people over which to wield power (Meyers 1988, 174, 175).

Meyers, writing in 1989 in Lesko's work *Women's Earliest Records*, discusses her concern that women held power within Israelite society that was often not legitimized with authority, which the men held (Meyers 1989, 269). She suggests that even though Israelite society became increasingly hierarchical, female power did nevertheless exist in pre-monarchic times and is evidenced in biblical texts (Meyers 1989, 277-278). One might question the idea that women's power decreased as society became less agrarian. Since women of ancient Israel continued to be involved in the running of households and domestic chores, their sphere of influence remained constant. Perhaps women's power even increased as they began to move about more freely inheriting wealth and performing monetary transactions.

Also in *Women's Earliest Records*, Bird writes on the religious involvement of women in ancient Israel. Although she explores a much earlier time period than the first century C.E., it is important to note Bird identifies women as key components of religious rituals, and in particular she distinguishes women who were more active during the time of goddess worship. Bird briefly addresses the informal power women exercised, suggesting this power was manifested in the influence women had over family decisions and the favours which they elicited. She claims women had authority in the areas of affection and wisdom, as displayed in their teaching and formation of values in their family (Bird 1989, 291). While her ideas are quite plausible and certainly are also supported by this model, they do not seem to be supported by much primary evidence from antiquity or anthropology.

Biale (1984, 69), in her work *Women and Jewish Law*, does not address the issue of power. She misses an opportunity to discuss power within her chapter on marriage. She writes that women were "passive participants" both in marriage and divorce, but does not expand on this idea. Women were passive in choosing their husbands, but based on our model we could question what role mothers played in arranging marriages, even on an informal level.

Even though the previous discussion of honor and shame might suggest otherwise, women in the Jewish culture did have some level of power. The traditional model suggests that power did not exist for women in the ancient world, that they had no access to it, or it was inconsequential to their lives. Yet the model which has been nuanced in this work suggests that women did hold power in the family specifically in the domestic sphere. They had power through the dishonor their actions could bring upon their family, and they also gained power through manipulation. A review of the literature finds that some secondary sources did address the issue of women and power whereas others missed this key cultural pattern entirely.

Given this review of the secondary sources there is a need to see more specifically what power was like for Jewish women and how it can be nuanced and better understood. Therefore, the following section will present this work's findings on women and power within the primary sources.

## Accounts of Women and Power

In this section we will look at women who appeared to hold power. We may not see it in traditional forms, but we will find women in power in places such as the family, the community and in governing roles.

Philo recounts the story of the daughters of Zelophehad. He had five daughters but no sons. After Zelophehad died his daughters were concerned about their inheritance: "since inheritance went in the male line they approached the ruler in all maidenly modesty, not in pursuit of wealth but from a desire to preserve the name and reputation of their father" (*Moses* 2.234). Philo tells us in his story that Moses went on to make some changes to the inheritance laws. Sons were first in line of succession for their father's inheritance, daughters were second if there were no sons in the family. The heirs of parents were their sons, but if they do not exist or have died, then their daughters become heirs. Philo says, "for just as in nature men take precedence of women, so too in the scale of relationships they should take the first place in succeeding to the property…". Virgins without a dowry would share equally with the male heirs of the family (*Spec. Laws* 2.125). Hence, we might consider that Jewish women who had no brothers may have, in fact, been in line to receive their father's inheritance. Jewish women were provided for in their dowry, and, thus, indirectly received their inheritance.

Philo reports that a wife had great power over her husband. In particular if she was a *wanton* she was viewed as one who manipulates him and he was described as unaware (Philo *Embassy* 39). Josephus wrote of other powerful women, some because of their wealth and others for their noteworthy actions. We also read of everyday women who performed courageous acts when their families were threatened. An account of Titus' attack on the Galileans describes the strength of Galilean women: "...the able-bodied fell upon the Romans in the narrow alleys, while from the houses the women pelted them with whatever missiles came to hand" (Josephus *J.W.* 3.301-305, Thackeray). These women fought physically for their homes and families.[10]

*Royal Women*

Queen Helena, during the administration of Tiberius Alexander, supplied money and grain to the people in a time of famine (Josephus *Ant.* 20.101, 102). The people accepted the help of a woman in time of such great need, her gender did not matter. Thus, Queen Helena's power was one of manipulation, based on her wealth and position.

We learn in Josephus that Alexander the Great bequeathed his kingdom to his wife Alexandra for he was convinced the Jews would bow to her authority as they would no other because of "her utter lack of his brutality and by her opposition to his crimes she had won the affections of the populace" (*J.W.* 1.107). Josephus recalls "this frail woman firmly held the reins of government, thanks to her reputation for piety" (*J.W.* 1.108). Alexandra was said to be a strict observer of the Jewish nation's traditions and would punish anyone who broke their laws (*J.W.* 1.107-109). She was said to be a good administrator, but it was also said she was ruled by the Pharisees (*J.W.* 1.111-112). Josephus eulogizes her saying she did not show the weakness of women. She was able to carry out her plans and rule effectively. Yet he also says her family lost power because, among other reasons, she desired "things unbecoming a woman" (*Ant.* 13.430-431). Perhaps she was not as powerful as she appeared, yet she was a ruler and we need to recognize both her position in society and her wealth which surely influenced the amount of power she wielded.

Josephus also gives an account of a group of women who were anything but quiet. It was said "a gang of women" at Herod's court, including the wife of Pheroras, her mother and sister and the mother of Antipater, created mischief in the palace. Josephus says, "these women domineered over the rest" (*J.W.* 1.569). Once they were told of Herod's displeasure, they began to meet in secret, holding "clandestine meetings and nocturnal carousals, and the knowledge that they were watched only bound them closer together" (*J.W.* 1.570). As a result, the king falsely accused the wife of Pheroras of convincing the Pharisees to work against him, of turning his own brother against him and of insulting his daughters (*J.W.* 1.571-572). These women seemed to wreak much havoc for supposedly having little or no power.

Mariamme, King Herod's wife, found many ways to exert her power in the palace. On one occasion she found herself a captive of the king, and in response, to learn of Herod's plans, manipulated the chief guard through kind words and gifts.

Soemus, the guard, believed the king to be ruled by his intense love for Mariamme (Josephus *Ant.* 15.202-207). There are two accounts of Mariamme's execution both in *Jewish Antiquities* (15.231) and *Jewish War* (1.442). In the version found in *Antiquities*, Salome and her friends are said to have influenced the king to dispose of Mariamme.

Josephus claims that Herod's love for Mariamme gave her great freedom of speech (*Ant.* 15.237-239). Mariamme used her influence to obtain the position of high priest for her brother (*Ant.* 15.23-32). Herod was said to fear that Alexandra, the mother of Mariamme, might interfere with his governing. Josephus writes that Alexandra had "a full share of womanly pride" (*Ant.* 15.44).

Salome, Herod's sister, along with her mother tried to influence his concerns about Mariamme and to add to his mistrust of her by spreading damaging rumours about her (*Ant.* 15.213ff). Salome continued in her manipulation of the palace particularly through her daughter who was married to Mariamme's son Aristobulus. Salome kept tabs on the king's sons and reported conversations to him to besmirch their characters (*Ant.* 16.200-205). According to Josephus, Salome gained a reputation among the king's wives as one who could not be trusted (*Ant.* 16.219). Salome, a woman who knew what she did not want, sent documents of divorce to her husband Costobarus. Josephus notes under Jewish law her acts were not possible because she was a woman. Yet we read that Salome disregarded the customs (*Ant.* 15.259) and "acted on her own authority and repudiated her marriage" (*Ant.* 15.260). Salome seemed to know the power she held by being in the royal court and the king's sister. She appeared unafraid to use it even though she lived in a society that did not view women as powerful.

Another royal woman, Herodias, sister of Agrippa, jealous of her brother's wealth and success, encouraged her husband Herod to appeal to Emperor Gaius to regain his royal birthright (*Ant.* 18:240-244). The plan was not to succeed, and Herodias was offered a deal by Gaius. She could keep her personal wealth and be indebted to her brother Agrippa or be exiled. She chose to stand with her husband and not align herself with her brother saying her loyalty to her husband was stronger. Josephus comments that Herod was punished by God for listening to a woman's frivolous chatter (*Ant.*18: 253-255). By attributing Herod's downfall to his wife's involvement in this controversy, Josephus must have felt she held some sway in the marriage.

Josephus tells us about another man who was under the power of women. We just read about his wife and the "gang" of women in the royal court. Pheroras, an advisor and brother of Herod, was said to be controlled by Salome and other women in Herod's court, for he needed their support to accomplish his goals (*Ant.* 17.34-36). Herod at one point asked Pheroras to state his allegiance to his wife or to his brother. Pheroras would not chose his brother over his devotion to his wife (*Ant.* 17.48-50).

As mentioned earlier, Herod's court inherited his wealth. Herod bequeathed money to Caesar's wife Julia and to Salome his sister, among others (*Ant.* 17.146-147). Along with wealth and property, Salome was given a palace in Ascalon by Caesar. Herod's two daughters, as yet unmarried, were also given additional money by Caesar (*Ant.* 16:321-322). Later when Salome died she left Gamala and its land to Julia (*Ant.* 18:31). Josephus tells us Agrippa borrowed quite a sum of money from Antonia (Josephus *Ant.* 18:167). Therefore, Antonia must have had sufficient money to make a loan and, thus, had some leverage and influence in her society.

## Babatha's and Salome's archives

We also find evidence of powerful Jewish women in archives which have been found centuries after their deaths. Babatha was a woman who in the early part of the second century C.E. had enough wealth to own land. A "Registration of Land" recorded her ownership of four groves of date palms in the area of Maoza. Her husband Judah was her transactional guardian (5/6Hev 16 papRegistration of Land gr, Lewis, JDS 2). There is also a document that appears to be a monetary transaction between Babatha and her husband Judah. He received 300 denarii from her that was repayable upon demand but a date for repayment was not specified (5/6Hev 17 papDeposit gr, Lewis, JDS 2). Babatha was a woman of her own means, she held property and even sold it. Yet her power was still dependent on the amount of legal freedom her guardian (Judah) gave her. Her decisions were not completely her own.

Also found in Babatha's archives is a reference to a second woman guardian, Julia Crispina. She was a guardian for Babatha's orphan nephews who filed claims against Babatha in court. It was unusual for a woman to be a guardian, as they were usually represented by guardians themselves. One assumes she could read and write and was viewed as a capable person to represent children. However, details of her guardianship are not given. Ilan (1992, 377), in her research exploring the identity of Julia Crispina, suggests there may be evidence indicating she was the granddaughter of Queen Berenice.[11]

We also read of Shelamzion, who was named heir to all her father Judah's property in En-Gedi. She was given half of the property eleven days after her marriage and the other half after his death. Lewis (1989, 19) suggests that it may have been her father's way of leaving her an inheritance. Not many women were left an inheritance, and this act suggests a measure of power that Shelamzion would have through financial wealth.

Salome is given the gift of a date orchard and half a courtyard from her mother Salome Gropte (XHev/Se 64, papDeed of Gift gr, Cotton, DJD 27). In her marriage contract it is her mother who gives her away and not a male kinsman (XHev/Se 65, papMarriage Contract gr, Cotton, DJD 27). We might question whether Salome's father had died and she had no brothers or male kin. It seems unlikely that there was no one who could represent her, but rather her mother seems to have had an unusually strong role in her life. Also in the Salome archive, there is a wife's deed of renunciation of claims against her husband, which may have been a possible call for divorce (XHev/Se 63, papDeed of Renunciation of Claims gr, Cotton, DJD 27). It is not clear whether this document represents a call for divorce, but if it should then this woman was in a rare position of power to even make such a request.

## Women and Power in the Apocrypha

We see numerous examples of powerful women in intertestamental literature, including the Apocrypha. Judith was one such woman to whom a whole book is dedicated. She was a widow who honored the name and reputation of her husband through her actions (Jdt 8:1-8). She had an inheritance which she was left to manage (Jdt 8:7,8). Her role among the people was similar to a prophetess who told rulers to direct the hearts of the people back to God (Jdt 8:11-17). Judith had wealth and, thus, power as well as the respect of the people, even the king (Jdt 8:29). Judith prayed for her people and risked her life for them (Jdt 9-11). Her power was one of deception and manipulation through which she killed the Assyrian commander (Jdt 13:6-10). Even though her power was sanctioned by the people she was still governed by the values of society and swore she had not been defiled or shamed by him, in order to ensure the honor of her actions (Jdt 13:16). Thus, despite her great victory she showed that she was still a modest woman and proclaimed that her shame had remained intact, otherwise her triumph would have been a defeat.

Amy-Jill Levine discusses how Judith leaves the private sphere, enters the public sphere and disrupts the status quo. Judith, thus, threatens the hierarchical pattern of male and female relationships. However, she dwells in the private sphere again after she alleviates the crisis. She returns to being a widow in the private sphere which is what one would expect in her society (A.-J. Levine 1992, 17-20). Levine suggests Judith does not fully return to her former way of life because she no longer expresses the depth of faith she once seemed to have. She has been changed by her experience (A.-J. Levine 1992, 27).

Due to the great respect she commanded, she was praised by the king, the high priest and the elders (Jdt 13:20, 15:9,10). The women and all the people also honored Judith for her actions (Jdt 15). Judith is remembered for her deeds and, thus, her fame is her only visible mark on the public world (A.-J. Levine 1992, 28). Her power is short lived and yet memorable. Judith is portrayed as an example of a powerful Hebrew woman who was not under the control of male kin. She even refused marriage and instead preferred widowhood. LaCocque calls her a hero and a heroine. Her role in Hebrew and Jewish literature is significant. Beyond the gripping story is a possible commentary of the Jewish reactions to Hellenization (LaCocque 1990, 46, 47). LaCocque suggests the Book of Judith reflects many parallels to significant women of the Bible including Jael, Naomi, Deborah, Rachel, Tamar and Abigail as well as others (1990, 35-37). Ilan asserts the stories of Esther, Judith and Susanna support and propagate the rule of Queen Shelamzion. They definitely promote women's ability to be political leaders not by being forceful or revolutionary but by presenting a great witness of women in powerful positions (Ilan 1999, 153).

Women in I Esdras are presented as having power even if it comes through their family relationships. I Esdras chapter 4 asks: "who is it then, that rules them, or has the mastery over them: is it not women?" I Esdras chapter 4 continues saying women give birth to kings and to all people, women raise boys to be men and women make the clothes men wear. A beautiful woman is preferred over even gold and silver. A man leaves his family to cling to his wife, living out his days with her, happy to give up mother, father and country. Of women verse 17 says "...they bring men glory; men cannot exist without women."

I Esdras goes on saying to men "...you must realize that women rule over you!" (4:22). When a man goes to war or labours he brings home the fruit to his wife. Wives are loved more than mothers and fathers. Men have died, sinned and stumbled on account of women. The king's relationship with the queen is similar. She is bold towards him and would even sit at his right hand, put on his crown and slap him. He wishes to please her (4:29-32).

Another example of women confronted by their need for power can be found in II Maccabees. When there was some concern over the money in the temple at Jerusalem, Simon who was "captain of the temple" (2 Macc 3:4) investigated the matter. The high priest said some deposits belonged to "widow and orphans..." (2 Maccabees 3:10). The money was to be confiscated for the king, for Simon said it might belong to him. The priests and people prostrated and prayed: "People also hurried out of their houses in crowds to make a general supplication because the holy place was about to be brought into dishonor" (2 Macc 3:18), and "...women girded with sackcloth under the breasts, thronged to the gates, and some to the walls, while others peered out of the window" (2 Macc 3:19). They all made "supplication" to heaven (2 Macc 3:1-21). Some women did hide in seclusion, but many responded to the crisis in a public manner. The concern for those who had given what little they had to the temple was paramount. Publicly women attempted to protect the powerless even though they too were numbered among them.

Thus as we have seen, women in ancient Jewish culture did have some limitations placed on them and yet still exhibited some power. They did not often rule in government, but did have a prominent and well-respected role in the royal courts, Jewish religion and social history. They seem to have held in tension both a sense of powerlessness and of power to make things happen and get their own way. These women may have been exceptions to the rule rather than reflective of the rest of society, or they might be example of a larger picture of Jewish women that is seldom painted. In order to further understand women's role in ancient Judaism we will need to explore the issue of public and private.

## Public and Private

Another significant cultural pattern is that of the public and private divide. Women in ancient Judaism were limited by such boundaries and their lives were shaped by them. Meiselman, writing from his own experience of the Jewish culture, suggests that public and private divides are necessary components of men and women's lives. He asserts that women are traditionally maintained in the private sphere while men are predominately focused on the public arena although they are able to cross the divide to the private (Meiselman 1978, 15).

Meiselman (1978, 2) suggests that while Abraham played a public role in the biblical narrative Sarah was a "private person." He emphasizes the importance of women's role in shaping the home within this private sphere (Meiselman 1978, 18). Swidler articulates a more modest divide with sharper differences occurring in the city than in the country. Women in the country would have to draw water from the well, work in the fields and poorer women would have to also earn money for the upkeep of the home (Swidler 1976, 118).

Archer, in *Women in Ancient Societies: An Illusion of the Night*, fails to address the public/private divide in her discussion of community. She suggests that girls did not enter into Jewish community as boys did through circumcision, but their acceptance in the covenant came through association with males and was passive (Archer 1994, 56). This view focuses on their dependence on their male kin, yet misses the point that women also functioned within their own sphere of influence. They had their own set of complex social relations and interactions that this research shows more clearly. They were not a part of the male "public" sphere, but they did have an active life within their own circles, more often called the "private" sphere.

Another work addressing public and private issues appeared in 1993 when Cohen edited *The Jewish Family in Antiquity*. Within this work, Peskowitz discusses the place of the family in Jewish life. She refuses to separate the family into public and private roles along gender lines and even challenges the idea of such lines, insisting such a divide is not as easily made in family life (Peskowitz 1993, 10). She looks at the concept of family in regard to differences in composition, economic standing, cultural needs for heirs and suggests that family was shaped by which member was defining it (Peskowitz 1993, 14-16, 20).

In support of her assertion that public and private spheres overlapped, Peskowitz (1993, 30) suggests work was performed in the home, thus blurring the divide. She further proposes that both men and women might work in the same trade (she cites Treggiari's work *Lower Class Women in the Roman Economy*). In Palestine she admits the evidence is limited to only one reference (Peskowitz 1993, 32). She relies on Roman and Greek data to talk about the Jewish family and, thus, does not adequately defend her argument.

Peskowitz suggests the idea of the public world as associated with men, law, politics and institutions is not all together accurate, nor is the private world held within the bounds of women and family. She suggests these ideas are formulated in our Western mindset (Peskowitz 1993, 25), and she has found evidence in inscriptions of men and women working side by side (Peskowitz 1993, 32). She views the Jewish family as a working unit that shared in its labours (Peskowitz 1993, 32, 34). Although she may take her point too far, and thus render it unlikely, it is probable that the family of antiquity was more nuanced than our "traditional" understanding of the Jewish family.

It is certainly likely that out of sheer necessity the lower classes of people had more overlap within men's and women's worlds. Ilan (1995, 132-133) seems to see the divide more clearly, citing the Apocrypha (Sir 42:11, 2 Macc 3:19, 3 Macc 1:18) and Josephus (*J.W.* 5.512) to support the view that women for the most part were kept in seclusion from the world outside their homes. The debate over the use of these terms and the reality of the existence of such divisions in the ancient world continues. However, for the purposes of this research they will continue to be referred to as public and private spheres and where possible there will be a nuancing of the traditional understanding.

As we have seen in the secondary sources, there is much discussion over the validity of these distinctions of public and private spheres. Some scholars clearly see a division while others suggest the divide was more blurred. The approach of this research is to suggest that these spheres existed for both women and men but they were not always as clear cut as has been assumed. Women's experience of them differed more greatly than men's experience. A better distinction, as has earlier been suggested in the model, is to divide these spheres into men's world and women's world, as each seemed to operate under a different set of rules. Yet, regardless of the terms used to describe them, it is undeniable that we see evidence of women moving in men's worlds when and where appropriate. We will now turn our attention to the primary evidence for the nuancing of these values.

## Public and Private in Josephus, Philo and Babatha's letters

In relation to these two worlds, public and private, we have found in the model that they more often distinguish women's world from men's world and are less about institutions and seclusion and more about who one talks to, interacts with and relates to while remaining modest and honorable. Jewish women were not as secluded or subdued as one might assume.

Josephus writes about how he was greeted in several cities by not only the men but also by the women and children. In Tiberias the men, believing their city would be destroyed, threw down their arms and "with their wives and children, implored me to spare it" (Josephus *Life* 329). In Galilee when his departure was announced, the men assembled with their wives and children to ensure no harm would come to their city (Josephus *Life* 207). When Titus entered the city of Gischala, the people, including wives and children, came out to greet him (*J.W.* 4.112-113). These women did not stay in complete seclusion, but were found out in public when it was necessary.

In *Questions and Answers on Genesis*, Philo writes that men are concerned about matters of the state while women are attentive to affairs of the home (Book 1.26). In *The Special Laws*, the different spaces where men function and women live are noted. Men are said to be suited for markets, courts, and public assemblies, while women are better suited for an indoor life. Philo suggests maidens may go so far as the middle door but those who have reached womanhood can advance to the outer door. He goes on to say that the lesser management of the world is considered household management which the wife governs. He suggests women should desire a life of seclusion (Philo *Spec. Laws* 3.31.169-170). If a woman should go to the temple (or other place of worship) she should do so as unobtrusively as possible. She should only go through the market when it is quiet and she will be unnoticed. Furthermore, she is considered shameless if she joined her husband in a dispute he is having (Philo *Spec. Laws* 3.31.170-172). It appears from these passages, whether exaggerated or closer to reality, that women's movements were restricted in some way. They were not as free to interact with the world as were men. Women moved within a world enclosed by boundaries dictated by their gender.

Yet, Babatha was a woman who did not keep to her private role as completely as one might expect. She held and sold property (5/6Hev 16 papRegistration of

Land, Lewis, JDS 2; 5/6Hev 21 papPurchase of a Date Crop, Lewis, JDS 2; 5/6Hev 22 papSale of a Date Crop, Lewis, JDS 2), argued and took to court her son's guardians (5/6 Hev 13-15, Lewis, JDS 2), and had disputes with her husband's first wife (5/6 Hev 26 papSummons and Reply, Lewis, JDS 2). Even though she did these things she did not act alone, but was always represented by a legal guardian (5/6 Hev 14 papSummons, Lewis, JDS 2) who was her husband until his death. She was able to voice her views in the public arena but in the end her son's male guardians still prevailed. Her influence was limited because of her gender, even though wealth and property seemed to be at her disposal (Lewis 1989, 24). She was, however, a wealthy woman and her wealth may have added to her additional freedoms. Yet within her archives we read of another exception—a woman we have already mentioned, Julia Crispina. At one point she filed a document independent of the other guardian saying he was ill and could not summon Babatha (5/6Hev 25 papSummons, Countersum, Lewis, JDS 2). She obviously moved more freely in public than most women. She is assigned to be the second guardian of Babatha's son Jesus (5/6Hev 20 papConcession of Rights, Lewis, JDS 2).

When it was appropriate, usually in times of great need, Jewish women were visible, not just to their kin and not just to women, but also to unrelated males in the community. Although it seems most Jewish women abided by the public and private divide, we have clear examples of women such as Babatha who did not fit such a profile. Jewish women certainly seem to have had no lack of involvement with and dedication to their families and to their religion.

## Women and Kinship Relationships

The model indicates that relationships were an important tool of social interaction between women. Women seemed to interact differently with other women than they did with men. Through relationships women were able to influence decisions, evoke limited power, maintain a link to the public sector, and function in their roles as daughter, sister, wife and mother.

Kraemer (1993, 89) acknowledges the sources are few, but the issue of mother-daughter relationships is important. She discusses Hebrew Bible examples, such as Naomi and Ruth, the narrator of Song of Songs and her mother, as well as important heroines whose mothers are not noted, including Deborah, Esther and Judith (Kraemer 1993, 90-91). Susanna's mother accompanies her to court, when her daughter is falsely accused, and Sarah's mother in Tobit helps to prepare her bridal chamber (Kraemer 1993, 91, 93). Kraemer notes that intimate relationships between women are often not the focus and are ignored in most biblical and early Jewish writings. She goes on to say that women are often portrayed with their servants such as in the book of Judith or with other female virgins/companions such as in the story of Seila in Pseudo-Philo's *Biblical Antiquities* (Kraemer 1993, 95). She points out that it is significant that Babatha's papers are found with her stepdaughters, suggesting perhaps a close tie between the two (Kraemer 1993, 100). In addition, Kraemer astutely mentions the New Testament examples of Herodias and her daughter Salome who plotted to have John the Baptist killed and the gentile woman in Matthew and Mark who begs Jesus to heal her demon-possessed daughter. She concludes that the lack of such examples of mother-daughter relationships suggests that they were not valued in the ancient world (Kraemer 1993, 101). It is not clear whether one would want to go so far as to suggest these relationships were unimportant, but lack of evidence is clearly a problem for the study of women in a variety of areas of antiquity.

Ilan (1995, 48) addresses women's relationships with their fathers, quoting from Ben Sira about the concerns a father has for his daughter. Yet more time is spent discussing "only daughters" or their "naming" than their actual relationships with their fathers (Ilan 1995, 50-56). Biale writes that marriage was a central component of the personal and communal life of Jewish culture. It functioned as a control over economics, procreation, sexual activity and social standing. It was a means of perpetuating a family line (Biale 1984, 68).

In discussing marriage, Archer relies heavily on rabbinical sources[12] (which this work does not address) to describe betrothal, bride price and bride meal. However, she does not focus necessarily on women's role within those activities (Archer 1990, 50, 166, 168). Drawing on the marriage contracts from Babatha's archive, Archer (1990, 171-175) points out that the documents have been written entirely from the man's point of view, and record his obligations and duties. The following research will address the important issues in marriage from a woman's point of view, how it impacted her, and how she was involved in the process both as a bride and a mother.

Regarding parenthood, Archer (1990, 17) rightly points out that male children were a precious commodity. Kraemer (1993, 108), in her discussion on women's relationships with their daughters, suggests that the relation to one's daughter was not as important, for the son was the one who would provide for his mother in old age and would function as her legal guardian once his father died. Biale (1984, 198) cites procreation as a primary element of Jewish family life and tradition. Family was an important component of Jewish life. The model contends that families were the heart of Jewish women's lives. Meiselman (1978, 16) writes that the Jewish woman was the "creator, molder, and guardian of the Jewish home."

Peskowitz (1993, 18) views the family as a cultural concept, with a set of values and relationships. She goes on to suggest the family was not as female-dominated as others have portrayed it, that men also had an active role in it (Peskowitz 1993, 27). Although her point concerning Western patriarchal thinking is valid, it is also undeniable that women were key players in the Jewish home of antiquity. In contrast, Ilan (1995, 122) supports the view that women played a submissive role in the family. She acknowledges women as needing a guardian as in the well-documented case of Babatha (Ilan 1995, 173). Women were thus secluded and submissive, yet critical to the functioning of the family.

In this review of the literature the secondary sources seem to agree that family, marriage and kin relationships were key components of Jewish life. Women's lives were inexplicably intertwined with the lives of their family members.

*Women and kin relationships in primary sources*
*Marriage and women's relationships with their husbands*

In Philo we read about the importance of Genesis and the creation of the male-female relationship. Philo says, "It is not good that any man (ἄνθρωπον-person) should be alone" (*Alleg. Interp.* 2.4, Colson and Whitaker). Philo reminds us of Genesis 2:24 where it says that the two shall become one flesh. Philo also states that the second person is associated with a helper, and this helper was created: "'let us make a helper for him'" (Philo *Alleg. Interp.* 2.5, Colson and Whitaker). Woman, it seems in Jewish thought, was interpreted to be an appendage of her husband and an important but lesser element of his life.

Philo notes the care of women who were not otherwise protected by male kin and who did not have a dowry already provided for them. He writes, "The charge of protecting the girls left thus desolate and superintending their development, and the expenses of providing anything required for their maintenance and education as befits maidens should fall upon the head magistrate." Suitable marriages should also be arranged for them considering, if possible, men of their kin's group (Philo *Spec. Laws* 2.125-126).

Philo also notes in *Hypothetica* that an Essene does not take a wife. He describes why the Essene remains single by writing that a wife is selfish, jealous, manipulative and seductive. When children arrive a wife has even less shame and boldly compels her husband to act as she desires. Philo says this man is altered and "has passed from freedom into slavery" (*Hypothetica* 11.14-17, Colson). Alternatively in his *Questions and Answers on Genesis* 1.29, the woman at creation was said to have taken the role of servant and was to be obedient to her husband. Women were thus expected to be submissive to their husbands and primarily concerned about meeting their husbands' needs. Women who were widowed and orphaned children were provided for through the tithes every third year of which one third was to be devoted to their needs (Josephus *Ant.* 4.240). Thus it was honorable to care for the needs of women. Kin were usually responsible to marry their women and provide for their needs. Yet if kin were not available, the community took on that role.

In *Against Apion* Josephus considers marriage laws. We learn that the only acceptable sexual relation is between a husband and wife and only for the purpose of procreation. In the choosing of a wife, men are not to be guided by a woman's dowry nor are they to take her by force. We are told that the woman is, according to the law, inferior to her husband in everything. Thus, she is to submit to him because, according to Josephus, God has ordained it to be this way. A husband is to remain faithful to his wife, and he will suffer the consequences of the law if he is otherwise (*Ag. Ap.* 2.199-201).

In the Archives of Babatha we learn that eleven days after Shelamzion was given in marriage she was named as heir to all of her father's property, to be received half immediately and the other upon his death (5/6 Hev 19, papDeed of Gift, Lewis, JDS 2). Women were well provided for at the time of marriage. It was perhaps the most important event in a woman's life. There has been some question as to whether Babatha was one of two wives thus making her dead husband a polygamist. Lewis (1989, 22-23) suggests that Babatha may have been forced to enter this polygamous marriage because that was the best she could do as a widow. Katzoff (1995, 128), however, does not agree and instead raises the possibility of serial monogamy. He cites a dispute between Miriam and Babatha over the property of their deceased husband Judah in 131 C.E. Katzoff suggests Miriam may have held on to property she was not entitled to after her divorce from Judah, and Babatha was claiming it now as part of what her deceased husband left her. In the end Katzoff is careful not to commit himself to either polygamy or monogamy in this case. Rather, he argues the Babatha document cannot unequivocally support polygamy when there are other plausible explanations for the relationship between Miriam and Babatha (Katzoff 1995, 131).

We read of a husband's legal relationship to his wife as we witness Babatha's husband as her legal guardian. Her own transactional guardian is called Judah, son of Khthousion, who is assumed to be her husband. Husbands would normally act in this role as guardian in legal transactions and documents (5/6Hev 15 papDeposition, Lewis, JDS 2). Women were not legally independent, they depended on their husbands to represent their interests, and ultimately men controlled the better part of women's lives.

## Women and kin relationships in the Apocrypha
### Marriage customs amongst kin

It was important in ancient Jewish culture to find one's bride among kin. Tobit told his son Tobias to "marry a woman from among the descendants of your ancestors" (Tob 4:12). He was not to marry a foreign woman from outside of Tobit's tribe (Tob 4:12-13). Tobias was led by the angel Raphael to the house of Raguel, when he met his daughter Sarah. He was told that he was the closest relative and should thus marry the woman. Raguel had no son and thus no heir and so Tobias could have claim on her and all her father's possessions. Tobias was described as having a right and an entitlement to marry Sarah. Raguel could face death under "the decree of the law of Moses" (Tob 7:13) if he refused. Tobias was worried because of her seven dead husbands supposedly killed by a demon in the bridal chamber. Raphael told him that he should not be afraid, "for she was set apart for you before the world was made" (Tob 6:18). Raguel gave his daughter in marriage to Tobias and "wrote out a copy of a marriage contract, to the effect that he gave her to him as wife" (Tob 7:13).

Tobias prayed to God saying, "You made Adam, and for him you made his wife Eve as a helper and support...you said, 'It is not good that the man should be alone; let us make a helper for him like himself'" (Tobit 8:6). Raguel said to Tobias, "...Take courage, my child. I am your father and Edna is your mother, and we belong to you as well as to your wife now and forever. Take courage, my child" (Tob 8:21). The family of the wife becomes as family to the husband, and vice versa. The ancient Jewish family appears to function in close and extended units as does the rest of the Mediterranean. Bow and Nickelsburg suggest that the Book of Tobit presents traditional gender roles where women operate in the domestic realm. Anna does go into the public world to work only because her husband is unable to work.

Anna also expresses her opinions and has conflicts with her husband while the other women do not initiate conflict. The males mostly deal with public matters of law, economics and ritual duties. They also take a large part in the religious life of the family (Bow and Nickelsburg 1991, 143).

In Sirach we read about wives that are valuable: "A silent wife is a gift from the Lord, and no thing is so precious as her self-discipline" (26:14); and "A modest wife adds charm to charm, and no scales can weigh the value of her chastity" (26:15). Sirach says there is beauty in a wife who keeps her home in good order (26:16). A good wife doubles the number of a man's days, and a loyal wife brings joy and peace to her husband. Sirach sums up his view of a good wife calling her "a great blessing" in 25:3.

Yet Sirach also describes the evil wife as bringing a "dejected mind, gloomy face and wounded heart" (25:23) to her husband. An "evil wife" should not be allowed "boldness of speech" (25:25). "Heartache and sorrow" (26:6) result from a wife who is jealous of a rival. Sirach calls a bad wife a yoke and compares her to a scorpion (26:7). He suggests a drunken wife is shameful (26:8).

Thankfully, Ben Sira does not represent all the views of Jewish wives. Certainly women were regarded with caution, as the model suggests, and they had real power to bring shame upon a family. Yet the marriage relationship was important to Jewish women and their role in it was more often than not one of esteem. Nevertheless, women were always in relationship to someone, they could not act independently. They were specifically affected by their relationships to their fathers, brothers and, later in life, their husbands. In order to survive, women needed to know how to control and order their relationships. Women were not simply guided by their relationships with their husbands and other male kin, but they were also impacted by their parental responsibilities.

*Parenthood*

The parental relationship was significant in ancient Israel. Both fathers and mothers were to be honored. Recognition is given to the woman for her part in raising the children: "Equality too divided the human being into man and woman, two sections unequal indeed in strength but quite equal as regards what was nature's urgent purpose, the reproduction of themselves in a third person" (Philo *Heir* 33.164, Colson and Whitaker). We also read in Philo of a view that seems to oppose this equality. According to Philo the sons of concubines had a lower parentage, which is traced through their mother and not by their father which would imply a higher pedigree (*Unchangeableness* 25.121). Women in some ways were not important in the tracing of ancestry, but at the same time Philo acknowledged God's plan to include both of them in reproduction.

We read about parenthood in Babatha's archive. Several documents cite the legal dealings of her young son Jesus. In "Extract from Council Minutes" Jesus has two guardians appointed (5/6Hev 12 papExtract from Council Minutes, Lewis, JDS 2). A "Petition to the Governor" from 124 C.E. petitions the provincial governor detailing her late husband's financial worth. Babatha was concerned because the two guardians appointed over four months prior had not given her enough funds and she asked the governor to force them to give her more from the estate for her son's benefit (5/6Hev 13 papPetition to the Governor, Lewis, JDS 2). She fought for the protection of her son's rights and for his maintenance.

One of the guardians was summoned to court in "Summons" (5/6Hev 14 papSummons, Lewis, JDS 2), and the complaint against the guardians is further detailed in another deposition (5/6Hev 15 papDeposition, Lewis, JDS 2). Babatha this time complained they had invested her son's money but are not turning all the profit over to him. Babatha wished to have control over her son's assets, and she said she will increase them. We read of a later document dated 19 August 132 concerning a receipt showing the amount had not changed (5/6 Hev 27 papReceipt, Lewis, JDS 2). Throughout Babatha's appeals process we see the strength of her concern for her son's well-being. We also see how tied into his inheritance she is, as we can assume she was receiving no maintenance for her own living, as her son was the heir of her husband's wealth. Babatha is an example of a woman who was exceptional in having some access to wealth. Yet her life was intertwined with the male kin who represented her and her wishes.

In the Apocrypha we also read about parental relationships. An important person in a woman's life was her father. In Sirach 42 we read that a daughter causes her father anxiety and loss of sleep. He fears she will not marry or that she will be violated or seduced while still in her father's house. We read, "a daughter is a secret anxiety to her father" (42: 9, 10). Other fears include her being married but barren. A father is warned to "keep strict watch" over a daughter who is "headstrong" because she has the potential of making one a "laughingstock to your enemies...and put you to shame in public gatherings" (42:10, 11).

The father is warned that his daughter should not flaunt her beauty or spend time with married women (Sirach 42:12). For the conclusion is drawn that wickedness comes from women: "Better is the wickedness of a man than a woman who does good; it is a woman who brings shame and disgrace" (42:14).

Fathers in the ancient world had the responsibility of ensuring a dowry for their daughters. They would want her to remain a virgin so that no dishonor might come upon their families. Women certainly had to depend on their fathers and the other male kin in their lives to ensure the maintenance of proper shame. Ancient Jewish women clearly valued their kin relationships, in fact, the quality of such relationships determined their basic survival.

## Women and Religion

Another area the model highlights for us is religion. The active role of women in religion appears to be a characteristic of the Mediterranean world. Yet it cannot be said that all religious involvement looks or sounds the same. Women's religious roles certainly varied from those of men, nevertheless they are noteworthy.

Brooten's work *Inscriptional Evidence for Women as Leaders in the Ancient Synagogue* broke new ground when published in 1982. Her study focuses on the possibility that women were active in the leadership of the synagogue beyond simply holding honorific titles. She looks at inscriptions from 27 B.C.E. through the sixth century C.E. not limiting her search to Palestine, but also covering Italy,

Greece, Thrace, Asia Minor, Egypt and Libya. She analyzes the titles of "elder", "leader", "president of the synagogue", "mother of the synagogue" and "priestess" (Brooten 1982, ii). She has uncovered a wealth of information supporting women's active involvement in the synagogue and questions the traditional view that Jewish women were passive and uninvolved in religion. Throughout her work on women in the synagogue, Brooten (1982, 5, 11-12) clearly addresses the issue of women's involvement in the Jewish faith.

Although her work suggests women had a greater role in religion than previously believed, it must be recognized that Brooten covers a larger range than this thesis, including evidence from seven centuries and a more geographically diverse region (1982, 1). Her work highlights the involvement of women in religion, yet is too specific and hypothetical to determine whether any of these roles were held by women and if they were more than honorific. If women were indeed presidents of synagogues we have no bases for understanding how their roles would have been enacted and how they might have differed from those of men. While Brooten's work is significant, it does not provide enough correlation with the intent of this thesis to warrant deeper exploration. Brooten is reconstructing history while this thesis is considering values and social patterns and is working with different material.

Ilan looks at women who took an active role in religion citing how several wealthy women were known to have taken the Nazarite vow.[13] She also suggests that women may have been responsible for the circumcision of their sons (1 Macc :60-61; 2 Macc 6:10; 4 Macc 4:25) (Ilan 1995, 181-182). As it was their sphere of influence, it is likely that women performed religious duties in the home.

Several other authors such as Bird and Archer consider the topic of Jewish women and religion, however, they explore much earlier time periods than we are considering, and, thus, their research will not be addressed here.[14] However, it is important to note they identify women as key components of religious rituals, and in particular they distinguish women who were more active during the time of goddess worship.

The model we have been building from social anthropology and ancient sources suggests that women had a role to play in the religions of their time. Greek and Roman women worshipped many gods and goddesses, but it is not clear how much this phenomenon influenced Jewish women. During the first century the Jews worshipped one God—Yahweh. As worship became more monolithic and moved away from pagan gods and goddesses that still existed during Hebrew Bible times, were women excluded from certain acts of worship? It is uncertain what role emerged for them within the worship of Yahweh.

As we can see, the secondary sources express a diversity of voices on the issue of women and religion. Jewish women did seem to have an active role in their society's religious practices, even if that role was limited to home-based celebrations. As we will find, this central point of focus for women perhaps influenced their role in the New Testament church.

## Women and Religion in Philo and Josephus

In Greek culture there is evidence that women were involved in the religions of their society, and we will find the same is true of Jewish women.

Philo tells us that after the miraculous Red Sea crossing the Hebrews set up two choirs, one of men and one of women right there on the beach. Moses and Miriam presided over the choirs as they praised God: "they led hymns, the former for the men and the latter for the women" (Philo *Moses* 1.32.180, 2.46.256, Colson, as reflective of Exod 15:20-21). We also see a great woman of God in Esther. Even though in the biblical account God is not specifically mentioned, in Josephus' retelling Esther is said to have supplicated God on behalf of her nation, praying and begging him to have mercy (*Ant.* 9.231-232).

Women were also willing to make the ultimate sacrifice for the God they loved. Josephus details how the Jews did not want their Roman overseers to place images of God or man in any part of the country. Petronius was sent to carry out this action asking the Jews if they were willing to go to war with Caesar over the issue. The Jews responded by saying if the emperor wished to set up these statues, he must first sacrifice the entire Jewish nation, "...and they presented themselves, their wives and their children ready for the slaughter" (*J.W.* 2.195-197).

Women were obviously important to the Jews in their proselytising and missionary efforts. Josephus recounts the conversion of Queen Helena of Adiabene (*Ant.* 20.17ff). A Jewish merchant called Ananias went to the king's wives "and taught them to worship God after the manner of Jewish tradition" (*Ant.* 20.34, Feldman). Helena's son Izates was "won over with the co-operation of the women" (Josephus *Ant.* 20.34-35, Feldman). Helena had received instruction by another Jew and was converted (Josephus *Ant.* 20.35-36). Later Queen Helena gave God credit for her son's success. She wanted to go to Jerusalem to worship and make a thank offering, and the journey was made with her son's blessing (Josephus *Ant.* 20.49-50). We read of Izates praying and fasting (with his wife and children) to be delivered from the Parthians (*Ant.* 20:89).

Bernice, the sister of King Agrippa, was another royal woman who was religious. She had visited Jerusalem "to discharge a vow to God" (εὐχὴν ἐκτελοῦσα τῷ θεῷ) (Josephus *J.W.* 2.313, Thackeray). Josephus tells us that those who suffered from illness or affliction traditionally made a vow to abstain from wine and shave their heads for thirty days before they offered sacrifices. Bernice was said to have undergone these rites (Josephus *J.W.* 2.313, 314).

Ilan writes about powerful Jewish women's attraction to the Pharisees. She discusses Queen Shelamzion and how she allowed the Pharisees to influence her governing perhaps because this very movement was opposed to her late husband's policies (1999, 23). We have already read of Queen Helena's conversion to Judaism. Helena is remembered in rabbinic literature and Ilan suggests this would not be so unless she had converted to pharisaism (1999, 25, 26). Ilan further postulates that wealthy women supported the Pharisee's movement because their patronage was accepted and, while the movement was not overwhelmingly supportive of women, it did not introduce negative rules against women until after the Pharisees gained more power after the Temple was destroyed (1999, 37). Later, in a further discussion of the position of women in Judaism, Ilan suggests that as rabbinic literature was formed into the canon, the position of women was continually reduced as the prevailing ideas won out (1999, 81).

*Worship at the Temple and Synagogues*

Josephus relates how in the Temple the sons of Eli "dishonored the women who came for worship" (*Ant.* 5.338-339, Thackeray and Marcus). Thus, we know that women may have gone to worship even at the risk of their own personal safety. We also read of their devotion in coming to worship learning that in a certain quarter of their temple courts "a special place of worship was walled off for the women..." (Josephus *J.W.* 5.198, Thackeray). In Josephus' description of the Temple we learn there were four courts. The outer one was open to men, women and foreigners. However, when women were considered unclean and in an impure state, they were not allowed to enter. In the second court Jewish men and their wives could enter, but women could not be unclean at any time. The third court was open to Jewish men only. The fourth court was open only to priests in their vestments. The sanctuary was only entered by high priests in their religious attire (Josephus *Ag. Ap.* 2.103-105).

In regard to the Temple, women could bring sacrifices to the outer court. They could bring their offering to the gate of the Levites and could participate in worship through hearing the blessings and songs of the Levites. They might have also been able to see the sacrifices due to a balcony in the court or a low wall they could see over (Sanders 1992, 57). When women brought sacrifices they communicated the meaning of it to the Levite or priest. Due to the location of the courts and when the laying on of hands took place, Sanders doubts that women would have put their hands on the sacrifice and confessed (1992, 109).

In *Jewish War* there are additional references to women's relationship to the Temple. Women were restricted in their entrance to the temple, but so were foreigners and those in an unclean state. Women worshipped in a separate walled-off area (Josephus *J.W.* 5.198). There was a separate gate that led to the women's court. There were fifteen steps up to the "women's apartment" (Josephus *J.W.* 5.204-206). This court was open to Jewish women of the Diaspora or of Palestine (Josephus *J.W.* 5.199-200). During the feasts people made pilgrimages to the Temple from everywhere (Philo *Spec. Laws* 1.69). Surely women were among their number. Thus, there was provision for women to bring sacrifices, make pilgrimages and experience worship. They were limited in their access, but not prohibited in participating in their religion.

Lee Levine tells us that by the mid-first century the synagogue had become a central meeting place for the Jewish community. It was the place of prayer services on the Sabbath and religious holy days. It was probably not until after the destruction of the Temple in 70 C.E. that it became a place of regular communal prayer (L. Levine 1982, 3).

Lee Levine also tells us that sacred meals took place in the synagogue on the Sabbath and holidays. We might assume that women had a part in preparing these meals (L. Levine 1982, 3). Ilan, using rabbinic sources and the Apocalypse of Baruch (T. Sheqalim 2:6), suggests women were the weavers of the Temple curtain. She further suggests this is an allusion to women weaving the curtain used in the desert sanctuary in Exodus 35:26. Ilan feels the role of women weavers was gradually eliminated out of the Mishnah (Ilan 1997, 139-141).

We know from Brooten's work that women's names were found on inscriptions as heads of synagogues, mothers of synagogues, elders and patrons, therefore, they must have attended and perhaps participated in worship. Brooten suggests women and men were not segregated in the synagogue (1982, 119). We cannot be sure they were separated from men, but even if they were, it is significant they attended at all.

We also read of women who joined the Therapeutae sect. Women were said to attend worship with passion and a sense of calling. They met along with men on the seventh day. Women and men were partitioned when they worshipped. The wall was not so high that it prevented women to hear the speaker, yet Philo notes that the division protected the modesty of the women (*Contemp. Life* 32-33).

We can see how women were active in Judaism in the Temple and synagogue worship even though they were limited in the ways they could participate. Jewish women clearly bypassed the barriers and worshipped Yahweh in their homes, synagogues and at the Temple. There are further examples of their devotion recorded in the Apocrypha.

## *Women and Religion in the Apocrypha*

An example of a woman concerned for the faith of her people can be found again in the story of Judith. At the beginning of the book the Israelites were in fear of Holofernes, general of Nebuchadnezzar, king of the Assyrians, they all, including wives, children, cattle, resident aliens, hired labourers and purchased slaves put on sackcloth. The women, men and children put ashes on their heads and prayed to God for help. They also fasted and the Lord heard their prayers (Jdt 4). Judith was said to fear God "with great devotion" (Jdt 8:8). When asked to pray for the people Judith put ashes on her head and "prostrated herself" (Jdt 9:1). Judith credited her success to the faith that she shared with the people.

We read of the priests and the women protesting Ptolemy's insistence on visiting the holy of holies of the Temple in 3 Maccabees: "Young women who had been secluded in their chambers rushed out with their mothers, sprinkled their hair with dust, and filled the streets with groans and lamentations. Those women who had recently been arrayed for marriage abandoned the bridal chambers prepared for wedded union, and neglecting proper modesty, in a disorderly rush flocked together in the city" (1:18-19). Mothers and nurses left their children behind and "crowded together at the most high temple" (3 Macc 1:20). The women were not slow to respond when there was a religious crisis. They considered it more important than their modesty or future marital arrangements.

There was a time when the Jews were told to adapt Greek customs. In response two women were brought in for having circumcised their children. The women with their children were publicly paraded and then killed (2 Macc 6:7-10). Women were not afraid of taking a stand for their faith.

A courageous mother with seven sons who were killed because of their faith also died for her beliefs (2 Macc 7). She was called "especially admirable and worthy of honorable memory," and she was said to bear her burdens with "good courage" (2 Macc 7:20). She trained her sons in the faith and when it came time for them to take a stand she was said to be "...filled with a noble spirit, she reinforced her woman's reasoning with a man's courage..." (2 Macc 7:21). She was a woman of noteworthy significance in Jewish tradition. Jewish women had a legacy of rich faith that they upheld with their words and deeds. The same story is further expanded upon in 4 Maccabees 13-18. She is called "...mother of the nation, vindicator of the law...", and she is said to be more noble and more courageous than men in her endurance (4 Macc 15:29, 30). It was written that she did not wail and lament at her losses like one might expect. Instead she urged her sons to die for their religion (4 Macc 16:5-13). After we read in chapter 17 of her own death by throwing herself into the fire rather than letting someone else do it, there is a song about her courage, piety and faith (4 Macc 17:1-5). 4 Maccabees chapter 18 goes on to tell us about the virtues of this mother with the seven sons. She was a virgin and did not leave her home. She was not defiled or made impure in any way. She tells of her husband's commitment to the faith. The mother and her sons are said to have immortality (4 Macc 18:6-24).

One must consider how strong a women's devotion was to rise above such obstacles. The picture of the Jewish woman being on one hand banned from certain religious activities and places while on the other being so fervent in devotion reminds us of women in the early Christian church and the obstacles they also overcame. Jewish women were clearly not mere passive participants in their religion. They may have entered the faith passively but they certainly had an important role to play despite the limits imposed on them. We will look for just a brief time at issues of clean and unclean, which certainly interplay with women's roles in their society and in religion.

*Clean and Unclean*

Issues of clean and unclean were very important to the Jewish people and they had a profound effect on its women. In this section we will refer to Hebrew Bible passages that address such issues as they lay the foundation for the understanding of these laws in the Second Temple Period. Many laws restricted women's movements during times when women were considered impure: "If a woman conceives and bears a male child, she shall be ceremonially unclean seven days; as at the time of her menstruation, she shall be unclean" (Lev 12:2). A time of "blood purification" lasted 33 days during which she was not allowed to come in contact with any holy thing or to go into the sanctuary. If she bore a female child she was unclean for 14 days and her time of blood purification was 66 days (Lev 12:2-5).

After this time of purification a woman brought to the tent of meeting a lamb less than a year old as a burnt offering and a pigeon or dove as a sin offering. The priest presented these offerings to the Lord on behalf of the woman, and afterwards she was "clean from her flow of blood" (Lev 12:7). This ceremony took place whether the child was male or female. If the woman was poor and could not afford the sheep she could bring two pigeons or two doves, one for each sacrifice (Lev 12:8).

Leviticus 15 catalogues more purity laws. When a woman was unclean because of a "discharge of blood" that was regular to her, she was considered impure for seven days. Anyone she touched, everything she sat on or laid down on was also unclean. If someone touched her bed they had to wash their clothes, bathe with water and still they were unclean until evening. If a person touched anything she had contact with that one also became unclean. This cleanliness issue was also extended to her sexual relationships: "If any man lies with her, and her impurity falls on him, he shall be unclean seven days, and every herd on which he sees shall be unclean" (Lev 15:24).

There were also many laws having to do with nakedness, propriety and purity: "None of you shall approach anyone near of kin to uncover nakedness…" (Lev 18:6). This law included all women in a family group. A woman could not be "uncovered" during her time of uncleanness due to her menstruation (Lev 18:19). Leviticus 19:29 says, "Do not profane your daughter by making her a prostitute." Sexual purity was to be protected at all costs.

The purity laws also addressed relations between neighbours and between family members. If a person committed adultery with a neighbour, both the man and the woman would be put to death. Likewise, if a man had sexual relations with his father's wife or his daughter-in-law he would also be put to death (Lev 20:10-12).

Josephus records the Levitical purity laws. After giving birth to a boy, women were "forbidden…to enter the temple or touch the sacrifices" for at least 40 days. This time period was doubled if she bore a girl (*Ant.* 3.269). Intercourse with a menstruating woman was also forbidden by Moses (*Ant.* 3.275). In the same way, intercourse with a pregnant woman was also considered unclean. Certain acts of purification were required in such instances (*Ag. Ap.* 2.202-203). Philo highlights Leviticus 18:19 and the issue of impurity during a woman's menstruation. Philo notes that a man must not touch a woman during this time and must refrain from intimacy with her (*Spec. Laws* 3.6.32).

The priests needed to abide by even stricter purity laws. They were not allowed to wed a harlot (τὰς ἡταιρηκυίας), a slave, a prisoner of war, or women who "gain their livelihood by hawking or inn keeping or who have for whatsoever reason been separated from their former husbands" (Josephus *Ant.* 3.276-277).

By the second temple period ritual baths became important for women after menstruation and after childbirth for purification. Both men and women bathed when they were considered impure (Sanders 1992, 220, 221). Pools of immersion were found in remote areas away from the Temple. Thus, it can be surmised that immersion began to be a practice as part of the purity laws not just when one went to the Temple (Sanders 1992, 228).

Sanders raises the important question concerning how strictly these impurity laws be kept. When a woman was menstruating, could she cook meals if she had to avoid contact with others? Where would she sleep during that time? How would houses that had such limited space be kept from impurity (Sanders 1990, 150)? Thus, we might conclude that while these purity laws existed they could not realistically be followed. In reality women probably had more freedom than the ancient sources would lead us to believe. Sanders suggests just this that purity was an ideal. Separation during times of purity was not practical given the size of homes and the necessities of ancient life (Sanders 1990, 161).

Niditch discusses the purity laws as well and raised a different issue. Does the fact that women are dangerous during their considered polluted times (monthly menstruation and after childbirth) make them more or less powerful in the religious realms? They were considered barred from worship at the Temple during these times—so if they disregarded this injunction what kind of havoc did the priest perceive them bringing? In developing these laws were the priests seeking to hold power over women by barring their participation in the daily activities (Niditch 1998, 30, 31)? Such questions raise issues of the inadvertent power women did hold and the dual significance of these purity laws. In some ways the laws prevented women from entering into daily life and worship, yet in other ways they afforded them a dangerous tool to wield if they should seek to endanger the purity of others.

Clearly, women were impacted by the purity laws of their culture. Their religion's involvement in the cult was limited by the state of their purity at any given time. Their devotion to God could not be limited by their outward purity of rituals. Even these barriers were not able to prevent Jewish women's active participation in their religion.

## Death

Death highlights another rite of passage in which women were active. The model seems to indicate that women participated in the preparation and grieving process.

*Death Rituals as Found in Josephus*

Death is the final stage of the life cycle where women play a prominent role. We read of their role in mourning the dead in Josephus who recounts the biblical story of a woman coming to David in "mourner's garb" because of the death of her son (Josephus *Ant.* 7.182). Josephus also tells us from Deuteronomy 21:10-13 that if a married woman or a virgin is taken as a prisoner she cannot be married again until she is permitted time to mourn "...until such time as, with shorn hair and in mourning apparel, she shall have made lamentation for the kinsman and friends whom she has lost in the battle, in order that she may satisfy her grief for them before turning to the festivities and ceremonies of marriage." This time of mourning was set at thirty days (Josephus *Ant.* 4.257-259).

The story of Elijah and the widow offers an example of women's self-mutilation during a time of mourning. Sometime after the widow had trusted Elijah and provided food for him, her son became ill and seemed to be dead: "She wept bitterly, injuring herself with her hands and uttering such cries as her grief prompted" (Josephus *Ant.* 8.325-326, Thackeray).

There does not appear to be much primary material evidence within the time confines of these sources. However, one only has to look to the New Testament and gospel accounts[15] of the women preparing Jesus' body for burial and following behind the cross wailing to be assured that such rituals did continue. Although we are not focusing on these texts it seems they fill an important gap in this section and are worthy of mention.

# Conclusion

Women in ancient Judaism clearly embodied the values of the Mediterranean which were also found in Greece and, as we will soon see, Rome. We have many examples of strong and powerful Jewish women in their history, however, they appear to also be secluded and controlled by their male kin. Jewish women made their mark on religion and the family as did women in other cultures. We need to keep in mind that much of our information has focused on wealthy women and therefore may not be representative of the culture as a whole.

Jewish women held many different roles in tension. They had honor when they represented the family and kept their shame, and dishonor when they lost their shame. They were both virtuous and vile. They performed important tasks such as supervising the household, caring for the family, raising the children and keeping religious devotion, and yet they were also viewed as under their husbands' control and objects to be sold into slavery or gained as "booty" in war. They were thus powerful and at the same time powerless.

Perhaps as we begin to understand this dichotomy of the respect and subjection they experienced we will better understand how women's role in the early Christian church vacillated. We shall hopefully see these questions more adequately answered as we begin to ask them of biblical texts in the coming chapters. After a brief look at marriage contracts in the appendix to this chapter, we will then consider Roman women in their ancient Mediterranean context in chapter five.

## Ch. 4 Appendix

*Marriage Contracts*

In this appendix we will review first-century C.E. marriage contracts found in Babatha's and Salome's archives. This information confirms that women in the first century did receive some inheritance and basic needs protections under the provisions of these contracts. They will be compared to marriage contracts found in Elephantine in the 5th century B.C.E. as a point of reference only. It is clear that the Elephantine documents are too far removed in terms of time and location to be of use in the building of our model. However, the documents from the first century might help shed some additional light on our understanding of the relationships between kin particularly when it comes to the ritual of marriage.

A marriage contract found in Babatha's archive tells of the marriage between Judah and Shelamzion, daughter of Judah son of Eleazar Khthousion and his first wife. She has a dowry of 500 denarii, 200 from Judah her father and 300 from Judah the bridegroom. The contract states, "Judah...gave over Shelamzion, his very own daughter, a virgin, to Judah surnamed Cimber son of Ananias son of Somalas...for the partnership of marriage according to the laws, she bringing to him on account of bridal gift feminine adornment in silver and gold and clothing appraised by mutual agreement..." (5/6 Hev 18 papMarriage Contract, Lewis, JDS 2). We notice in this brief statement that it is made clear that the bride is a virgin and the father is the initiator of the contract.

The husband is required to feed and clothe "both her and the children to come" (5/6 Hev 18 papMarriage Contract, Lewis, JDS 2). He is responsible for the care of his wife and their children. The contract ensures provision for her physical existence. A woman was dependent first on her father and then on her husband for her well-being.

In the document entitled the "Deposit" found in Babatha's archive we read that Babatha has received back some of her wedding money: "...over and above seven hundred ten "blacks" of sliver which your mother has received as [repayment of] her wedding money, which she had [as a lien] against Jesus your father" (5/6 Hev 5 papDeposit, Lewis, JDS 2). Thus when he died she received her inheritance, which was her own dowry! Babatha was able to receive an inheritance and thus had some individual wealth. The amount of her inheritance however, equalled her dowry and appears to be no more.

Another marriage document records the marriage of Salome also known as Komaïs to Jesus son of Menahem. "Jesus...acknowledged...that he has taken Salome also called Komaïs...and for Jesus to live with her as also before this time...to the said Komaïs as her dowry ninety-six denarii of silver." The bridegroom also acknowledged the receipt of "feminine adornment in silver and gold and clothing and other feminine articles equivalent in appraised value to the [state sum of] money...". He agreed to undertake the "feeding and clothing both her and the children..." (5/6 Hev 37 papMarriage Contract, Lewis, JDS 2). Again the dowry is the focus of the contract and the bride's future care in her husband's house. Women were viewed perhaps as commodities assigned different amounts of value, dependent on their family's wealth.

A similar pattern is seen in a marriage contract for Selanipious. A dowry is mentioned and 100 denarii given to the groom. The need to feed and clothe the bride and children to come is mentioned. 500 denarii are received from the bride and given to the groom (XHev/Se 69 papCancelled Marriage Contract, Cotton, DJD 27).

In crossing the centuries, marriage contracts did not significantly change. If we go back to the time of the Elephantine documents we see similar patterns in the rituals of marriage. A "Document of Wifehood" from 449 B.C.E. begins with "I [c]ame to your house (and asked you) to give me your daughter Mipta(h)iah for wifehood" (Porten, et al: *Document of Wifehood*, B28 TAD B2.6 Cowley 15 [Sayce-Cowley G], v. 3). The bridegroom gave the father five shekels of silver as a *mohar*, or gift, at the betrothal. The daughter came with two shekels, wool, a shawl, another garment, a mirror, a bronze bowl, two bronze cups and one bronze jug. Her possessions were given monetary value. Six other items—a bed, a tray, two ladles, palm-leaf castor oil and a pair of sandals—were not assigned a value (*Document of Wifehood*, B28, vv. 14-16). The monetary and goods transaction of marriage were an important legal and social component. Once again we see the importance of the dowry that we see centuries later in first-century contracts.

If the husband were to die and was without children, Miptahiah had the "right to the house...", and "[hi]s goods and his property and all that he has on the face of the earth..."(*Document of Wifehood* B28, v. 18, 19). The wife was able to inherit her husband's wealth if there were no children. If Miptahiah died without children her husband Eshor was to inherit all "...her goods and her property" (*Document of Wifehood* B28, vv. 21, 22). Thus the same was true for the husband in the event of the wife's death. Just as Babatha was provided for in her husband's death so was this 5th century B.C.E. bride.

If she wished to divorce her husband she had to give Eshor seven shekels and two quarters and she was to take away what she had brought. She was to "go away wherever she desires, without suit or without process" (*Document of Wifehood* B28, vv. 23-26). If Eshor wished to divorce his wife, "her *mohar* [will be] lost" (*Document of Wifehood* B28, v. 27). It seems divorce was also permitted, although we must recognize these documents came from Egypt and may not reflect Israelite society accurately even though they were based on Jewish Diaspora culture and families. These provisions were not made in the first-century documents.

She would be given twenty *karsh* of silver if she was expelled from his house (*Document of Wifehood* B28, vv. 30, 31). In verse 32 we also learn that Eshor had not been married previously and had no children. If he was found to have children and a wife then the bride was to be paid twenty karsh in silver. Thus in this marriage contract we learn that Miptahiah had some of her own resources which remained hers beyond the bounds of the marriage. She also was protected in the case of divorce and in the instance of Eshor having another wife. We know that Babatha had some of her own resources as well as evidenced in the receipt for palm groves in her documents and in the inheritance given her by her husband.

Another document of wifehood from 449 B.C.E. was found in the Ananiah Archive and is similar to the other marriage contract just described (Porten, et al: *Document of Wifehood*, B36 TAD B 3.3 Kraeling 2). The wording is similar, except this time the bridegroom is asking a handmaiden's master for the woman to be his wife. "She is my wife and I am her husband from this day and forever" (*Document of Wifehood* B36, vv. 3, 4) was a phrase also found in the other contract. What the woman brought into the marriage was her own and she did have the ability to ask for a divorce but could not go her own way because she was a slave. The language differs here from other documents of wifehood. She was also entitled to inherit his wealth which was gained during their marriage and the same was true for her husband if she should die, but this clause did not apply to wealth prior to their marriage (*Document of Wifehood* B36, vv. 3-14).

Throughout the different marriage contracts over the centuries all studied seem to indicate some transaction of wealth. There was a commitment for the husband to provide for his family. The arrangement of a marriage was clearly a legal and social transaction that involved the male kin and did not leave much of a voice for the bride, although she was protected in most cases by a dowry or some form of monetary settlement. In reference to the values of our model we see the importance of kin relationships upheld.

We see evidence that women had some power in their dowry but that power was very limited. We also glean that women were dependent upon the male kin in their lives to uphold their honor, attest to their virginity and provide for their needs. The values of honor and shame are clearly present in the first-century C.E. Jewish world and these contracts from Babatha's and Salome's archives provide us with another example of their existence.

# Notes

1. See Léonie J. Archer. *Her Price is Beyond Rubies: The Jewish Woman in Graeco-Roman Palestine* (Sheffield: Sheffield Academic Press, 1990); Bernadette J. Brooten. *Women Leaders in the Ancient Synagogue: Inscriptional Evidence and Background Issues* (Chico, Calif.: Scholars Press, 1982); and Ross S. Kraemer, "Jewish Mothers and Daughters in the Greco-Roman World," in *The Jewish Family in Antiquity* (ed. Shaye J.D. Cohen; Atlanta: Scholars Press, 1993).

2. For example, Josephus, *Ant.*; Philo, *Creation, Abraham*.

3. For more information on women in the Dead Sea Scrolls see Eileen Schuller, "Women in the Dead Sea Scrolls" in *The Dead Sea Scrolls After Fifty Years* (ed. Peter W. Flint and James C. VanderKam; Boston: Brill, 1999), 117-144; Eileen Schuller, "Women in the Dead Sea Scrolls" in *Methods of Investigation of the Dead Sea Scrolls and the Khirbet Qumran Site* (ed. Michael Wise et al; New York: New York Academy of Sciences: 1994), 115-131; Linda Bennett Elder, "The Women Question and Female Ascetics Among Essenes," BA 57 (1994): 220-234; and James Davila, "A Wedding Ceremony?" in *Liturgical Works: Eerdmans Commentaries on the Dead Sea Scrolls* (James Davila; Grand Rapids, Mich.: Eerdmans: 2000), 181-207.

4. See Cheryl Anne Brown, *No Longer Be Silent: First Century Jewish Portraits of Biblical Women* (Louisville: Westminster/John Knox Press, 1992); Richard Bauckham, "The Liber Antiquitatum Biblicarum of Pseudo-Philo and the Gospels as 'Midrash'" in *Gospel*

*Perspectives: Studies in Midrash and Historiography*, vol. 3 (ed. R.T. France and David Wenham; Sheffield: JSOT Press, 1983), 33-76; Betsy Halpern-Amaru, "Portraits of Women in Pseudo-Philo's Biblical Antiquities" in *"Women Like This": New Perspectives on Jewish Women in the Greco-Roman World* (ed. Amy-Jill Levine; Atlanta: Scholars Press, 1991), 83-106.

5. Philo also discusses Eve in *On the Creation* 55.156.

6. This dishonest behavior is again repeated in Abraham and Sarah's interaction with Abimelech (Josephus *Ant.* 1.207-209 and Gen 20).

7. Unless otherwise noted, all quotations from the Bible and Apocrypha are from the New Revised Standard Version.

8. To read more about Ben Sira's view of women, see Roger Tomes, "A Father's Anxieties" in *Women in Biblical Tradition* (ed. George J. Brooke; Lewiston, N.Y.: Edwin Mellen, 1992), 71-91; and Warren C. Trenchard, *Ben Sira's View of Women: A Literary Analysis* (Chico, Calif.: Scholars Press, 1982).

9. To read more about women in Pseudo-Philo, see Bauckham, *Liber Antiquitatum Biblicarum*; and Brown, *No Longer Be Silent* which compares Pseudo-Philo with Josephus to highlight the emphasis Pseudo-Philo places on women.

10. Other examples of brave women can be found in the account of the destruction of Gamala where many men along with their wives and children committed suicide rather than be captured by the Romans. No one escaped except for two women who were nieces of a commander-in-chief to King Agrippa (Josephus J.W. 4.79-83). These women were bravely the sole survivors yet others chose to commit suicide instead of being dishonored by the Romans. In the recording of the fall of Masada, Eleazar's speech to the people urges them to not allow their wives to die in dishonor and their children to go to slavery (Josephus J.W. 7.334-335).

11. For a detailed discussion of Julia Crispina and her possible connection with the royal family see Tal Ilan, "Julia Crispina, Daughter of Berenicianus, A Herodian Princess in the Babatha Archive: A Case Study in Historical Identification," JQR 82 (1992): 361-381.

12. Both Archer and Ilan make use of rabbinic material to support their understanding of Jewish women in the ancient world. This thesis does not include such a discussion because rabbinic material, while it sheds light on first-century society, is often removed by time and has weighty theological implications which need to be considered if it is to be correctly understood. Such a study is beyond the scope of this thesis.

13. In the second temple period Mariamme of Palmyra, Queen Helena and Queen Bernice were said to have made this vow (m. Ned. 6:11, m. Naz. 3:6, J.W. 2.313).

14. See Léonie J. Archer, "The Role of Jewish Women in the Religion, Ritual and Cult of Graeco-Roman Palestine" in *Images of Women in Antiquity* (ed. Averil Cameron and Amélie Kuhrt; London: Croom Helm, 1983), 273-287; see also Phyllis Bird, "Women's Religion in Ancient Israel" in *Women's Earliest Records: From Ancient Egypt and Western Asia* (ed. Barbara Lesko; Atlanta: Scholars Press, 1989).

15. Mark 16:1∥Luke 23:27; Luke 24:1.

# 5

# Women of Ancient Rome: Understanding Their Values and Behaviors

## Introduction

We now will spend some time considering ancient Roman women and will nuance our cultural context model, and specifically our understanding of Mediterranean women in Romans 16, in these sources. Much has been written on the status of women in ancient Roman society. Secondary works on women's relationships to their mothers, fathers and the culture around them abound. The intent of this work is to look within the primary evidence to discern what nuances exist in the Roman world that would impact the initial model we have developed. Thus, we will pay particular attention to the roles of honor and shame, women and power, public and private issues, family/kinship, and religion. We will seek to develop a fuller picture of the ancient Roman world by using these categories to classify the material we find. It is not the intent of this work to produce another "history" of Roman women but to look at broad concepts and see how they might have affected such women. Generalization will, of course, be necessary and will be approached carefully.

The term "Roman women" is so diverse that one needs to define the field. In this study we will attempt to stay within the confines of the first century B.C.E. through the end of the first century C.E., with some slight deviations. This time period corresponds closest to the New Testament era and studying it will help us to understand more clearly the context of Romans 16. The model presents a general view of the values and patterns of the ancient Mediterranean society. It does not allow for specific delineations of class and status. The plays of Plautus are specifically studied to see if any class differences can be noted, but ultimately their bases in Greek New Comedy (written at least 100 years prior to Plautus' work) make trying to separate material from the second-century-B.C.E. Roman world complex. Thus, it would be difficult to draw inferences about women in the first-century-C.E. world from Plautus' writings. Any findings on "common" women were skewed by the mix of the cultures and time periods. Some of the major primary sources, however, used in this study include Pliny, Dio, Tacitus, Livy and Appian. Sources representing a broad spectrum of literature were chosen from those works that might yield material that would nuance, affirm or critique the model in some way. As in the other chapters, the search is limited by space and time constraints. The multidisciplinary nature of this thesis makes it necessary to contain and focus discussions that could, in themselves, be a single dissertation.

We will concentrate only on literature that is either foundational to the study of Roman women or pivotal to our discussion. Each section of the model will begin with a review of the relevant secondary literature. Throughout this study of the primary sources we will refer to and interact with a variety of secondary literature. Yet most of the resources do not address the issues from the same vantage point as this thesis. Little work has been done in anthropology and cultural values, which this work will highlight.

## Honor and Shame

As we have established in the model, honor and shame are key values found throughout Mediterranean societies even today. Men receive honor from one another based on their actions. Their reputations precede them as does their families' status in the eyes of the community. Women in the family need to protect their shame or modesty in order to maintain the honor of the family. Men are responsible for protecting a woman's honor, but women ultimately play a part in whether their behavior brings dishonor upon their family. These values exist in the Mediterranean today, and they also existed in the ancient world. We are about to examine some of the evidence for their existence in the ancient Roman world. It is likely that Roman women also lived within the confines of such cultural constraints and values.

At this point we will question to what degree Roman women experienced the effects of both honor and shame. Did Roman women break with tradition? We cannot have as full a picture as we would like, but will do our best to discern where ancient Roman women are in this continuum of values, between honor and shame. Ultimately, we are searching to discover how these cultural values of honor and shame impact our understanding of New Testament texts that concern women, particularly Romans 16. We will proceed by exploring both the primary sources and the secondary literature.

There are many examples of honor and shame in ancient writings. In Dio's historical writings we find the concern for "proper conduct" a very real issue. In Rome a magistrate was appointed in 29 B.C.E. to insure the morality of senators, knights and their families (Dio 52.21.3-4). This officer was required to punish those who needed correction, and thus the state regulated for a time the morality of its people. The state was not only interested in the behavior of its men but also of its women.

Cicero writes of a woman called Sassia, the mother of one of the men he defended. He tells of her unwholesome behavior that led her to woo her daughter's husband into adultery. He notes that not even the loss of honor, modesty or the threat of family disgrace could deter her (Cicero *Clu.* 1.12). Even though Sassia did not abide by such rules, women were expected to adhere to a code of moral behavior and if they did not, their family's reputation was on the line.

We also read about Philodamus who was holding a dinner party for men when the women of the house were called to join them. Philodamus sensed the men wanted to violate his daughter and called his slaves to find his son to save them from this calamity. As soon as his son learned the news he proceeded home to save his father and to protect the honor of his sister (Cicero *Verrine Orations I: Against Verres II* 1.26.67). As we have observed in other cultures already, a woman's honor was protected by the male kin of her family. What happened to her affected the whole family and the family's reputation.

Cicero, in defending Caelio, discusses the "kind" of woman that is like a courtesan. This woman has no husband yet keeps her home open for men. She attends dinner parties with men she does not know and is considered shameless in her words and deeds (Cicero *Cael.* 20.49). Alternatively, he makes mention of maidens who would rather commit suicide than face dishonor or disgrace (Cicero *Prov. cons.* 3.6). A woman's shame was the paramount concern of her life.

Women were considered pure if they did not stray from their husband's bed. In an epigram of Martial we read about a daughter who looks like her father and is thus the image of her mother's virtue (Martial 6.27). Women were willing to go to any length to protect their virtue. Statius writes about a Priscilla who would rather die poor but chaste. She was willing to give her life to protect her honor (Statius 5.62-65).

We also read of women and their concern for chastity in Pliny's letters. We read of Cornelia, a Vestal Virgin sentenced to death by Domitian on the charge of incest. It was said that she protected her modesty and maintained her purity from even the pollution of the executioner's hand (Pliny *Ep.* Book 4.11). When Pliny writes of his own wife he proclaims that her love for him is of "a chaste nature" (*Ep.* Book 4.19, Radice).

Throughout the literature the virtues of chastity and modesty are extolled. Not only did women receive the benefit of their shame and good name but men also benefited from their morally upstanding behavior. Men "looked good" and were respected when women in their family behaved modestly and with shame.

Pliny in *Panegyricus* writes that men could be dishonored by their choice of a wife, damaging their reputation in their families and in the community. He notes that the empress Pompeia Plotina added to her husband's honor. She was a model of virtue and brought her husband glory on account of her modest behavior (Pliny *Pan.* 83.4-8). Thus, women not only maintained shame but also protected the honor of the family by preserving their modesty and chastity. Women were an important consideration in the determining of the honor of a family.

The imperial ruling families were also concerned about respectability. When Livia was asked how she had so much influence over Augustus, she answered what would have been traditionally expected of a woman in her culture and time. She said that it was by being chaste, pleasing him and not becoming involved in his affairs, both political and otherwise (Dio 58.2.5-6). Augustus, when asked in 18 B.C.E. what "admonitions" he gave to Livia, was concerned with her dress and adornment that she should always display modest behavior (Dio 54.16.5). Appropriate modesty and virtue all added to a woman's sense of shame and contributed to the maintenance of the family's honor.

When Augustus discovered that his daughter Julia took part in drinking nights at the Forum and Rostra, he told the senate about her behavior. Consequently, as punishment she was sent to the island of Pandateria to live in seclusion (Dio 55.10.11-15).[1] She died in shame, forever branded by her acts of licentiousness. Even a woman of wealth and stature was not immune to the bonds of chastity and modesty.

Another imperial woman with a reputation for loose living was Messalina. She was said to not only show her own licentiousness but also to have compelled "other women to show themselves equally unchaste" (Dio 60.18.1, Cary). Messalina was said to have committed adultery with many men (Dio 60.22.5). In contrast Agrippina, Claudius' next wife, was said to possess moral excellence, purity in character and proof of her fruitfulness (Tacitus *Ann.* 12.6). Thus, we see again how a woman maintains her identity through her ability to be a "good," modest, and chaste wife and mother. We must acknowledge that what was written by Tacitus or Dio is their versions of the accounts and, thus, may not reflect an accurate picture of women's worlds but rather their own interpretation of the events.

Fischler notes that imperial women may have been cast into the image of either Roman matron or the woman "gone bad" who does not uphold her modesty or shame (Archer, Fischler and Wyke 1994, 120). This tension between honor/shame and power will be explored in a later section. Women in the imperial family were in a unique position, and while they were expected to maintain their reputation, they were in some ways free from many of the everyday constraints of their gender. Yet Roman women in general were still expected to maintain their sense of shame or modesty in a manner like Greek and Jewish women.

## Nuancing Honor and Shame

It seems probable and almost inevitable that the women of ancient Rome were bound to the virtues of modesty and shame, as these values were clearly evidenced in their society. Yet women were not completely separated from the concept of honor. We will now explore how such women were able to receive honor, in what form it came and when. We unfortunately know little about "common" everyday women, particularly in the area of any honor they might have received. For the most part, our focus will be on the readily available examples that include a multitude of imperial women and the honors they received.

Women's funerary inscriptions show us how they were thought of in life and how they were honored in death. In an epitaph from the first century B.C.E. found in Rome, Albia Hargula was said to be chaste and "the soul of honor" (*Tituli Sepulcrales* 61, Warmington). Aurelia Philematium (c. 80 B.C.E.) was also known as a modest and chaste woman who had been faithful to her husband. She was lamented by her husband as "chaste in body," faithful and loving (*Tituli Sepulcrales* 53, Warmington). Tomb inscriptions of several Roman women during the reign of Augustus celebrated their virtues of modesty, fidelity and honor. Women on all social levels were held to similar standards (Fantham et al 1994, 318-320).

Women were also honored for their noteworthy behavior beyond their chastity and fidelity. Pliny expresses concern over Fannia's illness when he writes to Neratius Priscus. He does not want her country to lose her because she maintains purity, integrity and loyalty. He says that she is a model to their wives and that her courage is an example even to men (Pliny *Ep.* 7.19.4,7,8). Such women were honored by their husbands and the men in their lives. They were considered worthy to receive respect in the eyes of the community.

Cicero describes a certain Caecilia, a woman from a distinguished and honorable family, saying as she obtains honor from her family she also brings honor to them by her upstanding behavior (*Rosc. Amer.* 50.147). Valerius Maximus was even encouraged by Pliny to honor his wife with some public building or show as a funeral tribute (*Ep.* 6.33.2). Such women brought public honor to their entire family.

Women did not receive honor as men did, but they did receive tributes, respect and public recognition. Perhaps their recognition was not found within the public or "men's sphere," but that did not make it any less noteworthy. Imperial women may have been the exception, but they have much to teach us about the honoring of women in the ancient Roman world.

*Imperial women*

Imperial women were also honored in public. Augustus built a colonnade inscribing Livia's name on it rather than the patron Pollio who had provided the property (Dio 54.23.6). When the sister of Augustus died it is said that her body was to "lie in state in the shrine of Julius." A public funeral oration and funeral procession were given and a time of morning was publicly observed (Dio 54.35.4-5).

Livia had statues voted to her in an attempt to console her after her husband Drusus' death and she was awarded the status of a woman with three children. Such a person would as a consequence not be subject to the penalties of childlessness and could receive the full rewards of those of a large family (Dio 55.2.5-6). Livia's son Tiberius dedicated a precinct to her (Dio 55.8.2).[2] Tiberius also honored his grandmother Antonia by granting her the role of priestess of Augustus (Dio 59.3.3-4). He gave the privileges of the Vestal Virgins to her and his sisters (Dio 59.3.4). Such imperial women were acknowledged and celebrated for their contribution to the imperial family and to their nation.

Pomeroy also discusses the honors imperial women received. Catulus in 102 B.C.E. was the first to honor his mother with a public funeral oration. Julius Caesar did so as well, when some of his relatives died, and later Augustus took up this practice. Funeral orations became a way that imperial women were honored. Such women were also honored on coinage, through honorific titles, and the erection of buildings and monuments (Pomeroy 1975, 182-184).

All of the honors given to Livia were also bestowed upon Drusilla. In a time when women were not often eulogized in public, Drusilla had a public funeral and eulogy. It was agreed she would be deified and an effigy of her would be put in the senate house. In the temple of Venus a statue of Drusilla as large as that of the goddess was erected. A shrine was built in her honor with twenty priests and priestesses serving there, and a festival was held on her birthday (Dio 54.11.1-4).

Other imperials followed suit in honoring their family members. Gaius, when celebrating Drusilla's birthday, "brought her statue into the Circus on a cart drawn by elephants, and gave the people free exhibition for two days" (Dio 59.13.8, 59.24.7, Cary). When Claudius came to power he "granted games in the Circus" on the birthdays of his mother Antonia and father Drusus. He honored his grandmother Livia with equestrian contests and also deified her by setting up a statue of her in the temple of Augustus. The Vestal Virgins received the duty of offering her sacrifices, and the women of Rome were to use her name when they made oaths (Dio 60.5.1-2). Claudius' wife Messalina, because of his victories, was "granted the same privilege of occupying front seats" as Livia had been given (Dio 60.22.2, Cary).

We can see there were great honors conferred upon Livia and the women of the imperial family. They held a place in society which was probably not reflective of the overall treatment of women but which certainly signaled a change in the idea that only men could be recipients of honor. Women's sense of honor may have, however, been different than men. Women were surely aware it was not a status readily available to them, yet they did have honor bestowed on them in various noteworthy contexts.

We have touched on just a few sources out of the many we could have drawn from if we had widened the time period. There are many examples of women being held to the values of honor and shame. It is clear that these values, although nuanced during the Hellenistic period, were strong influences of culture. It would be unusual if these values did not show up in the biblical text since they are so pervasive in the culture. We now need to consider whether women in ancient Rome did or did not wield power, and if so whether it was direct or indirect.

## Women and Power

As we have seen in the last section, women of Rome had a different place in society than did Greek women. It could be suggested that they had some measure of power whether obtained inadvertently or directly. In most cases their power was still drawn from the important role they played within the family. They often gained their power indirectly through wealth or perhaps through manipulation.

Clark points out that women have often been studied in relation to what they have been able to achieve. Yet she emphasises that scholars too often assume that what we should study is acknowledged power. Women have been competent in many ways that acknowledged power misses or diminishes. The new role of women's studies should be to focus on what women have done even if patriarchy views it as "menial" (Clark 1989, 2). Clark goes on to discuss ordinary and elite women from a variety of angles. As always, the availability of information on "ordinary" women is limited, yet Clark does attempt to address it through a variety of sources, including ancient art.

Clark's interest in women and power is particularly relevant to this work. Although the section is brief she acknowledges that women's power is often indirect and temporary (Clark 1989, 29). Women's power looks different than societal or "men's power" and thus needs to be seen with fresh eyes rather than through the tainted lenses of traditional male-oriented scholarship. Women displayed their power through the manipulation of their families and relations, in their spheres of power within domesticity and the home.

Cantarella contends it was during the Hellenistic era that women began to receive more freedoms, as they had more mobility and access to participate in society (1987, 90). Women were no longer simply reproductive vessels but were considered important instruments of the continuation of their culture. Women were expected to pass on the values of the state to their children, and thus, to some extent, they had to understand the world of men (Cantarella 1987, 134).

Pomeroy suggests the freedoms Hellenistic women enjoyed were expanded in the Roman empire. The wealthy Roman matron is portrayed as having considerable freedom which was exercised against a traditional background (Pomeroy 1975, 149). Bauman also argues that Roman women did enjoy more social mobility particularly through the infiltration of Etruscan and Hellenistic ideas. Although women continued to be excluded from public affairs and did not have a vote in civic matters, they did begin to advance by taking stands politically in the last few centuries before the common era. They also began to acquire education (Bauman 1992, 1-3). Gardner, however, counters that the status of upper class women in Roman society is overestimated. She argues they were probably not as assertive and independent as it may seem. Certainly slaves or freed women experienced a much different reality (Gardner 1986, 1). While Gardner may help us to proceed cautiously when considering the freedoms of upper class Roman women, it would appear that evidence to the contrary is overwhelming. As we will see in this chapter, wealthy Roman women, and clearly imperial women, did wield a certain amount of power although it may have been indirect and manipulative at times.

Pomeroy discusses Cornelia (second century B.C.E.) who was a symbol of womanhood and the picture of the Roman matron. Cornelia was the wife of Tiberius Sempronius Gracchus. She was educated and even had her own letters published, with references to her found both in the works of Plutarch and Pliny. Her sons Tiberius and Gaius Gracchus were influential in Roman politics until their deaths. Cornelia was an example of a widow within the imperial class who wielded power through the influential men in her life (Pomeroy 1975, 149). She managed a large household and a male guardian was never associated with her name. Pomeroy (1975, 151) also notes that Cicero's wife Terentina was also not associated with any male guardian even though much is written in Cicero's letters about her financial transactions. She very well may have had a guardian, but there are no recorded instances of his involvement.

Pomeroy (1975, 151) also discusses the legislation of Augustus that allowed a freeborn woman who bore three or four children to be exempt from male guardianship.[3] Pomeroy (1975, 152) does however suggest that although Roman women had increasing freedoms they continued to seek men to be their advocates in legal situations. Pomeroy (1975, 168) claims that Roman women had the responsibility of sole supervision over their household, which mostly included the supervision of slaves.

Pomeroy (1975, 189) ultimately claims that as Roman men prospered, so did their wives. Roman women in her perspective were more mobile, powerful and visible than Greek women. It is not hard to understand how she might draw these conclusions. The evidence from primary sources seems to suggest that women did have a place of influence in their home and their society. Roman women obviously wielded some power. The question, however, remains as to what this power looked like and how it was used.

Fantham et al (1994, 280) in *Women in the Classical World* suggest that women during the time of Cicero and Caesar began to enjoy a new-found freedom. They assert that women no longer accepted the constraints of modesty placed on them (Fantham et al 1994, 289). The argument is centered on the fact that men were away at war and no longer able to "watch" their wives' behavior. Women may have been more promiscuous when their husbands had less control over them (Fantham et al 1994, 289).

In the preserved ruins of Pompeii much can be discovered about Roman women of the first century C.E. Women may have lent each other money and property, with interest (Fantham et al 1994, 336). It is argued that women in Pompeii moved about freely, were involved in business and patronage, held honorific and cultic office as well as owned property (Fantham et al 1994, 341). There is even a wall painting showing a woman holding a stylus, perhaps suggesting women were literate (Fantham et al 1994, 342).

Clark claims "real" power was acceptable for women only when it was temporary and was a reaction to specific circumstances. A woman was only temporarily doing a "man's job." A woman could gain political power only if she was the daughter or wife of the "right" influential man (Clark 1989, 29). Women would take power in most cases for the good of their family and only when it was an absolute necessity (Clark 1989, 30).

Hallett, in her work on the families of Rome, found that women were intricately related to the power base of the family. Women were central to the family's existence and an upper class powerful family provided them with the resources within the political structure to influence their society. The fact that the private sphere of the family impacted the public sphere of the political realm made the two areas difficult to separate (Hallett 1984a, 29).

Women were not only powerful because of the successful men in their lives but also because of their position of importance in the family (Hallett 1984a, 36). Hallett (1984a, 55) suggests that a woman's relationship with her father resulted in public recognition for her. She contends that from at least the classical period onward a Roman father was expected to provide materially for his daughter even after his death (Hallett 1984a, 78).

In Lucan we read of Julia who is said to have peacemaking abilities. It is written that if she had lived she would have been able to reconcile her husband to her father. According to Lucan she may have averted a military conflict by her powers of persuasion (Lucan *Phars.* 1.115-120). We might consider whether women gained power through the bridges they were able to rebuild and the alliances they repaired within the family.

Dixon suggests that a Roman mother held power in the family because of the training she gave to her children. If the children's father died, the mother gained even more power in their lives. Dixon (1988, 202-203) goes so far as to suggest that women may have placed their own political ambitions on their sons.

Treggiari (1991, 8) reminds us it was necessary for the state that marriage took place and new citizens were produced. Because women were involved in both of these processes they held some position of power. Women held sway over those institutions and social conventions that entered into their domestic sphere. Women interacted with decisions about marriage, family and kin relationships because their lives were embedded in these connections. Their power was not necessarily a legal right, rather a social expectation and custom.

## Power in Non-traditional Areas

During the Punic Wars, Gaius Oppius created the Oppian law limiting women's gold jewelry, colorful garments and rides in carriages. The very fact that this law was created shows that women were displaying their wealth and prestige. The enacting of it might suggest that men were threatened by women's sense of growing power (Livy 34.1.2-6).

As we have already read these laws were opposed. Many came to the Capitoline to speak for and against them. The matrons blocked all the approaches to the Forum, begging the men to repeal the law. Given the reality of a prosperous state, they argued their privileges should be returned (Livy 34.1.2-6). The crowd of women continued to grow each day. They came not only from the city but also from towns and the country, approaching consuls, praetors and other officials to appeal their cause.

However, Marcus Porcius Cato spoke in favor of keeping the laws (Livy 34.2.1-7). Cato saw in women coming together a sense of momentum which he seemed to feel would only take them further out of women's traditional spheres. Despite his and others' concerns the law did not survive. After all the speeches were delivered to the Forum the women appeared more in number the next day. The law was not changed at that time but was repealed twenty years after it was passed (Livy 34.8.1-3). Women seemed to gain a sense of power in the banding together it took to voice their outrage over these laws. Women began to find their voice in numbers.

In the later centuries women continued to gain power through wealth. The triumvirs (124 B.C.E.) required 1,400 of the wealthiest women to have their property evaluated and a portion of it would go to the war cause. The women decided to join together with the women of the triumvirs. The sister of Octavian and mother of Antony found them forcing their way into the "tribunal of triumvirs in the forum" (Appian *Bell. civ.* 4.5.32, White). Hortensia was their spokesperson, saying that they had tried to talk with Fulvia wife of Antony, but as she denied them they had no choice but to come to the Forum. Stating that they had not participated with their husbands in evil gain, they shouldn't share the blame if they did not share the guilt.

Hortensia asked why women should pay taxes when they have no part in the offices and honors for which men contend. She went on to speak of women's past contributions to the state saying they had given voluntarily from their own wealth. The triumvirs were angry that women were holding a meeting in public while the men remained silent. Yet despite their resistance, the following day the men voted to decrease the number of women to 400 and decreed that some rich men should also lend them money for the war effort (Appian *Bell. civ.* 4.5.32-34). Thus, because of their persistence women achieved some of their goal, and not all were taxed. Perhaps not all of Hortensia's speech can be seen as historical. Yet it seems clear that women were beginning to voice their concerns.

Common women, particularly mothers, also had more influence under the laws of Augustus. Under his family law and incentives, women were given more freedom and power. The Lex Voconia had previously said no woman was entitled to inherit property over more than one hundred thousand *sesterces*. Yet Augustus allowed women who fit within his program of increasing families, to inherit larger amounts. He also gave Vestal Virgins full privileges as though they were women who had borne children (Dio 56.10.1-2). Mothers and those serving the state in religious capacities were given privileges that the barren were not afforded.

We also read of women who had control of their family's finances. In Cicero's letter to Atticus regarding the behavior of his wife Terentia, we read that Cicero has left her in charge of the finances while he was in exile. He tells Atticus that she had sent him less money than he requested (Cicero *Att.* 11.24). Women were not without their own resources.

Many sources cite women who wrote wills and men who left them legacies. Just a few are noted here. Pliny tells of a woman called Aurelia who is termed a "noble lady" (*ornata femina*) who had a will and wished to add a legacy to it (*Ep.* 2.20, Melmoth). Additionally, upon her death Ummidia Quadratilla's "excellent will" left her grandson two-thirds of her estate and her granddaughter one-third (Pliny *Ep.* 7.24.1-2, Melmoth). Suetonius in *The Lives of the Caesars* refers to Galba who was left a significant sum in the will of Livia Augusta (Suetonius *Galb.* 7.5.2). Women also received inheritances from men as evidenced in Pliny (*Ep.* 6.3, 8.17.12 and Book 8.18.8).[4] This area of power was indirect, but nevertheless significant.

A woman's wealth did not necessarily insure her good standing in the community. In fact, it may have made her more questionable in the eyes of men who were threatened by her power. Martial in his epigrams writes about the danger of marrying a wealthy woman. He says he does not wish to be a "wife's wife." The matron should be below her husband and only in that order can such a relationship be rightly "equal" (Martial *Epigrams* 2, 8.12, Ker). Some were concerned that women might gain too much power from their wealth.

Women continued to use their wealth to their advantage. In Cicero's *Against Verres II* the wife of Xeno owns property and manages a business while also leasing the land (*Verrine Orations II: Against Verres II* III.22.55). In *The Lives of the Caesars* Otho is said to have worked his way into the good graces of a woman in high society. As a result of this alliance he found favor in the eyes of Nero and eventually gained more power for himself (Suetonius *Otho* 7.2.2). Women also used their money to honor the gods. Inscriptions describe matrons as having made a gift to Queen Juno and to Mother Morning (*Tituli Sepulcrales* 11-12).

Women used their funds to their advantage and to advance their own desires. Yet wealth was not the only form of power available to women. Status was also an important tool in the game of power, and as we will see imperial women were not shy about flaunting it.

## Imperial Women's Power

Imperial women were clearly influential and had great power in ancient Rome. Livia was a highly important figurehead in her day. She seemed to feel a burden to care for the people of the empire and a desire to see her husband act as a fair and just ruler (Dio 55.20.2-4, 55.16.1). Livia was unafraid to share her feelings and ideas with her husband who also happened to be the emperor. Livia said she shared with him in the troubles and joys of ruling (Dio 55.16.2-3). She spoke out against putting people to death and the need to educate people in the law. She was unafraid to tell Augustus to heed her advice and to change his course of action (Dio 55.20.2, 21.4). Augustus listened to the suggestions of Livia and released some prisoners on her account (Dio 55.22.1-2). She shared her opinions and yet also maintained her reputation and shame.

In Augustus' will Livia was possibly left a third of his assets, which he had approved by the senate (Dio 56.32.1). After Augustus' death, Livia began to gain more power. She honored Augustus by holding a private festival for three days in the palace, a practice continued by later emperors (Dio 56.46.5). The senate passed these actions for the memory of Augustus in theory, but Dio says it was "actually by Tiberius and Livia that they were accomplished" (56.47.1, Cary). Livia was obviously a woman of great influence, and was revered in the eyes of her husband and her community.

Livia was also said to receive senators and others in her home and was not hindered in any way, this matter being a part of public record (Dio 57.12.2). For a while the letters from the Emperor Tiberius also contained her name. Dio says that while, "...she never ventured to enter the senate-chamber or the camps or the public assemblies, she undertook to manage everything as if she were sole ruler" (Dio 57.12.3, Cary). While Augustus was alive she possessed great influence and she maintained Tiberius became emperor because of her. She had no direct or official power. Yet she was aware of the sway she held over her husband and the hand she played in propelling and maintaining her son's career.[5]

Messalina was also an important woman in the imperial family who held much power. When Messalina wanted someone killed she terrified Claudius until she was allowed to have her way (Dio 60.14.1). An example of Messalina's manipulative powers can be seen in the case of Silanus, when he was executed due to one of her supposed lies (Dio 60.14.3-4). Other people were tortured and executed at her provocation, even women. Yet those who may have been most guilty were spared through the help of bribes to Messalina and the imperial freedmen (Dio 60.15.6-16). Messalina was also said to sell prestigious positions within the state (Dio 60.17.8).

After Messalina's death Claudius married Agrippina who was later "dignified by the title of Augusta" (Tacitus *Ann.* 12.26, Jackson). Homage was paid to Agrippina as it was to the emperor (Tacitus *Ann.* 12.37). It was without precedent in ancient custom "that a woman should sit in state before Roman standards" (Tacitus *Ann.* 12.37, Jackson). It seems significant that Roman women were not simply appreciated for their husband's position but that they were given honor and power in their own right.

Future imperial wives such as Poppaea continued to wield power over their husbands. Poppaea was said to dominate Nero "first as an adulterer then as a husband" (Tacitus *Ann.* 14.60, Jackson). When she replaced Octavia as his wife, effigies of Poppaea were thrown from the Capitol. In protest the people carried "statues of Octavia shoulder-high," surrounded them with flowers and displayed them in the Forum and temple. Yet after this uprising "the honors of Poppaea were reinstated" (Tacitus *Ann.* 14.61, Jackson).

Poppaea herself died at the hand of her husband who kicked her during pregnancy in anger. A public funeral was held for her and she was eulogized by the emperor at the Rostra (Tacitus *Ann.* 14.5.1). In contrast, Octavia died in seclusion and shame.

The power women wielded was limited and based on the whims and good graces of the male kin in their lives. Women may have held some sway in the imperial court, but the men had the final say. Women, both common and imperial, were able to have some say in certain spheres. Even though they wielded indirect power they were still largely limited to the domestic or family sphere.

Women had more power in relationships and family affairs than they did in politics. Yet what they influenced in the family had the potential for impacting their role in the larger society. Women held much sway in the family which might translate to indirect power in familial or "fictive" kin relationships. The early Christian church with its familial ties may have been a place where women's power was also influential. We should also consider how the divisions of public and private limited women's power and also opened up opportunities to them such as leadership in house churches.

## Public and Private

Now that we are seeing a slightly different picture emerging concerning women's visibility in society, one wonders to what extent the seclusion and separation of public and private issues come into play for Roman women. Traditionally, as the model suggests, it has been understood that women were secluded and not active in the public world outside the home. There is a question, however, as to how secluded they were and if they actually stayed in separate rooms.

It is evident that women were able to move about more freely in Roman than in Greek society and were an important part of celebrations. When Tiberius celebrated victory by feasting with the people, Livia and Julia gave "a dinner to the women" (κἀν τούτῳ καὶ ἡ Λιουία μετὰ τῆς Ἰουλίας τὰς γυναῖκας εἱστίασε) (Dio 55.2.4, Cary). Livia held another banquet for the women after Tiberius gave one to the senate on the Capitol (Dio 55.8.2-3). Even though these women participated in important celebrations, they were seemingly limited to the company of other women.

Pomeroy, however, suggests Roman women did eat in the company of men, citing the first-century-C.E. writer Cornelius Nepos who wrote about the difference between a Greek and a Roman woman. He noted in his "Preface" that the chief difference between such women is that a Greek woman sits in the interiors of the house and is secluded while the Roman woman accompanies her husband to dinner parties (1975, 170). Nepos continues: "...what Roman would blush to take his wife to a dinner-party? What matron does not frequent the front rooms of her dwelling and show herself in public?" (Nepos' Preface to *Generals* 7, Rolfe). It seems likely that Pomeroy is correct in asserting that Roman women were freer than their Greek sisters. We find further evidence of women attending dinner parties with men in both Petronius (*Satyr.* 67) and Cicero (*Verrine Orations I: Against Verres II* 5.30.81). Roman women, at least matrons and wealthy women, were obviously not as secluded as might be expected.

This argument supports this thesis that the women of Romans 16 were not bound by the belief that a woman's place was to never leave the home. Roman women, if they moved about more freely, would likely have been patrons, leaders of churches, and leaders in the Christian missionary movement. The Roman empire and particularly the Hellenistic era afforded great freedoms for women. However, such freedoms can only be appreciated in light of the seclusion women had previously endured in prior time periods and under Greek rule. By any sense of modern or Western standards such women continued to live very much connected to the private interior world of the home and outside of males' circles of influence. This scenario only seeks to reinforce our thesis that the women of Romans 16 were active in early Christianity because house churches existed within their sphere of influence.

The evidence does not end with these examples. Pomeroy also suggests that "virtuous" women could move about freely and even participate in the education of their children. She notes the references Tacitus makes to such women including Livia, Agrippina and Julia Procilla (Pomeroy 1975, 170).[6] Pomeroy recounts the evidence of three women who spoke publicly and were remembered for their actions. Valerius Maximus cites the three examples from the first century B.C.E. These women included Maesia Sentia, Afrania and Hortensia (1975, 175).[7] Each woman was reacting to some specific situation and thus their acts seem to be exceptions. Their speaking out is focused on obtaining some need or resolving some situation. There seems to be no evidence that they continued their public speaking, yet the very act in itself suggests a blurring of the public/private divide.

Kampen sees the public/private issue in the art works of first-century Rome. Such works of art adorned buildings and public places, and it was here that history was also recorded (Kampen 1991, 218). She recognizes that women were often represented in private and domestic scenes. However, she argues that implicit within such art could be found women's central role not only in the family but also in the state (Kampen 1991, 243). Kampen (1991, 244) suggests that historical relief shows a confusion between the public and the private role of women. The lines between public and private were not as easy to divide in ancient Rome as they are today. The private and public spheres were often interwoven, because great importance was placed on the family as well as the state. The blurring of these lines again makes this thesis much more plausible. Since public events also occurred in the home, women were not barred from them but, rather, had some influence over their occurrence for they took place within the realm they supervised.

Balsdon, however, suggests Roman women never lived in seclusion as the women did in Greece. The woman of the household more often oversaw the domestic domain. She probably also shared with her husband the responsibility for the religious cults of the family (Balsdon 1962, 45). A woman's first place was in the home and domestic realm. Her social duties came only second (Balsdon 1962, 201). Balsdon (1962, 277) claims women went out of the house to shop, attend public games, worship, make social visits and go to the baths. Anthropological data presented in the earlier chapter on the model might suggest otherwise. Women in Mediterranean societies appear to still live in seclusion even today. Yet Roman women of this time period do appear to be experiencing more freedoms than in the past. They also seem to be not quite as free as Balsdon would like us to believe. Perhaps Roman women had more freedom than do the Middle Eastern women of today but the spheres still appear to be divided.

Often freed people of Rome lived above their workplaces, and in the lower classes women also needed to work alongside their husbands. Thus, the lines between public and private were easily blurred (Treggiari 1991, 379). Roman houses did not have a separate area for women and one for men. Particularly in small houses when there were only one or two rooms, these rooms held many purposes and were not used solely by either gender (Treggiari 1991, 415). Although women did go out into the public world and attended social events, their first obligation was to maintain their homes and families (Treggiari 1991, 424).

Even though women seemed to be much more visible in public, some were still concerned with this behavior and tried to stop it. In the time of Tiberius, Caecina Severus said that women were creating problems for men when they went on military campaigns. He claimed that since the repeal of the Oppian law, women had now "cast their chains and ruled supreme in the home, the courts and by now the army itself" (Tacitus *Ann*. 3.33, Moore and Jackson). Thus, based on Severus' concerns it seems evident that even though he did not like it, women had been accompanying their husbands on military campaigns and leaving the bounds of Rome. Their mobility was dramatically increased, and they were exposed to new cultures and ways of living.

Traditionally women's sphere had been in the home and in the midst of their kin relationships. Yet it seems evident that women of ancient Rome began to move out beyond the limitations of their culture.

## Nuancing Public and Private

As alluded to in the above discussion, women in ancient Rome became more visible despite what traditionalists allowed. There are many examples of women who began to step out beyond the boundaries of the home. We proceed in this section with caution, aware that incidents or exceptions cannot be generalized. Yet we cannot ignore the evidence that some women did indeed interact with men in public.

Lucan relays the story of Cornelia who wishes to die with her husband rather than be kept safe. In the narrative Cornelia reminds her husband that she followed him on campaigns both on the land and at sea (Lucan *Phars.* 8.649-652). She was not afraid to walk with him wherever he went, even if it was to his death. Cornelia clearly showed courage as well as increased mobility.

Cicero in his letter to Vatinius discusses the possibility of making a visit to Vatinius' wife Pompeia (Cicero *Fam.* 11.2). Roman women seem to have been able to interact with men other than their kin. Men and women in the time before Augustus sat together in the gladiatorial theatre (Plutarch *Sull.* 35.3). Dio says Claudius (41 C.E.) "banqueted with the senators as well as with their wives" (55.7.4, Cary). Agrippina reclined at the table next to her father-in-law Tiberius (Tacitus *Ann.* 4.54). Her actions were far different than women who did not even eat with their own husbands or male kin. It seems more than possible that at least imperial women and men did attend public events and meals together. The custom seems to have been evident prior to Augustus but may have become more prevalent in the first century C.E.

Women were not only having meals with men but they also interacted with them intellectually, politically and socially. Cato in addressing the Forum concerning the woman's protest of the Oppian Law in 214 B.C.E., tells us that women who used to need guardians to represent them and who were once under the control of their male kin, were now addressing issues and attending informal and formal sessions in the Forum (Livy 24.2.13-14). It is clear that women were no longer as confinable as they had been in past times.

However, as Lucius Valerius spoke out in favor of the Oppian law being repealed and suggests that the matrons' involvement in public affairs is not as new as it seems. He reminds them of women's involvement at the beginning in the legend of Romulus' kingdom when the matrons rushed the battle lines with the Sabines to stop the fighting. He also mentions the city being captured by the Gauls and how the women by unanimous vote offered their gold "to the public use" (Livy 34.5.7-11, Sage). Perhaps Roman women were always more visible than their Greek and Jewish counterparts.

Other examples of women who were publicly visible include Agrippa's sister Polla who built a portico in the Campus and attended the races (Dio 55.8.4). When Tiberius dedicated the shrine of Augustus he held a celebration that not only involved the men of the senate but also their wives (Dio 54.7.1-2). We read that when Gaius set out for Gaul he did not go alone but took with him many women among his other luxuries (Dio 59.21.2-3). We also read that Drusus travelled with his wife as did Augustus with Livia. Drusus said it would cause him pain to be separated from his wife, the mother of his children (Tacitus *Ann.* 3.33-34).

Imperial women were also present at the dedication of important civic projects such as when Claudius and Agrippina both presided over the completion of a building project (Tacitus *Ann.* 12.56). We also read about Cornelia, a daughter of Metellus Scipio, a widow of fine lineage and reputation whom Pompey married. It was said, "She was well versed in literature, in playing the lyre, and in geometry, and had been accustomed to listen to philosophical discourses with profit" (Plutarch *Pomp.* 55.1-3). She was thus a woman who was well-informed in her culture and society.

It seems quite clear from this evidence that Roman women were perhaps more publicly visible and active than their Jewish, and surely their Greek, counterparts. Many imperial women moved about with great freedom, but it seems likely that wealthy matrons benefited from a society that celebrated the female companion of the male ruler. Women of wealth held some sway in Roman society, they were not secluded in some back room. Thus, it seems plausible that Prisca, of whom we read in Romans 16, the leader of a house church, was also mobile because of her accessibility to wealth. It is not to say poorer women were not as mobile, or that Prisca was definitively rich. It seems evident, however, that wealthy women, particularly of the imperial family, were remembered more often in the public and written records of their time period. Such women were not quiet about their needs. Although we do not hear the voices of everyday women quite so clearly, we do read of them participating in large events. All of the evidence seems to point to the need to re-examine traditional interpretations of the primary data. Woman may appear silent and submissive at first glance, but upon further inspection one might be surprised. What power did women have in society? What did their power look like? We will now go on to see that women were powerful and active in many areas of their culture.

## Women and Kinship

Women and men in Mediterranean society operated with a different understanding of family than we do in the modern Western world. Kin was the sum total of one's tribe or clan, made up of near and distant relatives. There was a close connection between people who bore the same name, and women were well aware of these ties. Sometimes they used their role in the family to their advantage and other times they were manipulated on account of it. Women had a variety of roles to play in the family—daughter, wife, sister and mother. Each role had a unique expectation.

Dixon asserts that mothers were not necessarily depended upon only for nurture but also for moral strength and teaching. She discusses mothers in relation to their sons, their daughters, the family unit and the law. Women held unofficial power by the relationships they forged through motherhood. Dixon highlights the unique role of the Roman mother in her society, arguing that a woman's status was enhanced by her ability to bear and rear children. Her achievements also earned her respect within the culture, particularly if she had been widowed (Dixon 1988, 6). In addition to gathering primary data Dixon researched psychoanalytical theory, linguistic and cognitive development as well as ethnography (Dixon 1988, 10).

Hallett focuses on the relationship between father and daughter within the context of ancient Roman society. She also deals with the relationship between mother and daughter as well as between siblings. Hallett suggests that Roman daughters were a mere link in the process of marriages and relationships, serving the interests and needs of their husbands and fathers while their own needs were often ignored.

Yet a tension existed because Roman daughters were often highly valued by their fathers and were central figures in Roman society (Hallett 1984a, 107, 111). Motherhood was from almost the beginning of Rome a valued activity, and gestation almost had a religious quality to it (Hallett 1984a, 211).

Dixon (1988, 71) also acknowledges that fertility had a critical place in the well-being of the state and was considered a part of the general good. Hallett (1984a, 259) goes on to suggest that Roman mothers played a role in the choosing of their daughters' future husbands. Dixon (1988, 63) informs us that this involvement of the mother in her daughter's marriage was more a social issue than a legal right, for in reality the father had the final decision. Hallett notes the importance of the Roman elite family to the social, political and economic makeup of the society. Women in such families occupied a key position within the family and as a consequence society in general. Thus the lines between the public and private spheres were not so distinct as may first appear (Hallett 1984a, 310).

## Women and Marriage as Useful Tools

Women in some cases were pawns in the political game. To whom they were given in marriage, or from whom they were divorced, could be more a matter of political dealings than parental or personal choice. Livy says Latinus gave his daughter in marriage to Aeneas in order to further support a treaty between the Romans and Trojans (Livy 1.1.9-10). Marriage was not always between two families alone, but could also symbolize political and social connections. For example, Augustus wanted to put Agrippa into a higher position of power and so he "compelled him to divorce his wife, although she was the emperor's own niece, and to marry Julia" (Dio 54.6.5).

Once again women were used as political pawns in the role of marriage. Caesar was said to want the good graces of Pompey, so, although he had betrothed his daughter Julia to Servilius Caepio, he instead betrothed her to Pompey. In return Pompey's daughter, who was betrothed to Faustus, would instead be given to Servilius in marriage. Caesar also took a new wife, Calpurnia, daughter of Piso, and so Piso was made consul for the next year. Cato, however, "vehemently protested, and cried out that it was intolerable to have the supreme power prostituted by marriage alliances and to see men helping one another to powers and armies and provinces by means of women" (Plutarch *Caes.* 14.7-8).

Publius Crassus is said by Cicero to have established ties with the orator Servius Galba through the marriage of their children (Cicero *Brut.* 26.98). Cato also arranged for the second marriage of his own wife Marcia. She became the wife of Hortensisus. It was said she was given to Hortensisus because she had borne three children to Cato and fulfilled her duty. She was given to populate another household and "to ally the two houses by the maternal blood" (Lucan *Phars.* 2.332-333, Duff). Women had very little say in their choice of marriage partners. Marcia was, however, bold enough to approach Cato after Hortensisus' death and did secure a remarriage to him.

Men also used marriage as a tool to advance their own wealth, status and whims. We read of men who betrothed themselves to infant girls so that they might enjoy the benefits offered by the state to married men.[8]

Women were often sought after because of their status, what they could offer by way of their family or their beauty, charms and chastity. Yet all too often they became a disposable commodity, one that was quickly discarded when something better was found. Marriage did not symbolize affection, but was rather a political, social and economic union.

## Family Roles

Our study has so far revealed that the family was an important component in Roman society, if not for emotional ties, certainly for the security and well-being of the state. Women had an equally important role to play within the family. They functioned primarily as wives and mothers but also in important roles as sisters and daughters.

## Expectations of Wives

In the discussion raised by Caecina Severus over whether wives should accompany their husbands on their travels, it was agreed that the marriage relationship should not be broken, for what could be "more legitimate" than the consolations of a helpmeet? It was decided that even though a few women were corruptible this frailty could not be held against all of them. He asserted that husbands were often "...corrupted by the depravity of their wives," but that did not mean all men were without fault. It was said that it was not right that "...a sex frail by nature was left alone, exposed to its own voluptuousness and the appetites of others" (Tacitus *Ann.* 3.33, Moore and Jackson). It was not just out of desire to please their wives that the men wished to take them on their exploits but also because they inherently did not trust their wives' nature. Women were thus dangerous, weak and needed to be supervised.

In arguing against the repeal of the Oppian law, Marcus Porcius Cato said women should be restrained just as their forefathers made them "subject to their husbands." He said the "moment they begin to be your equals, they will be your superiors" (Livy 34.3.1-3, Sage). He seemed to fear women who might somehow overtake men, and no longer be so subservient. His attitude suggests that other men may too have held those fears.

Hallett writes on Latin elegy in *Women in the Ancient World*. She points out that women were expected to be obedient and submissive to their husbands. Chastity and fidelity were paramount virtues in the Roman world (Hallett 1984b, 242). She suggests, however, that the elegists were counter-culture and did not always uphold this view of women (Hallett 1984b, 246). Hallett asserts that they purposely inverted expected norms in their love poetry. Hallett argues that Catullus, in describing his interest in Lesbia, uses political language to communicate his love, thus raising her to the status of an equal intellectual partner (Hallett 1984b, 248). She cites the example of women who were often referred to in the sense of a slave to their lovers. However, to reverse the order and suggest that men were also enslaved to women—as in Catullus to Lesbia—was unexpected (Hallett 1984b, 250-251).

In 18 B.C.E. Augustus laid "heavier assessments" on unmarried men and women while he also offered rewards for married people with children (Dio 54.16.1-2). He told men they should "admonish" and "command" their wives to obey them, following his own example (Dio 54.16.4-5). Augustus addressed the group of unmarried and later married men (Dio 56.1.1). Augustus told the crowd he was disappointed that there were not more married men. He praised the men who were married, saying they had been obedient in the replenishment of their country. He tells them through their actions "the Romans of later days will become a mighty multitude." He seems to view the successive generation as a way of making their mortal beings to become immortal, he calls them "torch-bearers in a race" (Dio 56.3.3, Cary).

Dio recounts Augustus' views on wives saying a wife was to be chaste (ἄριστον), sexually pure and modest. She was also a wise housekeeper (σώφρων οἰκουρὸς οἰκονόμος), one who manages the home. It was also her role to raise the children, the progeny who were so important to Augustus. The wife's role then was even larger than all this, as she was to be a partner to the husband in sickness and in health. She was also responsible to "restrain" his passions (τοῦ τε νέου τὴν ἐμμανῆ φύσιν καθεῖρξαι) (Dio 56.3.3-4). Thus she was a moral agent, a keeper of the morality in the home. A woman was to be a man's perfect complement, to give whatever he needed and to even control his behavior that he might be respectable.

When Agrippina was with Germanicus at a camp during a time of war, there was much discussion over whether she should stay or flee with his child. She was the daughter-in-law of Drusus, a "wife of notable fruitfulness and shining chastity." Although Agrippina wanted to stay, saying no harm would come to them since her grandfather was the deified Augustus, he still sent them away (Tacitus *Ann.* 1.40-42). Agrippina showed a fierce independence and confidence in her safety but her husband Germanicus made the final decision to send her away. In the end he was the "protector" of his family despite Agrippina's differing opinions.[9]

In a letter to his wife Terentia and his family, Cicero writes from exile concerning his daughter's marriage prospects and reputation. He calls Terentia "the most faithful and best of wives," his daughter "dear" and his son Cicero "our last remaining hope." His concern for his daughter is of her marital state, his concern for his son is to prolong the ancestral line (Cicero *Fam.* 14.4). It is not surprising that Cicero wanted to protect and provide for his women kin even when he was in exile.

Alternatively, Pliny writes that a man's reputation can be ruined by his wife. He goes on to talk about a wife who is a "...supreme model of the ancient virtues..." and thus contributes to her husband's glory. Such a woman accompanies her husband in silence, shows him respect and is obedient to him (Pliny *Pan.* 83.4-8, Radice). Women were to show their husbands respect through modest and obedient behavior. Their actions had an impact on the entire family and in particular greatly influenced their husband's standing in the community. In one of Petronius' poems we read that a wife is expendable and that she is "...a burden imposed by law, and should be loved like one's fortune." He goes on to say that this love does not last forever (Petronius *Poems* 78.5, Hesteltine).

Women were bound to their role as wives just as it was the social expectation for men to marry. We read much in the New Testament concerning the "right" behavior of wives. This evidence also calls into question or highlights the more equal partnerships we read of such as that of Prisca and Aquila. Women were indeed embedded in the family throughout history. As a consequence, another important role they played was clearly in childbearing.

## Parenthood

Women throughout history were mothers. It is a role bestowed upon them by nature. In this role they shaped and molded their families and transmitted their culture to the children. Yet some women were not able to bear children, and, as we have seen over and over again, this situation caused great distress in the ancient world. Roman mothers were no different than mothers in Greece and Palestine who were also valued in their society. Parenthood perhaps was even more emphasized in Roman society, particularly at the time of Augustus and certainly when there was a declining birth rate.

Dixon (1988, 13) quotes from Ulpian's *Digest* asserting that the mother is the beginning and end of her family. In other words, the mother is the glue that holds her family together. Dixon argues that mothers were able to leave their children an inheritance by way of their dowries, although their intentions were not legally binding. They also were by social convention strongly involved in the matchmaking of their children's marriages. She uses citations from Cicero's letters and interactions with his wife and daughter to support her work on such matchmaking (Dixon 1988, 56, 57, 63).

*Augustus and Parenthood*

Augustus in his great concern about the importance of family describes the needs of the state. He says that a "multitude of men" are needed to keep peace and to run the state (Dio 56.3.6-7, Cary). To the unmarried men he says they cannot even be called citizens or men because they are not fulfilling the duties of such stations (Dio 56.4.2). He feels so strongly about producing children he tells the men they are committing "murder," "sacrilege," "are guilty of impiety," and more importantly are "destroying the state" and "betraying" their country (Dio 56.5.1-3, Cary).

Augustus, according to this speech, believed strongly in the importance of the family, saying it is human beings that make the city not the buildings within it (Dio 56.5.3). He noted that penalties would be increased for those who did not have children and incentives multiplied for the married with children (Dio 56.6.5-6). He repeatedly stressed the need for the state to continue through marriage and procreation (Dio 56.7.4). Augustus noted that women had a very important role to play in the procreation of children and in the moral stability of their families.

Whether Augustus' legislation was successful in increasing birth rate or reducing adultery is debatable. However, motherhood now was officially recognized by imperial standards. It was a celebrated role in the culture and government (Dixon 1988, 98).

Dixon asserts that the Roman mother was not necessarily known for nurture but more for transmitting morality and culture. She was a disciplinarian and had the ability to bestow her inheritance (her dowry) to her children. She wielded power inadvertently, and held an unofficial position of authority in the family (Dixon 1988, 233).

Cicero claims it was a moral obligation to procreate within marriage. Yet he explained that it was immodest to speak of it (Cicero *Off.* 1.35.128). Augustus spoke of it publicly and extolled the merits of it. Of course, Augustus was not just benevolent toward women, he wanted to build a strong state. Yet he was astute enough to know that women, and particularly mothers, were the key to its future.

*Imperial Women and Motherhood*

The Roman mother seems to have had more power than her Greek sister. In the imperial family there is evidence that bearing children was a key rite of passage for women. As already emphasized when procreation was not possible there were great problems. For example, Sempronia, wife of Scipio, was a suspect in his murder because she was described as "unloved and unloving," and "deformed and childless" (Appian *Bell. civ.* 1.3.20, White). Having children was significant to a woman's sense of worth and value.

Nero was dissatisfied with his wife Octavia and felt she should be content just to be the emperor's wife. He eventually wanted to marry someone else and because his attempts to murder Octavia did not succeed, he divorced her on the grounds of barrenness (Suetonius *Nero* 4.35.1-2).

Alternatively, women were treated with great esteem when they bore children, particularly boys. When Julia gave birth to Gaius, a boy, he was honored with a "permanent annual sacrifice on his birthday" (Dio 54.8.5). Thus the birth of Gaius was celebrated because he was a boy, a male heir. The birth of a daughter would have likely been received with shame. It was an important rite of passage for a woman to give birth to a boy. Ovid tells a story of a man called Ligdus whose wife was to bear a child. This man said to his wife, "There are two things which I would ask of Heaven: that you may be delivered with the least possible pain, and that your child may be a boy. Girls are more trouble, and fortune has denied them strength. Therefore...if by chance your child should prove to be a girl...let her be put to death" (*Metam.* 9, 670-679, Miller). Although this is a mythical story, the importance of male children over females is key.

Women played a significant role in shaping their children's lives. Gaius said he spared Marcus Octavius from becoming a magistrate a second time because his mother Cornelia had requested it. It was said that the people honored Cornelia not as much on account of her father but because of her sons. A bronze statue was even erected, bearing the inscription: "Cornelia, Mother of the Gracchi." Gaius used her on record in his forensic speech, when attacking someone, "what...doest thou abuse Cornelia, who gave birth to Tiberius?" And said to another, "Canst thou compare thyself with Cornelia? Hast thou borne such children as she did?" (Plutarch *Ti. C.*

*Gracch.* 4.2-4, Perrin). Cornelia was honored because of the respect she had gained from being the mother of successful sons. Had she not been a mother the honor would surely not have been as great if it existed at all.

Women who did not bear children were worthless in the eyes of their society. Additionally, if they never bore a male child they were also useless. The pressure was on for ancient women to show their worth and their value through their families. Thus, it is not surprising that such women found value in their church as the Christian family. There were no pressures to produce, yet family ties were of the utmost importance. Women were at the centre of the family, so why should we not expect to see them taking leadership positions in the church family?

## Women and Religion/Death

Women were not only visible, they were also, along with their Greek and Jewish sisters, active participants in the religions of the time. The model informs us that religion was a major outlet for women's need for public expression.

Clark says religion was the one area where women could freely participate outside of their domestic duties. They usually did not do away with their domesticity but rather their religious duties became an additional responsibility (Clark 1989, 33-34). However, one might argue that religion was also a domestic duty. There were household gods to worship and many of the rituals centered around fertility and family. Thus, indirectly it was still closer to the private realm than the public spheres of the marketplace and discussions at the Forum.

Scheid (1992, 375) suggests that although Roman women remained in a subordinate position to men they held an integral place in the Roman religions. He goes on to suggest that the "public" worship of any deity, even a goddess, was practiced mostly by men while women usually were excluded (Scheid 1992, 378). Two exceptions, according to Scheid, were the Vestal Virgins and wives that served with their husbands as a "priestly couple" (1992, 384). Women's role in religion was limited to certain areas. Matrons were considered the most appropriate women for religious activity, but Scheid contends they were not able to make "public" sacrifices. Women's religious activity revolved around the celebration of fertility and the life cycle. Only on special occasions were women able to officiate at sacrifices (Scheid 1992, 405-406). Scheid (1992, 408) ultimately finds that women when they were able to participate publicly in religious rites did so by imitating the male model.

Staples in *From Good Goddess to Vestal Virgins* also discusses the important role of women in the Roman religions. She suggests that religion and politics were one cultural institution and attempts to understand why women were active in religion but not in politics (Staples 1998, 3). She argues that Roman women had a central role in the religious life of Rome, and that they were not only involved in annual festivals but during other times of the year (Staples 1998, 7). She questions why women were "allowed" this public role and why men sanctioned their involvement in religion. She explores the cults of Bona Dea, Vesta, Flora, Venus and Ceres (Staples 1998, 8).

Staples (1998, 12) contends that the cult of Bona Dea separated men from women by establishing a boundary between them. The separation of male and females was enacted through rituals of water and fire (Staples 1998, 15). Again in the cults of Ceres and Floria the roles of women and men were central, and were in fact reversed. Men were not present at the Cerialia, but in the Floralia women and men were placed on equal footing (Staples 1998, 93). Women were clearly active participants in these rituals.

The worship of Venus, although not restricted to men, seems to have been enacted solely by women. Both matrons and prostitutes participated in the rituals (Staples 1998, 109). Staples (1998, 131-133) also spends a good deal of time addressing the vestals and their vow of chastity. She asserts that a vestal's virginity was of great importance to Rome by being the very life and death, stability or chaos of the state (Staples 1998, 135). She concludes that Roman women did not have a marginal role in the religion of their state, rather they participated publicly and during civic festivals throughout the year (Staples 1998, 159). She adds that all of their religious celebrations were in some way related to men or their relationships to them. They had no standing outside of their connectedness to their male kin (Staples 1998, 160). Even for the Vestal Virgins, their relationship to men still pulled the strings.

## Vestal Virgins

References to Vestal Virgins and their importance to the religious life of Rome are evident throughout the primary sources. Cicero recounts how Pompilius organized the Vestal Virgins (*Resp.* 2.14.27), and how they were to "guard the eternal fire on the public hearth of the city" (*Leg.* 2.8.20, Keyes). As Pontifex Maximus, Numa was an overseer of the Vestal Virgins, who were entrusted with the worship and care of the perpetual fire. In Delphi and Athens this perpetual care was given over to widows who were too old to remarry. Numa chose to develop this order of serving women. These women were charged with guarding the fire and perhaps other sacred objects in the temple (Plutarch *Num.* 9.5-6 and 10.1,2).

The vestals were to be chaste for 30 years. They would progress throughout that time, first learning, then performing their duties, then teaching others. After 30 years they could marry if they wanted to leave the sacred office (Plutarch *Num. 10*). Great privileges were given to them by Numa. They could make a will during the lifetime of their fathers. They could manage their own affairs without a guardian, a privilege reserved for mothers of at least three children. If they were to "accidentally" meet a criminal who was being led to execution, the person's life would be spared. Anyone who passed under a litter they were carried on was killed.

The virgins were held to very high moral standards. They were punished according to their offence. For minor offences they were beaten. If one broke the vow of chastity she was killed by being burnt alive (Plutarch *Numa* 9.5-11.2). The Vestal Virgins lived apart from men and were punished if they were guilty of any lewdness (Dio 56.5.7). Augustus however considered the Vestal Virgins to be so trustworthy that his will was stored with them (Dio 56.32.1).

Around 14 B.C.E. the temple of Vesta was burned. The Vestal Virgins carried the sacred objects up to the Palatine and placed them in the house of Jupiter's priest (Dio 54.24.2-3). As a result of the fire Lepidus the high priest gave the house of *rex sacrificulus* to the virgins (Dio 54.27.3).

At one time noble families did not show much interest in having their daughters become "priestesses of Vesta." As a result a law was passed that enabled daughters of freedmen to also become priestesses (ἱερᾶσθαι). Dio tells us "many vied for the honor" (55.22.5, Cary). One Vestal Virgin, Occia, had served Vesta for 57 years with "unblemished purity" (Tacitus *Ann.* 2.86, Moore and Jackson).

These Vestal Virgins were under great scrutiny. In Pliny's *Letters* we read about one of the vestals being accused of incest and being buried alive (Pliny *Ep.* 4.11). The penalty for impurity was high, even if it was a trumped-up charge. Suetonius also mentions this incident in *The Lives of the Caesars*. Cornelia, who as a "chief-vestal," had been charged one time before but acquitted. Domitian had her buried alive and most of her lovers beaten to death (Suetonius *Dom.* 8.4). These examples show how the virgins' interactions with men were to be curtailed by their modesty, and they needed to be beyond reproach.

Vestal Virgins were in a unique position, and they were afforded certain freedoms. Their involvement in the religious rite of Rome was key to their society. They held a place of importance because of their religious duty.

## Women and Other Religious Roles

Being a Vestal Virgin was not the only role a woman could play in religion. Augustus is said to have "made a vow with reference to the Megalensian games because some woman had cut some letters on her arm and practiced some sort of divination." It is said that he believed she had inflicted the wound herself and had not been possessed by any divinity. However, he went along with the display to keep the crowd appeased (Dio 55.31.2-3). Did some women use religion, a medium in which they had some legitimate public role, to their own advantage?

Augustus also encourages families to approach the gods together. He says that men, women and children should address the gods in partnership (Dio 56.9.2). After his death Augustus was declared immortal and Livia was called his priestess. She and Tiberius also had a shrine built for Augustus in Rome (Dio 56.46.1-2). The imperial family seems to have encouraged women to be active participants in the religions. The imperial family was worshipped among the gods and goddesses.

In Plutarch's *Roman Questions* there is an acknowledgement that there are many shrines to Diana in Rome and elsewhere (Plutarch *Quaest. rom.* 264 C.3). He mentions worship in the shrine of Matuta, where slave women were not permitted to enter (Plutarch *Quaest. rom.* 267 D.16). The women prayed to Matuta to bring blessing upon their sister's children (Plutarch *Quaest. rom.* 267 E.17). The matrons also founded a temple to Carmenta (Plutarch *Quaest. rom.* 278 B.56). They worshiped Bona Dea in their home, decorating with blooming plants and ridding the house of anything male (Plutarch *Quaest. rom.* 268 D.20). Women again are shown to be active in religious worship within their home, yet their worship in this case seems to be shared only among other women.

According to these sources, it seems clear that in ancient Rome women were active in religions and had a major role to play in their society in this regard. Religion provided women a legitimate outlet for service and public display. Roman women made the most of this cultural freedom.

Horace sings the praises of Phoebus and Diana mentioning the "chosen maidens" and "spotless youths" who sing hymns of honor to the gods (Horace *Saec.* 1, 6). Cicero writes of women's celebrations to the Benign Goddess, sarcastically suggesting a man has no reason to want to be there (Suetonius *Dom.* 40.105). In an inscription we read "To Helvia....priestess of Venus, from her sons at their own cost" (*Tituli Sepulcrales* 109, Warmington). Cicero in his rhetoric *Against Verres* describes how women were distressed and would wail when objects used for "divine service" were taken from them as bounty (*Verrine Orations I: Against Verres II* IV.21.47). He goes on to tell of the response of the people both male and female when the statue of Diana was removed from the city of Segesta at Verres' command. There was weeping and wailing (Cicero *Verres* IV.341.76). He recalls a time when the statue was brought back into town because of a military victory and remembers the great crowd of women that gathered and the matrons that crowned the statue with perfume and flowers (Cicero *Verres* IV.35.77).[10]

Roman women were clearly active in a variety of religious experiences. Religion provided them with an outlet for freedom of expression they were not otherwise allowed to experience. The obvious implications for this study are clear. It was not a far leap to Christianity, particularly if we consider it a religion in which women served equally with men as we see in Romans 16. It was surely an area of society that women would have been likely to be visible.

## Death

The passage and rites of death was another area in which Roman women played a key role. As the model suggests, women received the role by default, because it was a job no respectable man would want. Yet they turned this shame filled role into an outlet for their own religious and emotional expression.

When Horatius had won in battle for the Romans he came home displaying his spoils. His sister was betrothed to a man he had killed in battle. When she realized her future husband was dead she mourned her betrothed by loosening her hair, weeping and calling "on her dead lover's name." Her brother was angered by her lamentations at this time of great victory and so killed her saying she wrongly mourned a foe (Livy 1.26.2-5).

When Augustus died women took part in his funeral procession as they came with their senatorial and equestrian husbands and the rest of the city (Dio 56.42.1). Women were present and active in his burial and in mourning. After the ceremonies were over Livia stayed by his grave for five days and at the end of the time placed his bones in his tomb (Dio 56.42.4). According to the law mourning was observed for several days by the men but for an entire year by the women (Dio 56.43.1).

In *Satyricon* Petronius includes an account of a woman following her husband's corpse in his funeral procession. She is in the "common fashion" for a grieving wife—loose hair, beating her breast in front of the crowd and keeping watch over his resting place (Petronius *Satyr.* 111). Lucan describes Marcia's widow's weeds and how her purple band around her tunic is covered with wool of the funeral colour (Lucan *Phars.* 2.365-367). We also read of Cornelia who met the crowd weeping and with loosened hair (Lucan *Phars.* 9.172-173). Plutarch in his *Roman Questions* describes how women wore white robes and head-dress while in mourning. They also clothed the body of the dead in white (Plutarch *Quaest. rom.* 270 E.26). Thus, women must have donned particular clothing and costume at the time of mourning. Women apparently followed certain protocols when their kin died. Their dress and their actions were culturally conditioned.

There were also regulations for the mourning period. Numa regulated the period of mourning according to certain ages. There was a time during which women whose husbands had died remained in widowhood. If such a woman took another husband before that time was over, she was to sacrifice "a cow with calf" (Plutarch *Num.* 12.2, Perrin).

In Plutarch we also read of Sulla who would not have dealings with his wife when she was about to die. Sulla sponsored great feasting after he consecrated a "tenth of all his sustenance to Hercules." During this time his wife Metella was sick and dying at home. The priests advised Sulla forbidding him to go near Metella. He was not to have his house polluted by her funeral. So Sulla divorced his wife and had her carried from his house before she died (Plutarch *Sull.* 35.2).

Thus, although women were quite close to death and its rituals, men were more removed and more concerned about uncleanness. Men seemed to fear death and its impurity. Women, however, whether by choice or necessity, accepted death as a natural part of their existence and expressed their connection to it by the ritual of mourning the dead. The evidence for their acts does not seems as prolific in Greek society, but nevertheless, it was still present throughout each of the Mediterranean societies we have explored.

## Conclusion

Roman women may have been more "free" than their Jewish counterparts, and were without doubt more influential than their Greek sisters. Having had more wealth and mobility, they seemingly spoke their minds more freely, and they also played a greater role in the decisions affecting their families. Nevertheless, we must remember that many of our primary sources refer to imperial and wealthy women and, thus, our view of Roman women is skewed. Certainly a woman's class and wealth made a difference in the amount of freedom she had and power she exerted. However, regardless of their class affiliation it seems evident that Roman women were still very much embroiled in the Mediterranean cultural patterns of their time.

The one area not highlighted in this discussion of the model but in the other two cultures is women and relationships. While it was postulated that Paul had formed a network of relationships and women generally worked within the power structures of relationships, the evidence cannot be supported in Roman women. Perhaps in Jewish and Greek cultures relationships were a stronger network than in the Roman world where women had more individual freedom. Perhaps they did not need to rely on the support they received from other women as much as Greek and Jewish women. Roman women were still interconnected to their kin group and were embedded in those relationships. However, our findings will alter how we approach the topic of relationship networks as they apply to Romans 16.

This study has a clear impact on our understanding of women in the early Roman church. These women were more active publicly, in their families and in religion. It does not seem as far a jump to make that such women would be involved in this "new sect" of Judaism and that their role might seem more public than the women of Corinth or Ephesus. We will now turn our attention to the women of Romans 16 as we consider the text in light of these insights.

# Notes

1. See also Dio 57.18.1a.

2. Livia was also honored by the senate and the women of Rome at her death (Dio 58.2.1-3).

3. Pomeroy does not cite the reference to this citation, and this problem is one of the significant difficulties with this work. She obviously is well versed in the classics, but does not always freely share her sources with the reader. See the section on Parenthood at the end of this work for a reference. Once again she makes mention of Claudius' law in the first century C.E. that abolished automatic guardians over women but does not cite the reference (Pomeroy 1975, 152).

4. Pliny writes to Verus asking him to oversee the gift of a farm he has made to his nurse. He says it is worth 100,000 sesterces and wishes it to increase in value (Pliny *Ep.* 6.3). In his will Domitius Tullus leaves an inheritance to his daughter as well as legacies to his grandsons and great-granddaughter (*Ep.* 8.18.2). Tullus also leaves to his wife a substantial sum of money and a home in the country (*Ep.* 8.18.8).

5. It was said that she was not satisfied to rule on equal terms with Tiberius, but wished to take precedence over him. Many of the people believed she should be called "Mother of the Country" or "Parent." Some even suggested that Tiberius should change his name to reflect his relationship to her. Tiberius was subsequently angry and jealous, thus he tried to block the many honors afforded to her.

On one occasion Livia wanted to hold a banquet for the senate, the knights and their wives, but Tiberius would not allow it to go forward unless the approval of the senate was given. He went further so as to restrict Livia to dining with the women and he the men. He slowly moved her out of her visible role in "public affairs" and "allowed her to direct matters at home" (Dio 57.12.1-6, Cary). The idea that Livia not only dined with women but also with men and interacted with men outside her kin on a daily basis also signifies a change in gender relations. Because of their increasing power women did not seem to be as segregated from men as they once had been.

6. Other mothers Pomeroy references are Aurelia, Rhea and Atia in Tacitus *Dial.* 28 and Cornelia in Cicero *Brut.* 211.

7. See also Valarius Maximus 8.3, and for Hortensia, Cicero *Quint. fratr.* 1.1.6.

8. Augustus subsequently ordered that no man could betroth himself to a girl less than ten years old and that they had to marry within two years (Dio 54.16.6-7). He set the marriageable age of a girl at the end of her twelfth year (18 B.C.E.) (Dio 54.16.7).

9. An example of another independent woman is Scipio's daughter Cornelia (c. 183 B.C.E.), wife of Tiberius Gracchus. They had twelve children together and he died when she was still young. From then on Cornelia raised the children and controlled the estate. When

Ptolemy around 163 B.C.E. asked for her in marriage, "she refused him, and remained a widow" (Plutarch *Ti. C. Gracch.* 1.2-4). Cornelia was an example of a woman who survived despite widowhood and who refused the security of a second marriage.

10. Cicero tells us of another woman who was having her property stolen by an admiral. In the name of Venus she told the admiral that he was committing sacrilege. She claimed her property also belonged to the goddess (*Verrine Orations I: Against Q. Caecilius* 17.55). Cicero also speaks of wives, children and husbands celebrating at shrines together (*Cat.* 3.23).

# 6
# Romans 16: A List of Greetings or Evidence of Women Leaders?

In this next section we will overview the secondary literature on Romans 16 and discuss basic historical-critical issues about the text. As we move along in this discussion and into chapter seven we will begin to ask how the cultural context model will influence our understanding of the text. We will eventually review insights from the model and the values we have explored and will see where Romans 16 is highlighted and new questions are raised by this work. With these goals in mind we begin our study of Romans 16.

## Focus on Romans 16

### Introduction

At this point in our exploration of women in the ancient Mediterranean world we turn to the crux of our argument. As has been shown in Greek, Jewish and even Roman society, women held little power in the ancient world. However, they may have held some power in the spheres of the home and religion. While some exceptions in the wealthy or ruling classes existed, those women were certainly not considered equal to men. Our model has helped us to understand better their general status and yet has also upheld a more balanced picture of women's role in the ancient Mediterranean. Women in the ancient world clearly had a role in the family, community and in their religions. Mediterranean women were guided by honor and shame and public and private divides, but the shades of these values are made clearer as the various primary sources of the individual cultures nuance the model. We will suspend much of our discussion of these insights until we can get a solid picture of the text we are focusing on, Romans 16. We will resume the discussion of the model in the second half of chapter seven after gaining a good understanding of Romans 16.

We will use this model to cast more light on Romans 16, particularly in the area of cultural context. In a sense it will be used as an example for how such a model can help us to understand better other New Testament texts. We will also explore Romans 16 as a significant pericope in and of itself, beyond the use of the model, to inform our understanding of women in the early church. Romans 16 is a richly diverse text that can add much to the picture of women in the early church.

# Historical-Critical Considerations

## Author

Scholars[9] accept without discussion that Paul is the author of the letter to the Romans. C.K. Barrett writes, "That the Epistle to the Romans was written by the apostle Paul is a proposition which it is unnecessary to discuss because it is not in dispute" (1991, 1). Though some scholars may question whether Romans 16 is attached to the rest of the letter, they certainly accept Pauline authorship.[10] Paul is also connected with this letter by association and self-identification. Prisca and Aquila were indisputable co-workers of Paul, for he greets or mentions them in some of his other letters[11] and Luke also associates them with Paul in Acts 18. Timothy, his co-worker in the gospel, also sends greetings in 16:21.[12] Paul also identifies himself in the text as the author of the letter (Romans 1:1). However, it seems probable that he did use an amanuensis, Tertius (16:22), who penned Paul's words to the Romans.

## Date

It makes sense to also consider the dating of this letter in order to determine whether our cultural/historical analysis can be supported by other evidence contemporary with Paul. Paul was perhaps writing from Corinth, given his mention of the church at Cenchreae. The letter was most likely written on one of his stays in that city.[13] Harrison offers that Romans was probably written around 57, or the mid-50's C.E. (1995, 4). This date takes into account Claudius' expulsion of the Jews in 49 C.E. and his death in 54 C.E. The persecutions of Nero from 64-67 C.E. had more than likely not taken place yet, as there is no evidence for this scenario in the body of the letter. Dodd suggests Romans was probably written around 59 C.E., but 57 and 58 are also possibilities. The letter appears to definitely have been written prior to the Neronian persecutions (Dodd 1932, xxvi). Dunn suggests that Romans was written in the mid-50's, probably between 55 and 57 C.E. (1988, xliii).

According to Acts 28, Paul made it to Rome as a captive to face trial, spending two years under house arrest. He was met by fellow Christians in neighboring villages of the Forum of Appius and Three Taverns. He received both home and provision by some unknown donor(s) during the years he was under arrest. The story of Acts ends there. We do not know whether Paul ever made it to Spain or whether he was martyred first. We can surmise that he needed some financial help while living in Rome which this letter would have garnered. As is evident in its contents[14] the letter was written sometime before Paul's first visit to Rome. Thus the people who came to visit him probably had prior knowledge of his ministry and perhaps developed respect for him via his letter and his patron Phoebe. It does not appear in the Acts source that the Neronian persecutions had yet begun. Therefore, we can safely assume Nero was in power, but the persecutions had not yet become full-fledged (Suetonius *Nero* 5.16.2 and Tacitus *Ann.* 15.44). The dating of the letter somewhere between 57 and 59 C.E. seems most plausible because it was probably composed sometime after Claudius' edict was lifted and Nero would have been in power. Romans surely was written before the fires of Rome and the intense persecutions of the Christians which began in 64 C.E., as there is no indication in the letter that these persecutions were underway.

## Literary Analysis

Is Romans 16 an original part of Paul's letter to the Romans? There has been much debate over this very issue. In fact, chapters 15 and 16 are both problematic. The question of the doxologies appearing in 15:33 and 16:25-27 in a variety of texts is also one of contention.[15] There have been many theories, including at one time the belief that chapter 16 was never intended for Rome but was for Ephesus. Some scholars still hold to this belief, as does T.W. Manson in the revised edition of *The Romans Debate*.[16] Yet F.F. Bruce and Peter Lampe in that same work support a Roman audience. Both argue in varying degrees that Romans 16 not only supports a Roman destination but also paints a picture of the people who were a part of the Roman Christian community. There is increasing scholarly support for a Roman audience, including Dunn, Jewett, and Brown and Meier among others,[17] therefore, it is safe to assume that Romans 16 is connected to the Roman Christians and can provide us with a window into the early Roman church. We now need to ask how we understand this list of greetings and brief comments as a literary form.

## Literary Features

Romans 16 appears at the end of a rather intense and weighty letter. It contains an exceptionally long list of greetings, beginning with a commendation of Phoebe who was probably the bearer of the letter. There are the farewell greetings and then some final words of exhortation and a doxology. There are also greetings from people who were with the author. Yet this seemingly "standard" letter has some very unique peculiarities. In order to determine what is striking about this ending we need to first consider the usual components of ancient Greco-Roman letters.

### Greetings

Mullins (1968, 418-421, 424-425) notes that the greeting was used to establish a bond between the sender and the receiver. Greetings could be written in the first, second or third person. There is only one first-person greeting found in the New Testament, that of Tertius in Romans 16:22. Jewett suggests that the greetings of Romans 16 along with the unique opening indicate it is an ambassadorial letter.

Paul writes as an ambassador of the gospel hoping to gain support for his endeavor to Spain (Jewett 1982, 14). Letters of introduction are also mentioned in Acts 9:2, 18:27; 1 Corinthians 16:3 and 2 Corinthians 3:1,2. Passages of commendation are found mixed into some Pauline letters such as Philippians 2:25-30, 1 Corinthians 16:15-18, and 1 Thessalonians 5:12,13. 3 John is considered a letter of commendation (Stowers 1994, 155-156).

Other Pauline letters that close with greetings include 1 Corinthians (16:19-21), 2 Corinthians (13:12-13), Philippians (4:21-22), I Thessalonians (5:26) and Philemon (23, 24). Three include references to a "holy kiss" (Romans, 2 Corinthians and 1 Thessalonians). To several of his other letters Paul adds a final closing as a personal touch (Stowers 1994, 61).[18]

Gamble also discusses the readership of the letter. He states that the greetings mostly appear in the form of the second person imperative. The debate over whether Paul is asking the readers to greet others outside the readership is questioned.[19] Gamble suggests that the ones being greeted were also a part of the audience because they were to exchange a "holy kiss" with one another (1977, 92).

*Commendation and Recommendation*

According to Kim, there are three parts to Paul's commendations. The first includes an introduction with a petition and a reference to the one being commended. The second component includes a section where Paul praises or presents the credentials of the person being commended. In papyrus letters the person is recommended by describing the person's relationship to the writer. The third and final aspect is a statement concerning the "desired action." In this section Paul advises how he wishes the recipients to respond (Stowers 1994, 156).

In Aune's discussion on letters of commendation he underscores their relationship to Greek letters of introduction. Patronage, a relationship played out between people of different social classes, played a great role in the development of such letters (Aune 1987, 166). He further suggests that since letters formed the primary mode of communication between people, the language of reunion occurs repeatedly (Aune 1987, 190).

Gamble (1987, 85) along with Stowers says it is not unheard of to find letters of recommendation embedded within letters concerning other matters. It would thus not be surprising to find this recommendation of Phoebe as part of the body of the letter to the Romans in the concluding statements. The greetings of Romans 16 are both personal and private, as such they do not belong in the "official letter" (Gamble 1987, 91). They reflect Paul's personal relationships with some of the Christians at Rome.

*Familial Correspondence*

It seems useful at this point to consider a body of letters that were written within the time period of the New Testament. The best source available for such a comparison is Cicero's collection of letters. Some letters of Pliny are also studied. In a review of Cicero's letters to both Atticus and his friends it is obvious when he is writing to a family member or close associate. In writing to Atticus he often closes with greetings to Attica and Pila.[20] He sometimes sends greetings from those who are with him or sends greetings to a friend, although he does not name more than one or two people at a time.[21] There is a difference between Cicero's endings and those of Pliny's letters. Pliny does not greet anyone nor close with any familial or affectionate language. He sometimes closes with *Vale* or farewell, but does not expand his closings much more.[22] White (1986, 198) notes that in family letters and "friendly correspondence" the goal of maintaining relationships is accomplished in the opening and closing of the letter. He goes on to acknowledge that in the ancient world, the letter conveyed actual presence and conversation (1986, 202). Such letters also often mention future visits that would be mutually beneficial (1986, 202). The lengthy ending and extensive greetings of Romans seems to indicate that Paul wrote to his churches in a familial language and form. If we can make the case for such a situation then there are implications for the way we understand the relationships mentioned in the letter. Did the Christians of Rome consider themselves as "kin" to one another? The term "fictive kinship"[23] might express the relationships one sees demonstrated here.

Stowers, in his work *Letter Writing in Greco-Roman Antiquity*, points out that Pauline letters have a familial sense that was common to the papyrus letter of the ancient world. He notes that Paul maintains his ongoing relationship with the Christian family through his letters (Stowers 1986, 43). A familial or household letter was written to continue social relationships and show affection within the family (Stowers 1986, 71). It seems very probable that Paul's letter to the Romans falls into this category. White (1986, 19) in *Light from Ancient Letters* addresses the additional features of familial letters, noting that in such letters the opening and closings are more extensive.

*Postscripts, Autographs and Orality*

Could Romans 16:1-16 be a postscript added for emphasis to the end of a lengthy letter? Perhaps it stands out because it highlights the relationships via extension which Paul already had with members of various Roman house churches. Jervis (1991, 152) in *The Purpose of Romans* suggests that Paul identifies specific individuals within the Roman community whom he knew to "commend" himself to his readers. She also suggests that Paul sought to write this letter as a substitution for his own physical presence (Jervis 1991, 156). Paul was seeking to solidify his own relationship with the Roman church. Jewett (1988, 153) suggests Paul wanted to use his connections to ensure support for his mission to Spain, using his wealthy patroness Phoebe as the one to make the way clear.

Weima states that postscripts in ancient letters were not common occurrences but were often where the author placed his/her personal mark on the letter. These postscripts usually consisted of final remarks that for whatever reason were omitted from the letter and closing (Weima 1994, 52). If Romans 16 functions as a postscript could it have been added as a letter of recommendation for both Phoebe, the carrier of the letter, and Paul the apostle wishing to solidify his ministry in Rome in order to carry out his new ministry to Spain?

Gamble notes that there is often a "concluding autograph" in ancient letters. Writers would have an amanuensis copy most of their letter, but would add their own message at some point in the conclusion (Gamble 1977, 62). Could Paul have added his signature to the end of Romans and as a result what we have is disjointed? Gamble argues it seems likely and indeed befitting Paul's concern for the church at Rome (1977, 94). His argument seems sensible and a good possibility.

Aune notes that the original understanding of epistle also contained connotations of oral communication. He suggests that the letter functioned as a substitute for oral communication (Aune 1987, 158). Thus, Paul's letter to the Romans could perhaps be compared with a rather lengthy modern phone call or visit. Aune also makes an interesting suggestion that necessitates some consideration. He offers the possibility that Romans follows a diatribe style of Socratic method in pitting one opponent (the Jew) against another (the Gentile) (Aune 1987, 219). The implications, if he is correct, would be in conflict with this work's understanding of the audience. The audience reading this letter appears to have been made up of both Jews and Gentiles. The opponents do not appear to be imaginary but are real. It seems to be a letter sent to address conflicts in a specific time and place. The conflict between these two ethnic groups was not unique to Rome but was also found in Galatia.[24]

What then can we conclude about the literary form of Romans 16? It appears to be connected to the letter as a whole and not a later addendum. It is possibly a postscript that Paul added to commend the bearer of his letter and to lend credibility to his teaching by showing all of the Christians in Rome that he is connected with in some way. It offered Paul a chance to continue personal relationships and to develop a connection with Roman Christians he had never met. It may appear disjointed because it is Paul's own writing distinguished from the writing of his amanuensis. Romans 16 is an unusually lengthy list of greetings that Lampe (1991, 218) suggests is ultimately a commending of Paul himself to the Roman people. It is becoming apparent that the purpose of Romans 16 seems inherently tied to the occasion of the letter to the Romans. Discerning why Romans was written may help us to understand better the meaning of these greetings.

## Occasion of the Letter

Why did Paul write the letter to the Romans? There have been many theories over the years. Too often it has been seen as a major theological treatise rather than as a letter and has, as a consequence, lost its context. Jewett, however, puts forth the idea that Paul wanted to finance his Spanish mission which he mentions in 15:28.[25] Paul was sending Phoebe ahead to make the way clear for him to gain support and be sent out from Rome to evangelize the Western world. Paul was heading for Spain and wanted to garner support through Phoebe's contacts and power. Phoebe, clearly an influential woman who has been a patron to many, would be able to prepare the way for Paul's coming to Rome.

Fitzmyer summarizes Paul's reasons for writing Romans as multipurposed. Paul wanted to introduce himself to the Roman Christians and seek support for his future journey to Spain. He wanted prayers for his delivering of the collection to Jerusalem that he might be well-received. Yet he also deals with some very real problems in the Roman community among Jews and Gentiles. This letter was intended to provoke discussion and co-operation between the Jewish and Gentile Christians. It was also Paul's intent to present his gospel as available to the Jews and the Gentiles who were both equally guilty of sin and in need of redemption (Fitzmyer 1993, 79, 80).

It is likely that at least one of the purposes behind Romans is that it was written to unite the Roman Christians who were experiencing discord over their ethnic and cultural differences. Dunn believes Paul wrote to the Romans to intercede in the midst of possible divisions in the house churches. He says that the idea that individual churches were segregated along Gentile/Jew lines is simplistic. Rather, Paul may be writing to help the house churches individually be more welcoming of Jewish Christians who entered their fellowship (Dunn 1988, lvii). The conflict between Jews and Greeks is clearly a theme throughout the entire letter, as will be demonstrated later in our discussion of the text. Developing unity in the midst of diversity may have been another intention of the author.

*Specific Occasion/Purpose of Romans 16*

Why did Paul specifically write Romans 16? It seems likely that Phoebe carried the letter for him to the Romans. It was, according to Keener (1993, 262), important for him to establish her credibility in the eyes of his audience. It was also a way for Paul to make connections within a church he himself had not founded or visited. He desired to come and visit them soon (Romans 15:23-24), therefore, it would be a good way to pave the road. He knew many of them from his missionary travels and contact in other churches, so he was not going to a completely foreign place. Phoebe also needed contacts upon her arrival in the city. Goodspeed (1951, 56, 57) makes too much of this point by claiming she was in desperate need because she was a woman. Phoebe had been resourceful enough to get herself to Rome without any trouble, thus it seems provision for her was not the intent of this text. More than likely if Phoebe stayed at Rome for any length of time she would have wanted to continue the ministry she was involved in at Cenchreae.

She would perhaps want to serve the Roman church or at least minister among them while she was there. Otherwise why would Paul feel the need to discuss her ministry skills? She also might have become a patron of the Roman church if her resources were needed (Whelan 1993, 79).

It is not uncommon for Paul's letters to contain a list of greetings. It is, however, unusual that they would be this lengthy. Chapter 16 might be a cover letter to the rest of Romans. As has already been highlighted, Phoebe is commended and contact is made with a church that was fairly unknown to Paul.

There are many reasons why such an addendum to the letter would have been written. We have only considered several possibilities in this limited space. It does seem likely that regardless of any other reasons, Phoebe's visit to the recipients was primary. Paul's coming visit to Rome was also an important factor, for the personal connections in chapter 16 paved the way for his future work among the churches there.

A key to our interpretation of this passage will be found as we begin to unravel the picture of the audience of this letter. Yet we will hold off on that discussion and first focus on the text and its grammatical components.

## Grammatical Study of Romans 16:1-16

Translation of Romans 16:1-16*

(v.1) And I commend to you Phoebe our sister, who being also a deacon of the church in Cenchreae,
(v.2) in order that you might welcome her in the Lord in a manner worthy of the saints, also that you might assist her in whatever she might need a deed/work from you, for she has become a patron of many and of me as well.
(v.3) Greet Prisca and Aquila my fellow workers in Christ Jesus,
(v.4) who risked their necks for my life, to whom not I alone give thanks but also all the churches of the nations/Gentiles,
(v.5) also (greet) the church in their house. Greet Epenetus my beloved, who is the first fruits of Asia in Christ.
(v.6) Greet Maria/Mary, who toiled much for you.
(v.7) Greet Andronicus and Junia my kinsmen and my fellow prisoners, who are outstanding among the apostles, who also were in Christ before me.
(v.8) Greet Ampliatus my beloved in the Lord.
(v.9) Greet Urbanus our fellow worker in Christ and Stachys my beloved.
(v.10) Greet Apelles who is valued in Christ. Greet the ones from the house of Aristobulus.
(v.11) Greet Herodian my kinsman. Greet the ones in the Lord from the house of Narcissus.
(v.12) Greet Tryphaena and Tryphosa the hard workers in the Lord. Greet Persis the beloved, who worked hard in the Lord.
(v.13) Greet Rufus the elect in the Lord and his mother, also mine.
(v.14) Greet Asyncritus, Phlegon, Hermes, Patrobas, Hermas and the brothers with them.
(v.15) Greet Philologus and Julia, Nereus and his sister, also Olympas and all the saints with them.
(v.16) Greet one another with a holy kiss. All the churches of Christ greet you.

*Author's own translation from The Greek New Testament, United Bible Societies, 4th ed.

## Grammatical Analysis

In the next stage of our exegesis we focus on the text for grammatical nuances that might help give us a clearer picture of its meaning. Immediately following this section we will consider the variants of the text and the understanding of key words.

The first word to draw attention to in this first verse is οὖσαν, which is the present active participle of the word "to be." Thus, we understand that Phoebe is currently "being" a deacon, implying a durative, continuous activity. She was not at one time a leader in the church, but even as she delivered this letter[27] she represented the church of Cenchreae to the people of Rome, and continued in her role as deacon. She is described as both "our sister" and a "deacon."[28] Whelan (1993, 82) argues that Phoebe is also called "our sister," because she is not a patron who is on the periphery, as was often the case, but is an actual member of the group of which she is a benefactor.

In verse two this sentence carries on to include a ἵνα subjunctive purpose clause, suggesting a hypothetical situation which has not yet occurred. Thus the idea that Phoebe might be welcomed in a manner worthy of the saints and that the church at Rome might provide for her needs suggests an ongoing relationship Phoebe does not yet, but might possibly in the future, have with the Roman church. Schüssler Fiorenza (1986, 424) emphasizes the fact that Phoebe is described in regard to her ecclesiastical functions and not "wifely" duties or family responsibilities. She is a woman identified with the church, not with her family of origin nor with the family she might have been associated with via marriage (if she was not an unmarried virgin or widow).

The subjunctive is still operative following the καὶ, suggesting that both of the above described situations are a possibility for Phoebe. Paul is attempting to provide for her needs as she probably bears the letter and also is called his patron. The word προστάτις is found in the noun form only here in the New Testament.[29]

This final clause in verse two begins with two co-ordinating conjunctions that stress a connection to the rest of the sentence and emphasize this clause's importance. Phoebe should be welcomed and helped in any way because she is a patron to many, including to Paul. Her importance to the early church is thus underscored—not only is she a sister in the Lord, a deacon of a local church community, but also a patron to many. No doubt is left as to her importance to Paul or to other Christians within his circle.

Verse three begins a new thought, a command to greet Prisca and Aquila. Prisca's name does appear before her husband's name in the text, thus adding an interesting literary technique. It has been acknowledged by scholars[30] that women's names would often appear after their husbands, and not before, given their "subservient" role in society. Perhaps Paul is making a point of highlighting Prisca's importance to the Christian community. Of the other instances where she and her husband are mentioned in the biblical text, her name appears first all but once.[31] Also take note in verse three that Prisca and Aquila are referred to more personally than Phoebe. Instead of being "our" co-workers Paul calls them "my co-workers." Paul mentions they "risked their necks for him," and thus were clearly committed to his friendship. Paul focuses on both his thankfulness and that of the other Gentile churches.

In verse five we see that the church is referred to as meeting in "their" house, αὐτῶν, thus implying the church is led or hosted by both parties, not just the male. Throughout the text it is evident that Prisca and Aquila are equally greeted and honored by Paul. Recognition of Prisca in this way went against the grain of society.

The list of greetings continues, but becomes more brief and with fewer grammatical nuances. This work will highlight just a few of the important points. In verse seven we read of Andronicus and Junia and learn of a variant concerning Junia's name. This issue will be discussed in a later section on variants. Andronicus and Junia are considered "outstanding" among the apostles. As Keener (1992, 241) notes, they were not just of importance within their circle but were indeed apostles themselves. Witherington offers that ἐν plus the dative case of ἀπόστολος could have several meanings. Perhaps the two were outstanding in the "eyes of" the apostles. Witherington concludes the phrase most likely means "among," yet he goes on to raise the issue of what the word "apostle" meant to Paul. He suggests it meant "itinerant missionary" who might have engaged in evangelism and/or church planting (Witherington 1988, 115-116). A καὶ joins them together suggesting perhaps they are related in some way, either husband and wife or brother and sister. Keener (1992, 242) suggests it would be scandalous in that day for an unmarried woman apostle to travel with an unmarried male apostle, therefore the early church understood them to be a husband and wife team.

Our exploration of the grammatical nuances of the text reveals there are some insights that help us to understand the people greeted and the roles they played in the church and society. Yet our grammatical analysis needs to continue in order to investigate the issues that arise from variant Greek manuscripts. We will now consider such variants in the text and their implications for our understanding of women in the Roman church.

## Variants in the Text

One significant variant in Chapter 16:1-16 is found in verse seven and has already been mentioned. It concerns the correct spelling of the second name in the first phrase. Some ancient manuscripts and P[46] (the Chester Beatty Papyrus II, ca. 200 C.E.) read Ἰουλίαν but there is not much support for this spelling. The committee compiling the 4th edition of the United Bible Society's Greek New Testament was unanimous in rejecting it. However, it struggled a bit more with the decision over whether the name was the contracted Ἰουνιᾶν (Junias), the shorter form of the masculine Junianus. Metzger in his *Textual Commentary on the Greek New Testament* reports the committee leaned more towards the idea that Ἰουνίαν was the feminine accusative of Junia. Apparently some on the committee were influenced by the belief that it was "unlikely that a woman would be among those styled 'apostles'...." (Metzger 1994, 475). Yet the female Junia appears 250 times in Greek and Latin inscriptions found within the bounds of Rome. However, Junias (masculine) is not found in any inscriptions in any location, nor is it found in literature. In later centuries when the text began to be accented, scribes continued to identify the name as Junia. Metzger makes it clear that the committee's A decision on this variant "...must be understood as applicable only as to the spelling of the name Ἰουνιαν, and not the masculine accentuation" (1994, 476). Cranfield supports this interpretation, suggesting prejudice has led scholars to conclude the name is male because of context (Cranfield 1979, 788).[32]

Despite the work of scholars including Brooten, Schulz and Thorley,[33] the support for a masculine name continues to prevail among Bible translations. The only scholarly English translation to accept Junia as the correct interpretation is the New

Revised Standard Version, which still footnotes the name Junias. Yet the King James Version and the New King James Version do clearly use Junia and do not consider this partner of Paul to be a man. The New English Bible uses Junias but footnotes Junia. The New International Version, Revised Standard Version and the New American Standard use the masculine form and do not even footnote the feminine. It is telling that these standard English translations have not been able to include even the possibility that a woman might have been outstanding among the apostles. Yet it is equally important that some church fathers, including John Chrysostom, did not find the idea impossible and acknowledged and, in fact, exalted Junia in her position among the apostles (*Hom. Rom., Homily 31*).

Regarding Phoebe we also have many areas of debate. Several scholars have suggested that she was the bearer of the letter to the Romans.[34] It is important to note there is a textual variant that supports this possibility. In 16:27 a subscription sheds some interesting light on the identity of Phoebe. The earliest subscription found simply states "to Romans", yet other subscriptions refer to Phoebe and her role in carrying the letter to them. One manuscript reads "πρὸς Ῥωμαίους ἐγράφη διὰ Φοίβης ἀπὸ Κορίνθου,"[35] which tells us that the writing to the Romans has come through Phoebe from Corinth. Another subscription reads similarly but also calls Phoebe a deacon (Metzger 1994, 477).[36] The doxology "...the God of peace be with all of you. Amen" comes in 15:33 just before the start of Chapter 16. It seems an awkward place for the doxology and has been found in different places in various manuscripts (Metzger 1994, 475).

It is evident from this brief look at English texts that translators have found Romans 16 a troublesome pericope to tackle. It is an unusual list of greetings that seems to turn many cultural norms upside down. What it says is difficult to accept given the importance some ascribe to the theology and doctrine found in the letter to the Romans. Traditionally some scholars have understood Romans to be Paul's *opus magnus* or last will and testament in which he systematically and intentionally spelled out his theology. Perhaps its unique focus on the role of women makes the connection between his longest letter and his most egalitarian a hard one to understand. More evidence is needed and thus we will next focus our attention on the meaning of specific words within the text.

## Word Analysis

In this section we will explore several of the words that arose in the prior section. The words chosen are those which will shed more light on our topic or are ones that have raised questions in scholarly circles. The words we will specifically highlight are συνίστημι, διάκονον, προσδέξησθε, προσδέχξομαι, προστάτις, συνεργός, and ἐπίσημοι. Time will not permit a complete and exhaustive search of each word within its context in the primary sources. However, to gain some leverage in the discussion a broad range of primary resources have been reviewed in depth. The search tool used to locate the primary sources was the *Thesaurus Linguae Graecae* (TLG). All of the results have not been recorded, only those that help us to better understand the words' meanings. A significant number of examples from the TLG were examined in order to determine the meaning of the words. However, only the citations that nuanced or expanded the meaning of the words are mentioned in this study. Those words that have disputed meanings are highlighted.

Συνίστημι is the very first word of the chapter, a word that exhorts the Romans to accept Phoebe as one sent by Paul. The word does not appear in Greek literature until the first century C.E. In addition to Romans 16 it is also found in Josephus, where the historian refers to a man who was being "recommended" for an honor (*Ant.* 19.315-316). Chariton (second century C.E.) uses the word in relation to a child being "commended" to the care of another (*Chaer.* 8.4.8). One shade of the word is very different than the other. Phoebe might be "recommended" by Paul as he goes on to tell of her role in the church of Cenchreae. Yet Phoebe more likely is being commended to their care, as the next verse asks for the Romans to welcome or receive Phoebe.

The next word to be explored is one loaded with many presuppositions, hopes and frustrations—διάκονον. Phoebe is called a *deacon* of the church of Cenchreae. Many have argued this word means *deaconess*, others have argued for the meaning of *helper/servant* and still others *deacon*. The simplest analysis leads us to conclude the word is *deacon* and not *deaconess*. The word διάκονισσα (*deaconess*)[37] is not evidenced until later in the second or third century C.E. (Lampe 1991, 348; Whelan 1993, 68). The order of deaconess was an early church development for which we have no evidence in the first century C.E. The word διάκονος can be either masculine or feminine and can refer to help, service or ministry. The largest single source in the first century C.E. is the New Testament, where there are 29 references to this word throughout the various books. Philo, Josephus, Epictetus and Dio Chrysostom all use it as well.[38] It usually contains the meaning of servant, helper or attendant, yet some slight variations of its meaning include the idea of enslavement (Dio Chrysostom *4 Regn.*, 100), a ministry of care or task completion (Josephus *Ant.* 1.298, 11.255), minister (speaking as representative of God) (Josephus *J.W.* 4.626) and as an envoy or representative (Josephus *J.W.* 3.354). We can see how the word gets its underlying meaning of service. It is also possible that as the church began to adapt the word for its use, while it still meant service, it also had the meaning of representative or leader and one who brings the ministry of care, with the intent that everything is done in an attitude of service. In Phoebe's case we need to look at some of the other New Testament words to determine which nuance is appropriate.

Jesus referred to the need for his followers to become servants (using διάκονον) three times (twice in parallel passages).[39] Servants as a role in a household are referred to three times in the gospels (Matt 22:13 and John 2:5,9). In the larger text of Romans the word is found in two other occurrences. In Romans 13:4 it seems to mean "servant to God" and in 15:8 it again has the meaning of "servant to Christ." Διάκονος, used in Corinthians, Galatians, Colossians and Ephesians, continues to have the sense of servant. In Philippians 1:1 it is possible the word is referring to the early beginnings of an office because saints are mentioned as a separate group. The designation *saints* would seem a sufficient category if the term was meant to refer to servants. It is in the pastorals that we really begin to see distinction. In 1 Timothy 3:1-13 bishops, deacons and women are addressed. It appears these were categories of people in service to the Lord. In 1 Timothy 4:6 the word seems to be referring to servants in the church in general. Thus, there is no real sense that the word carries with it an office, yet in the case of 1 Timothy 3:8, 12 and Romans 16:1 there are some similarities. All three, according to the context, seem to indicate a specific function within the church at large and a particular church. Thus, there is a great possibility that the word in Romans 16:1 reflects the fact that Phoebe was a deacon of the church in Cenchreae. She was not simply "our sister" or a saint, but she had an acknowledged role in that church and Paul is highlighting it in his letter. Not only is the word hard to secure in the Greek, in English it seems much more elusive.

The New International Version describes Phoebe as a "servant." The Revised Standard Version and the New Jerusalem Bible describe her as a "deaconess." Once again, only the New Revised Standard Version describes Phoebe as a deacon. The word clearly has a complex history, and in the end we can only infer possible meanings.[40] It does mean servant, and yet in other instances throughout the New Testament text when referring to a man it is often translated "deacon" or "minister."[41] Cranfield writes that based on Paul's statements about Phoebe it would seem certain he is referring to a definite office held by her. He argues it is unequivocal that Phoebe is described as a deacon of the church (Cranfield 1979, 781). The question becomes whether there was an office of deacon so early in the formation of the Christian church or should all deacons be simply translated as servants. Clearly the word does imply servitude yet at times such as in Philippians 1:1 and here in Romans 16 there is a sense that the person being described is more than just another servant of the community.

The next word we will explore further is προσδέξησθε, which addresses the manner in which the Romans are to receive Phoebe. In Josephus' *Antiquities* we find προσδέξησθε in a variety of forms, as the word is used on at least four separate occasions. In 6.255 it seems to mean to receive or to welcome. In 6.42 we find it with the nuance of attending to or accepting. In 14.30 it has the nuance of accepting or receiving and later on in that same chapter (14.451) we see a shade of anticipation or expectation. Thus, in looking at these examples we see that it seems very possible that Paul is calling on the Romans to accept, receive and attend to his patron, sister and co-worker Phoebe. One would assume that the hospitality in the ancient world would be connected with this reception of Phoebe in to their midst. Phoebe would not be simply greeted but also provided for, and as Paul goes on to say, helped with whatever need she might have.

The next word we will explore is key to understanding Phoebe, but will be difficult to unravel. Phoebe is also called a προστάτις. This word is not commonly found in the Greek of the first or second century C.E. or B.C.E, however it does appear several times in the second century C.E. (in Aelius Aristides 054 68.2, Pseudo-Lucianus Soph. Charid 10.6, Lucian Bis. Accus 29 and Dio 38.17.5.3 and 54.8.4.2 [referring to one who has oversight]). It also appears in Graecae Magicae Papyri 7.699 and 36.338 (one offering protection). In the third century C.E. it is referenced by Porphyrius Phil. Deantro Nympharum 12.10 and Quaestionum Homericarum ad Iliadem Pertinentium Reliquiae 8.1.71. By the fourth century it came into common usage by John Chrysostom and Theodoretus. It is found only this once, in its noun form in the New Testament. It appears, in this case, to have the meaning of *patron*, or one that provides tangible support to another. When one looks at the masculine form of the word προστάτις, the meaning can be inferred. It appears in Josephus (*J.W.* 1.385.3, 1.633.5 and 2.208.2) with the nuance of protection referring to one who rules or oversees; in Appian (*Civil Wars* 2.1.4.11-12) with the sense of one who is a patron; in Arrian (*Epict. diss.* 3.9.3.1 and 6.3) again with the sense of patron; and in Dio Chrysostom (*4 Regn.* 118.5) among others.

Käsemann does not view προστάτις as leader or representative. Rather, he suggests Phoebe is more of a person to help with the personal care of Paul and others. Käsemann does not adequately support his reason for dismissing the idea of Phoebe being a patron who was also a person in leadership (1980, 411). The term was clearly chosen by Paul for a purpose, and Käsemann's discussion does not give adequate exploration of what the reason was.

Phoebe is called a προστάτις of many including Paul himself. However, the translations have difficulty deciding what to call Phoebe. The New English Version lamely calls Phoebe a "good friend," while the New International Version struggles to say Phoebe is "a great help." Along the same lines, the Revised Standard Version translates the word "helper." The New Jerusalem Bible notes that Phoebe "looked after" Paul. The New Revised Standard Version, however, comes the closest in citing Phoebe as a "benefactor." More than any other word the translators appear confused over the "correct" meaning of προστάτις. If one considers the usage of most of its variants, as discussed above, there seems to be a stronger meaning than "helper." The term would most likely be considered "benefactor" or "patron."

The next word we will look at is συνεργός, a word found in frequent usage during the New Testament time period. Over and over again the literature seems to indicate the meaning of "fellow worker" or "co-worker," one in co-operation with another.[42] Dunn discusses συνεργός as a term that is often used by Paul to refer to his associates. He cites references in Romans, 1 & 2 Corinthians, Philippians, Colossians, 1 Thessalonians and Philemon as evidence. In relation to Prisca and Aquila it is possible they used their business interactions and contacts as a forum for their working together with Paul in advancing the gospel (Dunn 1988, 842).

The final word to examine is ἐπίσημοι. It becomes critical if we consider that it refers to both Junia (feminine) and Andronicus and their work among the apostles. Josephus uses it in the sense of famous, well-known or notorious as applied to a description of a city (Josephus *Ant.* 15.296). Earlier in *Antiquities* 5.234 he uses it in this same sense of well-known as applied in this case to people. In Dio Chrysostom's *The Seventy-Fourth Discourse* (13), Josephus' *Jewish War* (2.428) and *Jewish Antiquities* (7.58), and Dionysius of Halicarnassus' *The Roman Antiquities* (8.52.1), it is used to describe men of distinction or note. Strabo uses it to refer to prominent or important settlements (*Geogr.* 5.3.9.C 237). It is a word that is also used to refer to elaborate, royal and brilliant outward markings.[43] It seems likely that this word refers to Junia and Andronicus as important and of note among the other apostles. If we understand Junia to be a female name, it is evident that we have a precedent for a female apostle who is of importance. It would seem to follow that there were other women in similar roles that did not get recognition. Junia was not considered outstanding because she is a woman but rather for her service to Christ.

We have learned from the study of these words that at times preconceived notions concerning women's roles in the early church have blurred our understanding of these terms. It takes some digging, but through such research we learn that women played a variety of roles in the Roman house churches. We now need to dig deeper and consider some issues of context.

## Immediate Context

Romans 16, as we have already noted, is a part of the final remarks of the writer. It is preceded by a discussion on the forbearance of the strong with the weak in Chapter 15. In verses five and six there is an exhortation to be one with Christ and with God as well as one another (v. 7). Paul talks about his call to preach to the Gentiles and explains he has been hindered in coming to them. His main intent is to preach where the gospel had not yet been heard. He says he has not gone to Rome for that reason, because a foundation had already been laid (vv. 20-22), in other words, the church has been planted by someone other than Paul. He now intends to visit them on the way to Spain, his next missionary journey (v. 24). Paul seeks their prayers and support against his enemies in Jerusalem.

Romans 16:17 continues after the greetings are concluded. Paul warns the believers to watch for teachers motivated by their own desires rather than those of Christ, people who might mislead them and cause dissension. This section appears to be a final exhortation, where Paul calls them to be faithful and encourages them that Satan will soon be crushed under their feet. Could Satan be exemplified by their enemy Rome? Why were the people being pursued by evil? What was happening behind the scenes? We know from early on the situation in Rome was not an easy one for Christians. In verse 20 Paul imparts grace to them passes on greetings from others. His amanuensis Tertius (v. 22) passes along his greeting, as does Paul's host Gaius.

In the letter to the Romans, Paul discusses sin and salvation, justification by faith, the grace of God and appropriate Christian behavior which are cornerstones of the Christian faith. It is indeed noteworthy that so many women are greeted and honored in a letter that contained the majority of Paul's theological underpinnings.

It is important to now begin to ask how the cultural context model interfaces with what we know about Romans 16. What new questions are raised? What new insights are gained? We begin this discussion by setting the cultural context through understanding the audience and the historical setting.

## Notes

1. Witherington cites uses of διάκονον in Acts and in Rom 16:1, Phil 1:1 and 1 Tim 3:8ff. See Ben Witherington, *Women in the Earliest Churches*. (Cambridge: Cambridge University Press, 1988): 113.
2. 1 Cor 3:5; 2 Cor 3:6, 6:4, 11:23; Eph 3:7; Col 1:23, 25.
3. Eph 6:21; Col 1:7; 1 Thess 3:2; 1 Tim 4, 6.

4. See my word study of διάκονον in the grammatical study of Romans 16 for further information on this variant.

5. For an exploration of the role of Joanna the apostle, see Richard Bauckham, *Gospel Women: Studies of the Named Women in the Gospels* (Grand Rapids, Mich.: Eerdmans, 2002), 109-202.

6. The references Whelan cites are second century C.E. sources which are later than this text, and she admits it was mostly amongst the aristocracy that women would have been afforded this privilege. Thus, some caution needs to be exerted when considering these findings. The majority of women were probably not free to hold property or to enter into free marriage. See Caroline F. Whelan, "Amica Pauli: The Role of Phoebe in the Early Church," *JSNT* 49 (1993): 67-85

7. It is not clear whether such titles were simply honorific or held any power within the structure.

8. See also Peter Lampe, *Die stradtrömischen Christen in den ersten beiden Jahrhunderten, Studien zur Sozialgeschichte* (Tübingen: Mohr-Siebeck, 1987) which addresses early Christians in Rome and connects Romans 16 to the earliest congregations in that city.

9. See C.E.B. Cranfield, "Commentary on Romans," in *The International Critical Commentary*, vol. 2 (ed. C.E.B. Cranfield; Edinburgh: T&T Clark, 1979); Ernst Käsemann, *Commentary on Romans* (London, SCM Press Ltd., 1980); James Dunn, *Word Biblical Commentary*, vol. 38B (Dallas: Word Books, 1988); Everett F. Harrison, "Romans" in *The Expositor's Bible Commentary* (gen. ed. Frank Gaebelein; Grand Rapids, Mich.: Zondervan, 1995); C.K. Barrett, *A Commentary on the Epistle to the Romans*, 2nd ed. (London: A & C Black, 1991); C.H. Dodd, *The Epistle of Paul to the Romans* (New York: Harper & Brothers, 1932); and Paul J. Achtemeier, *Romans* (*Interpretation, A Bible Commentary for Teaching and Preaching* (Louisville: John Knox Press, 1985).

10. See, for example, Whelan, "Amica Pauli": 67-85; and Peter Richardson, "From Apostles to Virgins: Romans 16 and the Roles of Women in the Early Church," *TJT* 2 (1980): 232-261.

11. See 1 Corinthians 16:19, 2 Timothy 4:19.

12. Timothy is noted as a co-worker of Paul in the following passages: Acts 17:15, 18:5; Phil 1:1; Col 1:1; Heb 13:23 and, of course, in 1 and 2 Timothy.

13. Romans 16:1 mentions Cenchreae as Phoebe's sending church. If Phoebe was bringing the letter from there it would make sense that Paul might have been in nearby Corinth.

14. Paul makes it clear in Romans 1:13 that he has not yet been to Rome.

15. For more information see Bruce Metzger, *A Textual Commentary on the Greek New Testament*, 2nd edition (New York: United Bible Societies, 1994), 470-473.

16. For further reading see Edgar J. Goodspeed, "Phoebe's Letter of Introduction," *HTR* 44 (1951): 55-57; and Ray R. Schulz, "Romans 16:7, Junia or Junias?," *ExpTim* 98 (1987): 108-110; See also Whelan, "Amica Pauli," 67-85.

17. See Barrett, *Romans*, 257-258; Raymond E. Brown and John P. Meier, *Antioch and Rome: New Testament Cradles of Catholic Christianity* (New York: Paulist Press, 1983), 109; Dunn, *Romans*, ix; Robert Jewett, "Romans as an Ambassadorial Letter," *Int* 36 (1982): 5-20; Jewett, "Paul, Phoebe and the Spanish Mission," in *The Social World of Formative Christianity and Judaism* (eds. Jacob Neusner, Peder Borgen, Ernest S. Frerichs and Richard Horsley (Philadelphia, Fortress, 1988): 147-148; Robert H. Mounce, Romans. In *The New American Commentary*, vol. 27 (Broadman & Holman Publishers, 1995): 27-30

18. 1 Cor 16:21, Gal 6:11, Col 4:18, Phlm 19 and Rom 16:22.

19. See also Terrence Mullins, "Greeting as a New Testament Form," *JBL* 87 (1968): 418-426; and Chan-Hie Kim, "Form and structure of the familiar Greek letter of recommendation." Published by Society of Biblical Literature for the Seminar on Paul, [Missoula, Mont.], 1972.

20. Cicero *Att.*, vol. 4, letters 332.13.24.4.2-3, 357.14.3.2.7-8, 372.14.19.6.6-7, 413.16.6.8-10, 414.16.6.4.10-11.

21. Such greetings also appear in letters 255.12.17.11-12, 263.21.24.3.1-2, 265.12.26.2.10-11, 266.12.27.3.5-6, 267.12.28.3.15-16, 272.12.31.3.4; *Fam.* 16.4.8-9, 7.29.2.4-5; *Att.*, vol. I, 35.2.15.4.5-6.

22. For example, in *To Nepos* 3.16 Pliny ends with *Vale* (farewell) as also in *To Calpurnia Hispulla*, 4.19 and *To Velius Cerealis*, 4.21, *To Arrius Antoninus*, 5.15, *To Verus*, 6.3, *To Macer*, 6.24, *To Fabatus*, 6.30, *To Cornelianus*, 6.31, *To Quntilian*, 6.32, *To Maximus*, 6.34.

23. Although the Roman Christians were not blood relatives they acted and functioned as though they were "kin". Therefore, women could interact with men without the fear of their modesty being challenged. We will explore this concept further in our final section on the cultural context of Romans 16.

24. See Acts 15 and Galatians.

25. See Jewett, "Paul, Phoebe": 142-162.

26. This statement assumes that Romans 16 was intended for Rome. See prior discussion in the literary analysis section. Hereafter, the audience will be referred to as the Romans.

27. This statement assumes Phoebe was the bearer of the letter. See Jewett, "Paul, Phoebe": 142-162; and Jewett, "Ambassadorial Letter": 5-20.

28. The meaning of the word διάκονος (deacon) will be discussed later in this section.

29. Προστάτις appears in its verbal form in Romans 12:8, 1 Thessalonians 5:12 and 1 Timothy 3:4-5, 5:17. See Richardson, "From Apostles to Virgins": 239; and Elisabeth Schüssler Fiorenza, "Missionaries, Apostles, Coworkers: Romans 16 and the Reconstruction of Women's Early Christian History," *WW* 6 (1986): 426.

30. See M.B. Flory, "Where Women Preceded Men, Factors Influencing the Order of Names in Roman Epitaphs," *CJ* 79 (1984): 216-224; Ramsay MacMullen, "Women in Public in the Roman Empire," *Historia* 29 (1980): 210; and Wayne A. Meeks, *The First Urban Christians: The Social World of the Apostle Paul* (New Haven, Conn.: Yale University Press, 1983), 59.

31. See 1 Corinthians 16:19.

32. For a detailed analysis of this topic see Bauckham, *Gospel Women*, 166-169.

33. See Bernadette Brooten, "Junia...Outstanding among the Apostles," in *Women Priests: A Catholic Commentary on the Vatican Declaration* (New York, Paulist Press, 1977); Schulz, "Romans 16:7": 108-110; and John Thorley, "Junia, A Woman Apostle," *NovT* 38 (1996): 18-29.

34. See Jewett, "Paul, Phoebe": 151.

35. This citation can be found in the following: manuscript 35 (201 omitting πρὸς Ῥωμαίους) (Metzger 1994, 477).

36. 42, 90, 216, 339, 462, 466* 642. 337 go as far to say that the letter through Tertius was sent through Phoebe from the Corinthians (Metzger 1994, 477).

37. By the fourth century C.E. *deaconess* came into more common usage. It is found in numerous references of the *Constitutions of the Apostles* (001 3.11.6, 001 6.17.12, 001 8.28.15, 001 8.28.20 and 001 8.31.6), Flavius Justinianus (013 604.19, 013 615.1, 013 616.17, 013 620.26, 013 620.29, 013 623.26, 013 624.9 and 013 662.24), Callinicus (001 8 14.5) and in Epiphanius' *Panarion* (3.522.18).

38. See Philo, *Spec. Laws* 3.201.2; Didorus Siculus, *Biblio. Hist.* 5.26.3.11; Strabo, *Geogr.* 16.7.26.12; Josephus, *Ant.* 11.228.2 and 12.187.7, *J.W.* 4.626.2; Epictetus, *Diatr.*, 3.7.28.2, 3.22.63.4, 3.22.63.4 and 4.7.20.5; Dio Chrysostom, *Orationes* 4.99.4.

39. Matt 20:26||Mark 9:35; Matt 23:11||Mark 10:43; John 12:26.

40. For further discussion see Florence M. Gillman, "Phoebe," *ABD*, vol. 5. (ed. David Noel Freedman. 6 vols. New York, 1992): 348; and Whelan, "Amica Pauli," 68.

41. Eph 6:21 *minister* (NRSV, NASB); Phil 1:1 *deacons* (NRSV, NIV, NASB); Col 1:7 *minister* (NRSV, NIV), 1:23 *minister* (NASB), 1:25 *minister* (NASB), 4:7 *minister* (NRSV, NIV); 1 Tim 3:8 *deacon* (NRSV, NIV, NASB), 3:12 *deacon* (NRSV, NIV, NASB), 4:6 *minister* (NIV).

42. See Philo, *Alleg. Interp.* 3.112., *Names* 259.2, *Spec. Laws* 1.29.2; Didorus Siculus, *Biblio. Hist.* 1.8.9.4, 1.50.1.5, 4.5.4.3, 4.49.3.10, 4.77.5.4, 5.39.2.12, 11.69.4.5, 12.80.3.1, 15.25.2.5, 15.70.3.3, 15.71.4.6, 16.66.5.2, 17.2.4.6, 18.53.7.4, 20.91.8.33, 32.26.3.7, 36.8.4.8; Dionysius of Halicarnassus, *Ant. rom.* 7.7.1.1, 7.11.4.4, 7.63.3.10; Strabo, *Geogr.* 6.3.4.25, 8.3.33.54, 10.3.11.10, 15.1.48.3; Josephus, *Ant.* 1.156.5, 7.346.3 and *J.W.* 4.149.1; Epictetus, *Diatr.* 4.1.104.2.

43. See Diodorus Siculus, 17.53.3, and Dionysius of Halicarnassus, 7.72.7 and 6.95.4.

# 7

# Romans 16: Cultural Context and Interaction with the Mediterranean Model

## Reconstructing the Roman Church through the Text[1]

In this chapter we will attempt to create a picture of the Roman Christians who received Paul's letter. We will reconstruct who they were by studying the text as a whole, the chapter as a pericope and external sources that speak to first-century Roman Christianity. We will begin by noting a few external references to Christianity in Rome. We will then go on to listen to the text and to discern what light it has to shine on our understanding of the audience.

## Audience

The Roman emperors appear to have had a running interaction with the Jews and subsequently with the Christians. Tiberius was reported to have abolished foreign cults and forced the Jews (as well as Egyptians) to burn their religious clothing and items (Suetonius *Tib.* 1.36). Barrett explains the Jews came to Rome through captivity in 63 B.C.E. From that time the community increased in number despite some oppression by the government. He highlights the upheaval that took place when the message of Jesus as the Messiah was preached in Roman synagogues (Barrett 1991, 5, 6).

Dio recounts that in 41 C.E. Claudius came into conflict with the Jews. He notes their numbers had been growing, and as a consequence Claudius forbade them to hold meetings but did not force them to leave Rome (Dio 60.6). However, prompted by the disturbances the Jews "constantly" made at the instigation of Chrestus (Chresto), Claudius later did expel the Jews from the city altogether (Suetonius *Claud.* 5.25.4). There has been much debate over whether Chrestus is a misspelling of Christ, with most scholars taking it as such. There continues to be debate as to whether the two incidents reflect the same expulsion or two separate occurrences. Dunn asserts that Claudius may have expelled the Jews on two occasions (41 and

49 C.E.). The first expulsion was probably more limited, while the second was more substantial (Dunn 1988, *xlix*). He goes on to say that the Jews lived in an environment of hostility having also been oppressed in 19 C.E. by Tiberius (Dunn, 1988, *li*).

It seems likely that some level of expulsions did occur under the leadership of Claudius, with one resulting in the other. Perhaps Claudius' frustration had been building for some time before he made the final expulsion. We have confirmation of this in the New Testament. Acts 18:2 records Priscilla (Prisca) and Aquila who had recently left Rome because of this very expulsion and were at the time in Corinth where Paul met them. Brown and Meier assert Luke exaggerated the statement that "all" Jews were expelled from Rome. Josephus is silent about the issue, and Dio declares that Jews were not generally expelled. Brown and Meier suggest perhaps only the most troublesome of the Christian Jews (such as Prisca and Aquila) were expelled (1983, 102).

The difficulties the Jews faced in Rome are of key interest to our text. If we contend (as we will in the next section) that there were two groups in the Roman church, Jewish Christians and Gentile Christians, then this expulsion has a bearing on the whole dynamic of the Roman church. Fitzmyer discusses the return of the Jewish Christians after the expulsion. These believers would have encountered a different fellowship than the one they had left. Returning as a minority to a church they once led would have made for a difficult situation (Fitzmyer 1993, 33). Lampe (1991, 225) also suggests it was likely the Jewish Christians were in the minority. The Roman church, composed of many house churches (also see next section), was not one unified body, either in ethnicity, locality or theology. Thus, when the Jews were exiled from Rome for at least five years until Nero's reign, the church functioned as a mostly Gentile entity. Therefore, much of the later controversy Paul is addressing after the Jews (Priscilla, Aquila and others) returned to Rome is clearly related to cultural differences and diverse theological interpretations. As we will see when we explore the composition of the audience, the struggles the early Roman church had were over custom, culture and ethnic difference. This edict of Claudius is a key to understanding why these differences were so profound. The Jew/Gentile controversy was by no means foreign to Paul but was of a different nature in this text because the two groups had been separated and then brought back together. In the midst of all of this friction there is a call for unity and harmony that runs throughout the letter.

The persecution of the church did not end with Claudius' reign. It was, in fact, just beginning. Nero was reported to have later persecuted the Christians (Suetonius *Nero* 4.2 and Tacitus *Ann.* 15.44). The letter of Romans was written before these persecutions, probably during Paul's stay with the Corinthians in the late 50's. Yet, these references were precursors to the struggle that was yet to come and was mounting even during the time the letter was written. Only ten years or so later when the Temple was destroyed we read that Titus wished to wipe out the entire religions of both the Jews and Christians. The theory set forth by Tacitus is that Christians came forth from the Jews and, therefore, its root—understood as the temple at Jerusalem—needed to be destroyed (*Frag. Hist.* 2). When the temple was destroyed in 70 C.E. the separation of the Jews and the Christians became wider.

As we have seen, the environment surrounding the Roman Christians was one of impending doom and danger. Persecution may not have been imminent but the tensions were clearly growing.

*Reconstructing the Audience of Romans 16*

Before we begin to reconstruct the context of Romans 16 it is important to note this section proposes a rereading of the text to draw a fresh understanding of the audience of Romans, and in particular Romans 16. There are other scholars whose work is much more detailed who will be referred to throughout this section. Scholars such as Peter Lampe[2] and Robert Jewett[3] have spent laborious hours scouring the names and origins of the people mentioned in the text. It is clear their labors have been fruitful and thus do not warrant needless repetition. However, they will be referred to throughout this study, which will focus less on outside sources and more on the richness found within the letter as a whole.

As has already been intimated, a basic reading of Romans reveals that it was not sent to a monolithic audience. Harrison raises a concern about Romans that has plagued many scholars through the years: Is Romans addressed to a Gentile, Jewish or mixed audience? He notes that in Romans 1:13 the audience appears to be Gentile, yet further along in 4:1 it appears as though Paul is talking to those who share his heritage. Also, one cannot forget the fact that chapters nine through eleven are devoted to Israel. Yet despite these references seemingly directed at Jewish Christians, Harrison decides that Paul's use of the Hebrew Bible comes from his commitment to reinforce to the Gentiles Christianity's roots in and connection with Judaism and the Hebrew Bible (1995, 9). Moo also raises similar questions but comes to somewhat different conclusions that appear to be more accurate. Moo asserts in some places (such as Rom 1:18-4:25) Romans is a dialogue or even a debate with Judaism, yet the intended audience may not be Jewish. Perhaps Gentile Christians were intending to learn about the heritage of the Christian faith. Yet Paul's challenge to the "weak" and the "strong" would imply that he was addressing a mixed audience of both Jewish and Gentile believers (Moo 1996, 12). It does seem likely that both Jewish and Gentile Christians are addressed in an evolving situation of social and political turmoil.

Rome, already a diverse and cosmopolitan city, was challenged by the peculiarities of its Christian population. Williams points out the Jews of Rome probably lived near one another in separate communities or quarters apart from Gentiles. They probably sought one another out because of shared values, culture and a need to give one another support in an environment that may have been hostile (Williams 15). As we have already acknowledged, Jewish Christians were expelled around 49 C.E.[4] only to begin returning several years later after the death of Claudius. In the years the Jews were in exile, the Roman house churches developed without much direct influence from the Jewish Christians. This letter written by Paul was sent to the "beloved" in Rome sometime after the Jews have begun to return to Rome. It was not written to only one church of Rome but to the many house churches that existed in this diverse city.

It is now to the house churches that we turn our attention. If we accept Romans 16 as addressing the Roman congregations then we can look within it for evidence of the early Christians at Rome when this letter was written. A close reading of the text seems to indicate there are at least four natural breaks in Romans 16 that suggest the addressing of at least four house churches.[5]

Within such groupings we read of males and females in a variety of church leadership roles. Phoebe was a deacon at Cenchreae near Corinth, a patron and probably the bearer of the letter. Prisca and Aquila hosted a church in their home. They are called Paul's co-workers and are referred to in Acts and in some other letters of the New Testament. Schüssler Fiorenza (1983, 177-179) makes an interesting comment that Prisca may have influenced Apollos' theology. In a different study Schüssler Fiorenza points out that Prisca was a travelling missionary who, along with her husband, worked to support her ministry (1986, 429). Paul also commended four others, Mary, Persis, Tryphosa and Tryphaena, who were involved in working hard for the gospel in evangelism and leading the community (Schüssler Fiorenza 1986, 430).[6] Certainly these women did more than merely attend worship. They also seem to be involved in the spread of the gospel.

A variety of other women and men are greeted. In total 26 people, two households, two additional groups of believers and one *ekklesia* are greeted. Seven women are greeted and commended by name. An additional two are mentioned in relation to male kin. Seventeen men are named and greeted.[7] As already noted, there is a dispute over whether Junia(s) is female or male. Most ancient commentators including, John Chrysostom,[8] understood her to be both a woman and an "apostle." It was not until medieval times that her gender began to be hotly disputed. Brooten (1977, 14) cites Aegidius of Rome (1245-1316 C.E.) as the first commentator to have taken Junia's name as masculine.

There is much to learn from this list of greetings. Yet, first in order to frame the context one needs to place them within their whole book context. We will thus study the entire letter in the hope of extrapolating information about the readers, how they related to one another and what issues the letter highlights for their attention.

*Audience/Readers*

Let us begin by drawing a picture of the audience to which this letter is addressed. In this section we are not trying to interpret Paul's content but, rather, look for clues about the people to whom he was writing. In Romans 1:6-7 the recipients are described as "called," and Paul says they "belong" to Jesus Christ. He refers to them as "God's beloved in Rome" and "called to be saints." In 1:8 their faith is proclaimed throughout the world. Paul has not been to see them before, yet in verse nine he prays for them, and in verse ten he says he longs to visit them. They seem to be people of faith worshipping in churches Paul himself did not establish.

Chapter eight begins to discuss life in the Spirit. In 8:9 Paul says they are not found in the flesh but are in the Spirit. The Spirit of God is said to dwell in them. In 8:4 Paul reminds them if they are led by the Spirit they are children of God. They are adopted into the family (v. 15) and do not have to fear. Paul says the Spirit confirms they are children of God and have an intimate relationship with the Father (v. 16). He also calls them heirs of God and joint heirs with Christ. They have the privileges of sonship, which in the ancient world afforded them a privilege of one first born and as Christians an inheritance of eternal life.

Chapter 16 reveals much more about the audience, at least about those who are greeted. In verse 19 Paul says they have been obedient and that this report has reached "all." Prisca and Aquila had a church that met in their home, and they risked their lives for Paul. They were his companions, referred to elsewhere in the New Testament.[9]

The readers are exhorted to welcome Phoebe as she was commended by Paul to their care. They are told to greet one another with a "holy kiss" (v. 16), a greeting mentioned in two other New Testament letters.[10] Perhaps a sign of shared unity was needed. Thus Paul tells them to go out from their own house church and greet one another. That all the churches of the Gentiles greeted Prisca and Aquila's church indicates there is a global connection among the congregations. These Christians lived in the metropolitan city of Rome, not in an isolated bubble. They were known by Christians throughout Paul's circle of influence.

Paul says Epaenetus, who is also among their group, was the first convert in Asia. He singles out Mary, calling her a hard worker. Andronicus and Junia are identified as relatives or as kin of Paul and so is Herodian. Did these people represent the Jewish population along with Aquila (who is identified as a Jew in Acts) and possibly Prisca? More than likely there is a mix of ethnic compositions in this list.[11]

Paul says Andronicus and Junia were in prison with him and they were prominent among the apostles. Paul identifies them as having been "in Christ" before him. They were possibly a husband and wife team as they are paired together along the same line as Prisca and Aquila.

Paul calls Ampliatus beloved in the Lord and he says the same of Stachys. Urbanus is called a co-worker in Christ and Apelles is said to be approved in Christ. The family of Aristobulus is specifically mentioned so perhaps Aristobulus was not himself a Christian. The same might have held true for the family of Narcissus. Paul considers Tryphaena and Tryphosa workers in the Lord. Persis is called beloved and is also singled out for her hard work.

Rufus is called "chosen" and his mother has been a "mother" to Paul as well. Perhaps she was a wealthy patron of Paul or simply a warm supporter and motherly encourager. Two other groups of people are greeted and then Paul informs them that all the churches of Christ greet them.

If Romans 16 is taken as connected to the Roman letter, intended for the Roman people, it becomes quite clear that we are speaking of a substantial and influential group of Christians. Rome as a capital city was full of movement, trade and commerce and seems from this list to have held at least four and probably more distinct house churches. How would this letter have been delivered to such a diverse group? It was at least a circular letter but may have been orally presented to the various groups. What type of demographics can be inferred from this list of greetings? Certainly some of the readers were wealthy enough to be patrons or to support a house church. Yet some of these people were likely to be impoverished. The assembly was also made up of men and women, two groups that in ancient society did not mix unless they were of the same kin. Roman society was a little freer in this respect than the Greek or Jewish cultures. Yet for the majority of society the "fictive" kin groups that developed as an outgrowth of these house churches were uncommon. New gender, ethnic and class relationships are evident in this text.

Regarding the social composition of the women found in Romans 16, we can draw a few inferences. We might assume that certainly Phoebe was a woman of wealth and influence in that she was a patron to Paul and others. In addition she was probably the bearer of the letter to the Romans, and she probably had the means to travel from Cenchreae to Rome. Dunn suggests that Phoebe would have likely had some influence useful to her church of Cenchreae (1988, 889). He suggests that Phoebe may have had a dual role in the church of Cenchreae as both a patron and a deacon. It was known that in Greek cities there were patrons who looked after the need of foreign residents. Perhaps being that Cenchreae was a busy port Phoebe may have been a patron to foreign visitors that might have included visiting Christians and Jews that were residents (Dunn 1988, 889).

Prisca also may have been wealthy. We certainly know that a church met in her and Aquila's house. We learn in Acts 18:3 that she was a tentmaker with her husband, and we also know through various scriptures (Acts 18:19, 26; 1 Cor 16:19) that she and Aquila were able to travel. Dunn cautions that even though she certainly had some wealth due to the business she shared with her husband, we do not know the level of Prisca's social status (Dunn 1988, 892).

As Dunn surveys the list of greetings in Romans 16 he finds some important points regarding social composition. The names found are mostly Gentile but a significant number of Jewish Christians do appear. These names could be found among slaves and those who were free. There were also tradespeople like Prisca and Aquila and people who worked hard like Mary, Tryphaena, Tryphosa and Peris who many have had some independent means or wealth. He also notes that these people had the ability to travel since Paul seems to know them and he has not yet visited them in Rome (Dunn 1988, 900).

Junia's name seems to indicate a slave origin (Dunn 1988, 894) surely having implications on her social status. Julia was a name commonly found in Rome particularly among slaves in the imperial household (Dunn 1988, 898; Sanday and Headlam 1902, 427; and Bruce 1974, 275).

Persis also has its origins in a popular female slave name (Dunn 1988, 897, Bruce 274). She—along with Tryphaena and Tryphosa—was probably a freedwoman (Sunday and Headlam 1902, 426; and Dunn 1988, 897). The names Tryphaena and Tryphosa are also found in inscriptions in connection with the imperial household (Bruce 1974, 274).

It seems that the women of Romans 16 and also the men (even though we did not look at them in detail here) were diverse in their social status. Some were perhaps former slaves, business people or women of wealth. Certainly wealth and connections influenced women's ability to serve in the early Jesus movement. Yet it does not seem to have hindered the service of those who were not in positions of influence, at least not in this snapshot of the Roman Christians found in chapter 16.

Paul's audience was diverse. It consisted of Jews and Greeks, males and females, slaves and free. Gillman (1992, 50) suggests it was common for Greeks and Jews to take on Latin names while living in Rome. There is some debate over the meaning of Μαριάν in verse six as to whether it is the Jewish Miriam or Mary or the Roman Maria. Keener (1992, 241) points out that Andronicus was a Greek name borne by some Diaspora Jews and Junia was a Latin name also used by Jews. Fitzmyer notes that of the people found in Romans 16, two—Aristobulus and Narcissus—appear to be leaders of pagan households. Two names may be of Hebrew origin, ten are Latin names and 18 are Greek names (Fitzmyer 1993, 36). Thus, it seems we have a mix of ethnic origins. The audience was a diverse group, one that would be expected in such a large and important city as Rome. Rutgers supports Philo's view that many of the Jews in Rome were slaves who had become citizens after given their freedom (1998, 97). Jeffers asserts most Jews and Christians in Rome would be found among the poor. Included in their group would be some citizens, but most would have been non-citizens composed of slaves, freed slaves and freeborn (not of Roman origin). Most foreigners were slaves and had come to Rome not of their own will. They were often able to earn their freedom at some point in their lives (Jeffers 129). Sanday and Headlam address the status of the Romans listed in chapter 16, finding that many were probably slaves and freed slaves. They suggest Narcissus may have been the freedman of Claudius, and Aristobulus might have been associated with Herod's household. Philologus is thought to be a cultured name. Sanday and Headlam point out that some Greek and Oriental slaves were more educated and cultured than the masters they served (1902, xxxiv-xxxv).

In addition to the ethnic and social composition of the audience, there are several other factors to consider when trying to understand who Paul is addressing. There may be some husband and wife teams in this list in addition to Prisca and Aquila, including Andronicus and Junia (v. 7) and Philologus and Julia (v. 15), based on the connection of male and female names with a καί. Other familial ties are suggested in pairs such as Tryphaena and Tryphosa (v. 12), whose names are similar in sound and form and who could possibly have been sisters. Rufus is mentioned with his mother (v. 13), and Paul refers to her as his "mother" also. Nereus is greeted along with his sister, who is not named (v. 15). It is clear from the language used in this list of greetings that family ties, whether biological or fictive, were an important component of the early church. Their relationships were not just with one another but also extended to the larger Christian community.

*Jews and Gentiles*

In order to understand fully the audience from within the text, one also needs to look for evidence of relationships between these diverse groups in the letter as a whole. The clearest example of such relationships is between Jew and Gentile. Beginning in the very first chapter Paul says salvation has come first to the Jew and next to the Greek (v. 16).

Again the parallel relationships are repeated as Paul says anguish will be had for both parties who do evil and glory will be given to those who do good. In 2:11 Paul tells us that God does not discriminate but treats both groups without partiality.

Paul discusses the law throughout the letter but initially in Romans 2:12-16. He tells them not only to be hearers of the law but also doers. The Gentiles are able to follow the law even though they do not have it (v. 14). The law should now be written on their hearts (v. 15). Just because one might be a Jew does not mean that one can assume to know God's will. Verse 23 reminds the Jews they also break the law. In verse 27 Paul makes clear that even an uncircumcised Gentile who keeps the law will condemn the Jew who does not abide by it. A little further on we come to understand that circumcision is no longer physical and thus only for the Jews, but is now spiritual or internal.

The comparison of Jews and Gentiles continues in Chapter 3. The advantages of being a Jew are outlined, and yet Paul says all people are under sin. In 3:23 he states all have fallen short of God's glory. Paul then speaks in the third person saying, "we hold that a person is justified by faith apart from works..." (v. 28). The law is not overthrown by faith but rather it is upheld (vv. 30, 31).

In the introduction to his Romans commentary, Dunn discusses Paul's treatment of the law. He suggests Paul is freeing the law from its narrow interpretation of rule-keeping yet is also showing the law does have a role in faith. The law has a social function as an important piece of Jewish pride and heritage. Paul is ultimately using the law as an expression of covenant theology which is no longer to be understood in regard to Judaism but now functions differently in Christianity (Dunn 1988, *lxxii*).

To further illustrate the point, the great Jewish patriarch Abraham is appealed to in Chapter 4. Paul says Abraham and David were both given God's righteousness by grace and not by works. The Jews obviously knew these stories and yet it does not appear Paul writes to them alone. More Jewish traditions are mentioned in Chapter 9 where Paul recalls promises to Sarah and Rebecca and refers to the hardening of Pharaoh's heart. In verse 24 this dichotomy of talking to both Jew and Gentile is evident when Paul writes, "...including us whom he has called, not from the Jews only but also from the Gentiles...". Paul uses scriptures from Hosea and Isaiah as examples of how God brought salvation to others, yet how there is still a remnant in Israel.

By Chapter 10 Paul seems to refer to the Jews when he states it is his desire that "they" might be saved. He once again highlights that whoever calls on the name of the Lord will be saved regardless of whether they are a Jew or a Gentile. In Chapter 11 Paul repeats his self-identification as a Jew and his argument that God has not abandoned the Jews. In verse 13 he remarks that he is speaking to "you gentiles." He begins the discussion of being grafted into the tree. The Gentiles are not to get haughty because they are, after all, grafted in and supported by the root. In verse 23 we read that the Israelites can also be grafted in again. They are only partially coming into this mystery because their hearts are hardened. It will remain this way until the full number of Gentiles are brought into the fold. Brändle and Stegemann point out that we cannot be sure whether house churches were composed of both Jew and Gentile Christians or if they were separate. They do note that the problems addressed in chapters 14 and 15 suggest that the two groups did interact (Brändle and Stegemann 1998, 125). They go on to mention the relationship between the two groups was clearly strained after the expulsion of the Jewish Christians by Claudius. When these same believers returned to Rome it was more than possible that new tensions arose (Brändle and Stegemann 1998, 126, 127).

When Romans is looked at in light of all of this internal evidence, it seems quite probable that Romans 16 reflects the controversy between the Jews and the Gentiles. The Jew and Greek congregations may have been mixed or separated, but they were clearly experiencing some difficulties. There were tensions between them, particularly if some were holding onto the law and were not living by the edict of freedom.[12]

*Evidence of Tensions*

It seems these tensions could have easily grown up around the Jews being expelled from Rome and then later migrating back. Dunn suggests Romans 1:7 gives reason to believe there were tensions among the house churches. The specific emphasis in the greeting "to all who are in Rome" might make one question why the greeting is not simply to "the church in Rome" (Dunn 1988, 19). Other conflicts and tensions also appear present in the Roman churches during this time. In chapter one Paul identifies ungodliness and wickedness as associated with those who are suppressing the truth. He says they do not honor God, and they claim to be wise but are really fools, not following God's truth but accepting a lie.

In 5:3 Barrett suggests that the idea of exulting in one's afflictions is related to Paul's belief that the ministry of Jesus bought into existence the last stage of world history. Many Jews believed this time would be fraught with intense affliction. Jesus had taken this pain on the cross, but it was not so complete that his followers would not deal with any afflictions. Paul might see these hardships as signs of this last time which point out their future hope (Barrett 1991, 96, 97).

Paul says in chapter eight that all things work together for good and, thus, if God is with them who can be against them? Paul senses a need to encourage these saints, to remind them of God's promises in the face of suffering. In 8:33 Paul asks, "Who will bring any charge against God's elect?" He affirms that nothing can separate them from the love of God. What would have been threatening to separate them? What was happening in the Roman church that such discouragement is evident? Psalm 44 is the next quotation referring to many being put to death, like lambs being led to the slaughter. If Nero was now in power, it is apparent that the Christians in Rome were not at the height of their persecutions, but were beginning to suffer for their faith. Alternatively, Barrett suggests that Paul's writing in Romans 8:35 about persecution reflects his own experiences of suffering. Yet he does affirm that the text may describe "the general insecurity and unpopularity of Christians, which, in Rome, were to culminate in Nero's attack…" (1991, 162).

By Chapter 12 we can also discern that there were other tensions among the believers. Paul tells them not to think too highly of themselves and that they are members of one body. They are each given different gifts to exercise accordingly. Paul exhorts them to love without hypocrisy, to hate evil and to hold to what is good. He calls them to be devoted to one another in "brotherly" love. This familial love implies loyalty and protection of honor. There is a depth to such familial love that understanding the culture highlights.

Paul urges them to honor one another and to give to the needs of the saints. Roman culture was committed to protecting the honor of the family at all costs, so it seems likely that the Christian church would also take on such behavior.

Paul admonishes them to accept the weak in the faith and not to quarrel over opinions. They are not to judge the weak but to leave them to God. Paul discusses in 14:6 the day one observes and what one eats as being done to the Lord. They are not to put a stumbling block in another's path, for the issue of what was clean and unclean is not meant to divide. Paul calls them in verse 19 to pursue peace and to build one another up. Again, in verse 20 they are exhorted not to tear one another apart on account of food differences. Paul does not want the differences in their ethnic and cultural practices to separate them.

In 16:17 the topic of conflict arises again. Paul tells them to watch for those who cause dissension and hindrances, those who teach what is opposite of what they have learned. They are told to turn from such troublemakers. Paul describes these people as satisfying their own appetites, and having smooth and flattering speech that deceives the hearts of those unaware. Brown and Meier discuss the possibility that the conflicts referred to in 16:17 may have to do with Paul's reputation among those who have ministered with him and others who are from the Jerusalem contingent who are adversarial towards him (1983, 113).

*Unity in the Midst of Diversity*

In Chapter 15 Paul again calls for unity and for the people to be of one accord, to have one voice in glorifying God. He tells them to accept and welcome one another with a holy kiss. Moo highlights Paul's "pleas for unity" in 14:1-15:13. Paul encourages his readers to accept and not judge one another (Moo 1996, 826, 827). Lane also suggests the Romans are being called to unity. He particularly points to 15:1-13 which exhorts believers to accept one another in the Lord, as evidence for such a need (Lane 1998, 198). He notes that Paul is highlighting real tensions and struggles of a church divided along cultural lines. Paul is aware that he will have to deal with this same controversy in Jerusalem (Lane 1998, 202). He suggests that one of the main reasons why Romans was written was to reconcile a broken church divided between Jews and Gentiles (Lane 1998, 214). Dunn writes that chapter 14 and Paul's discussion of the strong and the weak reflects the diversity that can be seen in the body of Christ. In order for there to be real freedom there also must be the acceptance of different perspectives. This diversity can truly be displayed in Christian fellowship while unity can be maintained (Dunn 1988, 834).

Paul acknowledges that he has spoken to them boldly on some points. He then moves into his ministry and commitment to see them as well as to go to Spain. He tells them that the Gentiles are indebted to the Jews and they are sending an offering which he will deliver. Indeed, Paul points out there is a need for accord within a larger unity of the Christian church. Being in unity does not mean agreement but rather a common commitment to the Christian faith that superseded their differences.

It is evident from a basic reading and attentiveness to the whole letter that Jews and Gentiles were struggling over differences in worship, daily living and culture.

Throughout this letter Paul calls them to live in peace and unity. They were not to make their differences a stumbling block, but to live in one accord. Thus, whether they were Jew or Greek, slave or free, male or female they were to strive for peace and find their common bonds. Women did not present a stumbling block to their fellow men. They were able to serve their Lord together, and we are called to the same standard today.

We now need to go on to our final level of exploration—that of cultural context. Using the insights we have gained from our model, we will attempt to discern what nuances exist in our text which are brought out by a study of Mediterranean and ancient Roman culture.

# Context

It is in this section that we will begin to consider the relationship of the cultural context model to the text of Romans 16. What questions does it raise, where does it provide insight or highlight the need for further exploration? In order to aid and refresh the memory of the reader a summary of the values of the nuanced model now follows. It will be followed by a study of our text.

## Cultural Context Model of Ancient Mediterranean Women Key Values and Norms

The following discussion represents a brief synopsis of the Mediterranean model developed in this thesis. This summary is not intended to discuss all the nuances or insights of the model, but it is to serve as a bridge to the discussion on Romans 16 and the insights that this model brings to it.

### *Honor and Shame*

Women are to protect their shame, their modesty or virtue. If a woman's chastity or morality is called into question she can bring shame rather than honor to her family. What happens to one woman in the family affects the entire identity of the family. If a woman is violated by a man other than her husband she is considered unclean and is blamed for the incident as much as the perpetrator. The male kin of her family will seek vengeance against the perpetrator and his kin. Women are thus to keep to themselves and to avoid contact with men outside of their kin group, in this way they will bring no suspicion upon themselves or their family.

Women can also receive honor from other women, although this possibility is not as well documented or frequent. Women receive honor by what they serve their guests, how they welcome them, what they wear and how they provide for their families. Women rarely receive honor from men, except perhaps in the case of royal or wealthy women who had statues or plaques erected in their honor.

## Women and Power

Women do not hold direct power. They are in most cases not able to contract business or represent themselves in legal dealings. They attempt to influence such interactions and life choices via manipulation and indirect tactics. They can influence their relationships with their husbands and can uphold or tear down the honor of the family in a single action. Women hold inadvertent power through their ability to maintain their shame. They could easily bring dishonor upon their family through acts considered inappropriate such as talking to an unrelated male. This section of the model is new to the social scientific discussion of women in the text. Women have often been discussed as an appendage to their male kin. While they clearly function within a rigid framework, they do move beyond silence. Women in the domestic/private realm held considerably more power than is often thought. Some rare women received power through wealth or position such as those who were rulers or who were married to rulers.

## Public and Private

Women exist mainly in private space which is distinct from men's space. Their interactions with other women and children are different from interactions with their male kin. They function mostly in the home where they run their households. They train and provide for their children. They interact with their female kin and also in some instances with neighboring women. They relate to the male kin in their life but do not venture to interact with males not from their kin group.

Men exist mainly in public space which is distinct from the world of women. They interact with men in the marketplaces and gathering places outside the home. They may interact with men outside of their kin group. Most of their interactions are in some way connected to the protection of their family's honor or as an attempt to earn honor in their community.

Our model has encouraged us to consider the distinctions between men's world and women's world as something other than simply a public and private divide. Women were able to have mastery and rule in their area (in the home and with other women). Who makes the distinction between public and private? We need to question why men's world is public when they simply interact with other men. A new way of conceptualising these terms has arisen from our model.

## Women and Relationships

Women function in a myriad of relationships with neighboring women, their kin, their children and their husbands. They visit other women, have women visit them and participate in life cycle occurrences of other women. During a birth or at the time of a wedding women will gather to prepare and support other women. They do not function in isolation but rather in community. The roles they play in the family as wife, mother, mother-in-law and sister are important to the running of their household. They gain much strength from these relationships and are also able to wield power through them. Women continue to be defined and contained by the relationships to their male kin. If they should have no male kin, then they have a bit more freedom. However, they are not afforded protection of their modesty which is so important in Mediterranean society.

*Kin Relationships*

Women receive their identity from their relationships first with their father and, if he dies before they are married, their eldest brother. Once women are married, their identity shifts to that of their husband. They are represented by these relationships and any business such as marriage, property, divorce, etc. is carried out by their male kin. Women move from their natal home to their husband's home and have little contact with their family of origin once the transition is complete. What happens to even one member of the family affects the entire group for good or for bad. The family functions as a unit rather than as individual parts. Women often orchestrate the workings of these kin relationships.

*Women and Religion*

Women are active participants in the religions of their culture. They pass on religious beliefs to their children and participate in religious festivals with the community. They uphold the religious beliefs and practices for their family. They were found in all three cultures to be involved in expression of their religion even when barriers were placed in their way to deter them. Women found an element of freedom in the exercise of their religious beliefs. Often cultural restrictions were released for a woman to move about more freely in this realm.

*Women and Death*

Women are seen as capable of preparing a body for death because they are already considered unclean. They wail and lament a death. They express the grief of the entire family, either before the community or in their homes. They see the family through the life cycle from birth to death and are almost like guides for this journey.

*Insights from Roman Women Context*

Earlier in this work we considered extensively the role of women in Rome. We compared their lifestyles to those of Jewish and Greek women. In this section we will draw those insights together. Women in Rome seemed to have had more freedom than their Jewish and Greek counterparts. Their movements were not as restricted although modesty and shame were still important components of their lives. Women were active in the religions and in their families. Their power was obtained indirectly via their role as nurturer and shaper of culture in the family with their children. The home was their zone of influence.

## Social/Cultural Context of Romans 16

Up to this point, we have built a model of the predominant values and roles of Mediterranean society. This model has been nuanced by primary material from the ancient world and considered in Roman, Greek and Jewish contexts. Each of these cultures had a bearing upon the first-century New Testament world, as it was Hellenized, Greek speaking and Roman ruled. It is the hope that this nuanced model will help us to better understand various New Testament texts and women's roles within them. With this intent in mind the text of Romans 16 will now be used as an example of how we might glean insight from such a model and apply it to our understanding of women in the New Testament world. This passage was also chosen because it includes a remarkable number of women who seem to have been in roles uncharacteristic of the time. Exploration of this text will allow us to not only apply the model but also learn more about the role of women in the first-century church and why that role evolved and changed as time passed. We will look at a variety of values including honor and shame, women and power, public/private, women and kin relationships, and women and religion.

## Honor and Shame

A core set of Mediterranean values is honor and shame. In Romans 16 we see women moving about without much attention to their modesty. Phoebe's movement and position seemed to exist without the fear of reprisal for immodesty. We have acknowledged that women of the Greco-Roman world were less concerned about their movements and, although they were still bound by the values of honor and shame, they were less constrained by them. For Phoebe was not accompanied by any male kin that are mentioned, and thus we wonder how her modesty was assured. The study of Greek women in chapter three made us aware that the concern for a woman's shame was an essential part of Greek society. Surely Phoebe left herself vulnerable as she stepped out of this prescribed role. She clearly broke the cultural barriers of her society.

Yet the issue of honor went beyond the protection of shame. Men were honored for their lifestyle and behavior. Honor, according to Peristiany (1966, 21), is esteem in the eyes of another, traditionally men to men. Yet as we have nuanced this model we have seen that women too were capable of receiving honor from one another and even from men, particularly if we look to the honors bestowed upon the imperial women in Rome.

Rome testifies to the imprint of Prisca and Aquila offering evidence of their existence in the city, even to a traditional site of their home. There is a church built over the Catacombs of Priscilla, an early burial site and place of Christian worship (Spence-Jones 1911, 262). It is quite possible that the tradition surrounding Prisca and Aquila was so strong that this site was preserved or manufactured in their honor. It is also possible that there is no validity to the tradition, yet this seems unlikely. Research into the background of this catacomb and its connection to the pair cannot be adequately covered in this work, nor would it significantly impact the direction of this thesis.

Prisca and Aquila were honored by later Christians and by Paul, yet they were not the only two commended. As Paul goes down his list of greetings he addresses men and women who have worked with him, whom he wishes to greet. He gives them honor when he notes some have worked hard in the Lord and when he calls others "fellow workers." Women are given this honor almost every time they are mentioned. Paul does not distinguish among genders when he honors Christians for their service to the Lord. Mary is called a hard worker. Tryphaena and Tryphosa are honored and Junia is noted as outstanding among the apostles. Women are more frequently commended in this passage than are men.

What unusual actions for Paul to take. Women were unimportant according to his culture, yet he makes a point of commending and honoring them. He turns societal expectations upside down. Not only were men capable of receiving esteem in the eyes of others, but so also were women.

One note of caution needs to be sounded. Women in Romans 16 may not display any characteristics of protecting their shame or being modest, but this does not mean these concerns were non-existent. Such women were more than likely still operating within the bounds of their society; it is just not explicit in this text. Yet it is clear that women are noted and honored for their Christian service. They receive the same commendations as the men Paul greets.

*Women and Power*

Another area where women in Romans 16 interface with our model is in the area of power. They appear to demonstrate more power than was usually given to women in their culture. For we cannot sweep aside the fact that Phoebe is called a patron, a benefactor (προστάτις). Schüssler Fiorenza suggests the church functioned as a voluntary organisation and was involved with patron-client relationships. She argues that Christians like Phoebe acted as guardians for other Christians before both court and the government. Such wealthy patrons had connections among the upper strata of society and introduced other Christians to influential people (Schüssler Fiorenza 1983, 181).

Schüssler Fiorenza suggests that these wealthy women could not receive much power politically yet they had great influence. She suggests that when they joined religious associations or the Christian movement they gained religious influence and power. By opening up their homes and providing financial resources for church groups women were able to improve their self-worth and increase their religious authority (Schüssler Fiorenza 1983, 183). Did women get their self-worth from their sense of personal power? One might question whether this hypothesis is more of a twenty-first-century thought imposed upon the text. The model would suggest that women gained their sense of value from having children, running their households and keeping their religious beliefs. Women did exert power indirectly in the home and amongst their kin which probably gave them a sense of control missing in the rest of their lives.

Later in the passage we are reminded that a church met in Prisca's and Aquila's home (αὐτῶν), implying they were both responsible for its well-being. We then again question Prisca's equal involvement, could Prisca have had more freedom because she was in her sphere of control, her realm of power? Another piece of our model has been to look at the Greek, Roman and Jewish cultures separately. Although Prisca and Aquila are often viewed as Jewish, it is also believed they were living in Rome both before and after the expulsion of the Jews by Nero.[13] Thus, even though they would be influenced by the Jewish culture and its restrictions on women, they had lived and been shaped in large part by the Roman culture, which as the model suggests was much more open to women in positions of power, honor and leadership. Women in the early Christian era did have some level of influence; one only needs to look at Romans 16 to find a variety of women who broke the mould and stepped over traditional boundary lines.

*Public/Private*

We recall that we found that the public-private divide was a separation between the world of men and the world of women. Each gender operated in opposite societal realms: males functioned in the public, outside of the domestic domain, while women centered on the home and private world. We noted in ancient Rome that women were not as secluded as Greek and Jewish women were, and we may ask whether this difference affected the Christian community, with specific attention to the churches highlighted in Romans 16.

In Romans 16:1 we meet Phoebe, who is called a sister (τὴν ἀδελφὴν) and a deacon/helper/servant (διάκονον) in the church of Cenchreae. Our earlier work on the meaning of this concept seems to suggest that she was a leader in the church at Cenchreae. Our model questions how she rose to such a position of power within a public setting.

Using first-century eyes we may wish to question whether the church was a public entity at this point in history. From what we know of the church in this time period it was home-based, a fact verified in verse 3 where Paul greets Prisca and Aquila and notes they have a church meeting in their house.

Thus, perhaps because the church was indeed not public, but rather met in private places, Phoebe was able to be a leader. However, this theory breaks down with regard to Phoebe because we read of her not in Cenchreae but in Rome as probably the bearer of the letter to the Romans and obviously travelling in public spaces. There are other examples of women who were probably not bound to ministry within the worship service. Prisca spreads the gospel with her husband Aquila not only in Rome but also in Corinth and Ephesus. Junia is noted as outstanding among the apostles, and perhaps she also had an itinerant ministry. Mary, Persis, Tryphaena and Tryphosa are all honored for working hard for the Lord. Such labors in the gospel more than likely extended beyond the house churches to which they were associated.

Prisca and Aquila seem to be leaders in the church as their names appear together, and the text says the church met in "their" house. Although the church was meeting in a private home it is called an ἐκκλησίαν, the word which came to mean "church" or "gathering place." One would assume there was a public component to such a meeting, particularly if the gathering was composed of people outside the kin of Prisca and Aquila. This couple also taught Apollos and corrected his teaching as evidenced in Acts 18:26. We can acknowledge that, based on this model, perhaps Prisca was able to also teach and lead because Aquila her husband accompanied her. Yet that does not explain why she usually appears first when her and her husband are mentioned by Paul.[14] It is particularly interesting that her name appears first when we learn that the couple becomes teachers of Apollos. Again we may go back to the idea that they were a part of a house church movement, which met in the private sphere. In Romans 16:5 Paul greets the church that met in their home. Having a church meet in their home meant they were in some position of wealth, they had the space to offer, and they were in some way significant in the Christian community.

Torjesen argues that women were viewed as the "ruler of the household" and that this societal stereotype may have helped women to gain initial leadership roles in the early church. She suggests that the Jesus movement was more egalitarian than the society at large and certainly more than the later developed church. She goes so far as to suggest women's leadership in the church was not just acceptable but also viewed as natural (Torjesen 1993, 82). While this may take the point too far, it is important to note women did rule the domestic sphere. However, women were not viewed in the larger society as "natural" leaders of public happenings. Thus the church walked a fine line of becoming a public entity while contained in a private dwelling.

Torjesen elaborates further by discussing the development of the basilica, which did not occur until about the fourth century. It is then, when the church moved out of the private space of the home, that Christian worship truly occurred in "public" space. Up until this point the early church had met in private homes and by the third century had begun to purchase homes specifically for that purpose (Torjesen 1993, 127). Torjesen's point is clearly important to our argument. The changing private-to-public nature of the church may explain why women were significantly moved to the periphery in the later centuries. Culturally, the role of women in the public sphere was much more limited than in the private. Perhaps the church, further away from its founding roots, was not willing to take such a risk when it had finally won its legitimacy after the time of Constantine. While it is an interesting proposition, the exploration of such ideas is beyond the scope of this thesis and is for another time and place. It is sufficient at this point to note that our model highlights a possible explanation for why women did not seem to continue their active involvement in the Christian church after the first few centuries.

*Women and Kin Relationships*

As we know from our model, women were embedded in relationships with their male kin. They did not exist (legally, socially and culturally) apart from their male counterparts and were also enmeshed in relationships with their extended families. Thus, given the significance of these relationships it seems prudent to also consider how these connections interface with our text.

Phoebe is not mentioned with any male kin, which is unusual. We would expect her to be associated with her husband or at the very least her brother or father. Certainly given what we learned about Greek women in chapter three and their lack of freedom, it is significant that she appears to be of her own means and free to move about. We might presume she was a widow, for she would then have a legitimate reason to be unmarried. We might also consider 1 Corinthians 7 and ask whether this practice of remaining unmarried, or a "virgin," was active at this time of the church.

We finally might go on to ask why Paul exhorts the Romans to welcome Phoebe in the Lord as is fitting the saints. Did she accompany the letter, bring the letter or was she in some way associated with the Roman church or Paul? Many have speculated over the nature of Phoebe's association with the Roman church. Several theories have been proposed, and a particularly intriguing one is that Phoebe may have been the bearer of the letter to the Romans. Was she trying to prepare the way for Paul to visit? Was she, as Jewett (1988, 5) suggests, using her connections and wealth to raise money to finance Paul's missionary trip to Spain? As we have seen in an earlier section we have many good questions but few solid answers. We will probably never clearly know the identity of Phoebe or what her relationship was to the Roman church, but we can be sure she demonstrated there were exceptions to the rule. Women did have the potential for moving about freely, serving publicly and were entrusted with great portions of the message to the nations. Despite the barriers in society the early church appears to be countercultural in this regard.

Yet carrying on in our discussion of women and relationships another peculiar relationship exists in verse 7 between Junia, who is considered outstanding among the apostles (ἐπίσημοι ἐν τοῖς ἀποστόλοις), and her counterpart Andronicus. If they were married we would have another husband and wife team in ministry together. Paul greets other women including Mary, Tryphaena, Tryphosa and Julia, some in connection with male kin and others are mentioned independently. Mixed groups of men and women are greeted as well (vv. 14, 15). Yet it seems unlikely that women would fraternize with men outside their kin, or that they would be in positions of authority such as in the example of Junia as an apostle. Given what the model has told us about women's subordinate relationship to men, particularly in the public sphere, how can these apparent differences be reconciled? One thought to ponder might be the idea of "fictive kinship."[15] It seems possible that the New Testament church functioned as its own unit, certainly it was its own group, with its common norms, functions and values. If we accept that the church functioned as a family, as many New Testament passages lead us to believe, then we may have discovered an important point. If believers functioned as fictive kin to one another then it would not be inappropriate to have fellowship together, even men and women of different blood kin groups.

Another way to understand women's roles in the early church is to consider their role in the family. The model shows us the Roman mother or matron was quite powerful within the boundaries of her family. We might want to argue that this phenomenon only took place within wealthy families, but that seems unlikely. It would seem that women would have had an even more equal role in poorer families, where living divisions could not be made, and each person was dependent on the other, when the whole family unit was necessary to function together for its financial, social and material survival. Based on these probabilities it would seem feasible that women operating within a familial role, within the private realm of the home church, were able to assume roles of authority without much resistance. In fact, it may have been almost natural for women to function in such roles.

It seems likely the church as an emerging group was based on the family, but a new type of family, one established on the freedom Christ offers each individual regardless of ethnicity, class or gender. Yet as the church grew, familiar patterns of the family and the public world began to slowly take over so that the role of women became more subsidiary than central.

*Relationships*

Relationships are another area upon which the model sheds some light in Romans 16. We discussed the idea that women functioned within relationships with their husbands, brothers, fathers, mothers, etc. They were dependent on these relationships for survival. This system of relationships functioned both to their advantage and disadvantage. The homeostasis of the system was affected when anything changed within these relationships. For example, the death of a father profoundly affected the unmarried daughter, who still needed her dowry provided and her marriage arranged, thus her care went to her brothers. If she had no brothers then she had to depend on her nearest male kin, and so the situation could continue. One change could improve or completely alter a woman's existence since she was so dependent on these relationships. It is no surprise then that women were vitally important to Paul in his network of friends, for they knew how to support one another and to work through relationships to get what they wanted and needed. Since the relationships women formed and acted within were crucial to their existence, it is no wonder the early church was based on associations and group connections, sharing common goals and working together for a common good. It is interesting that our look at the Roman world did not suggest relationships were as valued in that culture as they seemed to be in the model as found in the anthropological sources. Yet there is evidence that such relationships ties were important to Paul in his co-workers in Romans 16. Perhaps the Jewish or Greek cultures brought out the importance of relationships more, or, alternatively, they may have been equally important in Rome but simply not as obvious in the primary sources.

*Women and Religion*

One final element of the model clearly evident in Romans 16 is the notion that women were active participants in the religions of all three cultures. They were shapers of the religious values in the home and participated actively in the rites and rituals of their cultures. It is no wonder that they would be involved in this new religion of Christianity. Thus it is not surprising to finding Phoebe as a deacon, Prisca organising a home church, Junia as an apostle and others as hard workers and co-laborers with Paul in the cause of the gospel. Romans 16 seems to reflect what we would expect to see in the culture, namely women actively participating in religion. What is unusual was the level of their involvement in leadership, their lack of embeddedness in male kin, and the freedoms they seemed to enjoy, perhaps as a consequence of their involvement in this new religion.

## Concluding Insights

As we have seen, Romans 16 provides us with a text very different than the rest of Paul's letters. Romans 16 does stretch the model on several points. Women are throughout the text found in uncharacteristic roles. Women exerted leadership, and served and supported the church and missionary activities. Women functioned in many cases independently of men. Women were not concerned about the immodesty of travelling alone or being mentioned before their husbands. Yet they walked a fine line between the public and private nature of the church. They may have been allowed some of their freedoms in leadership because of their traditional position in the home. They might have been able to relate freely to their "brothers in Christ" because they were fictive kin even though they were not related by blood or marriage. Despite the ways the text describes this unexpected voice and role of women in the early church, we do need to question why this relationship is not evident in more, specifically later, writings of the New Testament.

Perhaps two insights can be drawn. As time progressed the church moved more clearly from the private realm to the public arena. As this transition took place women were slowly pushed to the sidelines and seemed to move out of leadership positions. Hence, a later New Testament writing, 1 Timothy 2:11-15, may show evidence of this shift. We also need to recognize that Paul's letters and the other writings of the New Testament were set in a variety of locations. Rome was probably the city allowing the greatest freedom, while some of the Greek cities including Ephesus and Corinth may have been more constrained in the freedoms afforded to women given the history of women under Greek rule. The Jewish, Greek and Roman models have helped us to be sensitive to the diversity of settings in the New Testament and in relation to women's roles in the early church.

From this model we have come to recognize women's important roles in religion, their families, relationships and in their homes. In the end we have developed a more multidimensional view of women in the early church. As a result, our interpretation of Romans 16 has become a sharper and a more accurate reflection of the ancient Mediterranean world.

## Notes

1. Some sections of this chapter appear in the author's essay (and may be exact quotes of) "Unity in the Midst of Diversity: The Early Church at Rome, as Reflected in Romans 16," in *Who Killed Goliath?: Reading the Bible with Heart and Mind* (eds. Robert F. Shedinger and Deborah J. Spink; Judson Press, 2001): 88-103.

2. See Peter Lampe, "Junias," *ABD*, vol. 3: 1127, and "Prisca," *ABD*, vol. 5: 467-468 (ed. David Noel Freedman. 6 vols. New York, 1992); also see Peter Lampe, "The Roman Christians of Romans 16," in *The Romans Debate*, revised and expanded edition (ed. Karl P. Donfried; Peabody, Mass.: Hendrickson, 1991): 216-230.

3. See Robert Jewett, "Paul, Phoebe and the Spanish Mission," in *The Social World of Formative Christianity and Judaism* (eds. Jacob Neusner, Peder Borgen, Ernest S. Frerichs and Richard Horsley; Philadelphia, Fortress, 1988): 142-162; and R. Jewett, "Approaching

the Cultural Diversity of Roman Churches: A Proposed New Identity as 'Beloved of God'." Typescript. January, 1996.

4. As earlier cited in Suetonius *Claud.* 25.4.

5. Church of Prisca and Aquila; of Epaenetus (v. 5) and others—Rufus and his mother (v. 13); of "Asyncritus, Phlegon, Hermes, Patrobas, Hermas and the brothers with them"; of "Philologus, Julia, Nereus and his sister, and Olympas and all the saints with them."

6. A study of the New Testament texts where forms of ἐργάτης (2 Cor 11:13; Phil 3:2), ἔργον (50 references found in Romans, 1 & 2 Cor, Gal, Eph, Phil, Col and 1 & 2 Thess), συνεργός (Rom 16:3, 9, 21; 1 Cor 3:9; 2 Cor 1:24, 8:23; Phil 2:25, 4:3; Col 4:11; 1 Thess 3:2; Phlm 1, 24) and συνεργέω (1 Cor 16:16; 2 Cor 6:1; Rom 8:28) were found did not yield any specific nuances to the model.

7. In this counting Junia has been accepted as a female.

8. See John Chrysostom's Homilies 31.

9. Acts 18:18, 1 Cor 16:19, 2 Tim 4:19.

10. 2 Cor 13:12 and 1 Thess 5:26.

11. See Lampe, "The Roman Christians"; see also Jewett, "Approaching the Cultural Diversity."

12. For further discussions on the ethnic issues in the background of this letter, see James C. Walters, Ethnic Issues in Paul's Letter to the Romans: Changing Self-Definitions in Earliest Roman Christianity (Valley Forge, PA: Trinity Press International, 1993); and William Campbell, Paul's Gospel in an Intercultural Context (New York: Peter Lang, 1992).

13. See previous chapter on the reconstruction of the audience of Romans 16.

14. See Acts 18:18, Rom 16:3, 2 Tim 4:19.

15. See John H. Elliott, *What is Social-Scientific Criticism?* (Minneapolis: Fortress Press, 1993): 82-83, 131.

# 8

# Concluding Thoughts

We began this journey seeking to understand the women of Romans 16 in their ancient Mediterranean culture. We first gathered anthropological material on Mediterranean women. Then, after a comprehensive reading of the material, a model began to take shape. This model, although it closely resembles the approach employed by Bruce Malina, was nuanced and focused on women in the Mediterranean. It was informed by the classic works in this field by Pitt-Rivers and Campbell but also by female anthropologists such as Dubisch and Fernea.

This model became the framework by which we studied ancient women in their Roman, Greek-speaking and Jewish worlds. The themes of honor and shame, public and private, power, religion, death and kin relationships began to raise new questions, and as the model was nuanced, new insights emerged from the text of Romans 16. The model also highlighted cultural nuances we would surely have missed if we had been operating out of our twenty-first century Western mindset. The gap between the ancient Roman world and ours was narrowed as the values of their society became distinct from our own. The values of any society are what drive people to act, react and interact. Understanding ancient Mediterranean values helped us to see our own values and the text more clearly.

As we survey what has been accomplished in this thesis, there are many insights that rise to the surface. The first and most obvious achievement is the development of a nuanced cultural context model which sheds light on New Testament texts concerning women. Although this model was used specifically with the text of Romans 16, it could be easily employed to help raise questions about and provide understanding of additional New Testament texts including those found in the Gospels, other Epistles and even Acts. This model can be a tool to look at the text from a range of perspectives including historical-critical, and even feminist critique. It is not meant to be used to interpret a text alone but rather to complement existing methods of interpretation.

As noted all along, there are few dialogue partners in this journey. There is some work by feminist scholars that begins to use social-scientific criticism,[1] yet the work only scratches the surface of the vast resources that are available through the consideration of anthropology and Mediterranean values. This thesis is the first in-depth examination of women and the values of the Mediterranean world as illuminated through anthropology. Taking it one step further, this model does not stop with a look at anthropology but also consults the primary sources and attempts to make some distinctions between the Jewish, Greek and Roman worlds to look for nuances. It is in this back-and-forth discussion that the model adds to what Malina has accomplished. Malina cites some ancient sources in support of his model, but this thesis surpasses his treatment of the subject and others writing in the field who have not systematically laid out a reliable cultural context model.

Malina looks at examples of these values in primary sources, yet his choice of examples is neither systematic nor thorough. Alternatively, this work broadly surveys primary sources and pinpoints areas of connection with the model. This approach to nuancing the model is intentional and detailed. By going to the primary sources and thoroughly surveying them, the outcome is both extensive and distinct. This work is comprehensive in its approach to the material because it looks broadly at the available sources and considers a multitude of examples of values found in the culture. It is also a unique approach because each culture—Greek, Jewish and Roman—is considered separate from the other. Thus we see differences in the nuancing of the model according to what values are most pronounced in each culture, and we discover new insights into each culture as a result of this study.

Greek Egyptian women (as we studied from Plutarch and papyri) often reflected the values found in the traditional model of honor and shame and public and private. For the most part Greek women were expected to comply with standards of keeping their shame, remaining in the private sphere and having their lives dictated by their male kin. Greek women did have a sense of mobility, wealth and limited power in their personal relationships.

Jewish women, like their Greek counterparts, seem to fall into the traditional values highlighted by the model. They were at times secluded, were held to strict honor and shame codes, and were expected to function for the most part in the private realm. As with Greek women, they too had their exceptional women, particularly royalty such as Queen Berenice, Salome, Mariamme or the Apocryphal heroine Judith. Again the emerging theme suggests that the later the time period studied the more freedoms are evident. Such is the case with Babatha (2nd century C.E.), a wealthy woman who owned property, and Julia Crispina who was a guardian to Babatha's son. Yet Jewish women did not appear as secluded as Greek women. They did at times garner power even if it was by indirect means, and they surely showed themselves to be active, particularly in their religion.

Roman women did, however, appear to be freer than their Greek and Jewish sisters. They seemed to speak their minds more openly and they were more mobile. Wealth seems to be a factor in giving them more of an advantage over women in the other cultures. They were still embedded in male kin and in the same Mediterranean values the model lays out. However, they were not as constrained by them as Greek and Jewish women. Thus, it is not surprising that one of Paul's most supportive letters concerning women is written to the Roman church. Even though all three cultures are represented in Romans 16, the context of living in Rome seems to suggest such women were more mobile and more powerful than those women living elsewhere.

All three cultures testify to the fact that women were active in the religions of the time. It is, therefore, not surprising they would be a part of this new sect later known as Christianity. It is helpful to look at these cultures distinctly and not just for the light they shed on Romans 16. No other work has been found which examines these cultures using such a model. Perhaps our knowledge of these cultures is more complete when we understand the values that governed women within various contexts.

As noted in the beginning of this thesis, according to Esler a model cannot be proven. Yet this work suggests it can be nuanced and shown to be reliable. This study has made it clear that there are common patterns of values that existed in the Mediterranean two thousand years ago and in some form still exist today. It is necessary to understand these values, which in many cases are different from the Western perspective, so that we might better understand the New Testament texts. The model might also be used to illuminate Hebrew Bible texts, although in a much more general way, since the primary sources studied were geared to understanding the first-century C.E. world. The Hebrew Bible texts cover a more expansive time period and genre, thus making the task of employing the model more difficult although not impossible.

In addition to further developing a model that will be useful in exegeting the biblical text, there was the work of applying the model and the fruits of that labor. Some significant insights were gained as we studied the text of Romans 16. Our original question asked what the role of women was in the early church. Romans 16 has given us some insight into women's roles in first-century Roman Christianity. While other studies have highlighted the unusual distinctions of these women, this work offers some explanation and context for considering their non-traditional accomplishments. We discovered that Phoebe played an uncharacteristic role for a Greek woman, and she could even be considered a barrier-breaker in Roman society. She was a benefactor of Paul, a deacon at the church of Cenchreae, and probably the bearer of the letter to the Romans. She was unusual for her culture because no male kin was attached to her name. As stated in the model, women in the Mediterranean culture were embedded in their male kin and would be looked down upon if they were unattached. They were often identified with their fathers, brothers, husbands or sons. In this case there is no indication that Phoebe has a relation to any male kin. She is only identified as one who has provided a man, Paul, with probable financial support. She is unique in that she is described in relation to her ministry to Paul and to the church rather than in any domestic role. She defies the expected societal norms by appearing to travel on her own and to carry a letter of prime importance to the Roman Christians. She is honored by Paul through his commendation of her.

Several other women are commended by Paul in these greetings, including Tryphaena, Tryphosa and Mary. There are many women in this list honored for their service to their Lord, not to their male kin. In such a society if women received honor at all it was from other women and rarely, if at all, from men. Such thinking was not even a part of the Mediterranean culture, and it was highly unusual for a man to honor a woman as Paul commended these women. Thus, it appears evident that the early Christian movement flowed against the tide of its society. Women found a place where they were honored and were allowed to take part unhindered by their gender.

We learned that Prisca probably led a house church with her husband Aquila. Again, a woman in a leadership role was certainly not expected in the ancient Mediterranean. She is identified with her husband, but the text does not seem to indicate any subservience to him. She seems to be a co-sponsor of the church and is honored along with her husband, as they have both risked their lives for Paul. She is unusual in the Mediterranean world in that, although married, she seems not to be restrained by her role as wife, and children are not even mentioned. One might be more likely to explain away any of the other women mentioned because they are noted apart from male kin and could be assumed to be virgins or widows and thus free from the obligations of marriage. Yet with Prisca one cannot brush aside her status as wife, missionary and co-leader of a house church.

Junia is another woman who is out of place in Mediterranean society. She is called an apostle and is perhaps married to Andronicus or related to him in some way since their names are joined in a grammatical construction. She, like Prisca, is perhaps a married woman who is not constrained by traditional expectations but is able to serve in this emerging group's missionary circles. She is also shown honor and commended by Paul. Might we again ask if the emergence of these strong women is due to the setting being in Rome?

The model does indicate that Roman women had more freedom than Jewish or Greek women, however, it does not suggest that they were unhindered by their gender. Women in Rome were still bound by Mediterranean values and cultural expectations. They interacted more freely with men, and there were some who obtained power outside of their kin groups. Yet, Prisca, Phoebe and the others go beyond what one would expect to see in Roman society. They hold positions in this new movement that would usually be closed to women in their culture. Thus, what are some reasons the model offers which might explain these discrepancies between culture and the early Christian movement?

One point the model highlights, which may have helped women to be included in the early church, was the growing possibility that early Christians related to one another as "fictive kin." The language that we see in other New Testament writings suggests the early Christians considered themselves as brothers and sisters. Paul writes earlier in Romans that those who believe become sons of God and co-heirs with Christ (Rom 8:14, 17). He clearly uses kinship language to describe their new relationship with God and one another. They were perhaps able to interact with each other on a familial level which meant women could interact without fear of being shamed or violated. Related in this way, they, therefore, could protect each other's honor and function like a kin group or clan.

Yet another more significant point is the model suggests women ruled the domestic realm. They interacted freely with others and even ordered the household the way they wished. Since the church initially met in homes, women, who were already operating in the private realm, would have been more comfortable there than in the public world of men. They would have naturally been allowed more freedom within their own sphere of influence. This possibility is supported even more by the fact that women began to disappear from church leadership as the church became more public and viable in the sphere of men. One would need to take this trajectory further to discern whether the pattern continued to prevail and prove true as the church advanced in status and in its public nature. A further study might examine how women coped with the changing public character of the church, particularly when it became legitimized during the era of Constantine. It would seem likely that women's roles would diminish as the church became more public, as indeed history can attest. Romans 16 and our model highlight the importance of women and the house churches being located in the private sphere.

It is also evident from an understanding of the Mediterranean culture that women were viewed as subservient, perceived by males as needing protection and embedded in the male kin of their family. Their power was obtained indirectly through relationships and manipulation. Only wealthy or socially prominent exceptions such as Cleopatra and Salome wielded any direct power. Yet the text suggests that Christian women, at least the women of Romans 16, were able to wield some level of influence by the various roles they played of deacon, benefactor, apostle, hard worker and leader of house churches. The model aids us in seeing how strikingly different this community was from the Mediterranean society around them. The model informs us women were traditionally active in religion. It makes sense they would then be welcomed to participate in the development of this growing Christian community.

The model also highlights the fact that women interact through a network of relationships. They manipulate, scheme, plan and live through the relationships they had with particularly their male kin, but also with neighboring women. Hence, we see these networks of connectedness becoming a part of the circles in which the apostle Paul also travels. It is unusual that women interacted so freely with men outside of their families. Paul says to the Romans that, although he himself has never been to Rome, he knows people such as Prisca and Aquila (along with the 26 others he greets) who are well established and can vouch for his character. Women were not as secluded as one would expect from the model. They interacted with others and with men, including people outside of their kin group.

Finally, the implications that can be drawn from this text for the Christian church today come out of the cultural context of this letter. The epistle to the Romans was a letter written to the Roman Christians in the first-century church. Although it contains principles that form a portion of today's Christian theology, it is not to be understood as Paul's systematic theology, written to all people in all times in all places. The message, as the text was looked at culturally, seems to be the emphasis Paul places on unity within diversity. Paul calls the Roman Christians—Jews and Gentiles—to unite and be of one accord. He exhorts them to put away their differences over when they worship and the food they eat. The model has shown us not even gender stood in the way of the roles the early Christians played in the church. Paul clearly spells out the essentials of the gospel and how to live the Christian life, probably because the Roman church was arguing over points of tension that no longer are relevant if one is to embrace the Christian message fully.

Thus, for the Christian church today there is much to be learned. First of all, exegesis needs to include the cultural context of the text. The Epistles are letters to people in a specific time and place, two thousand years removed from our own and in a different cultural context (even as East is different from West today). In attempting to understand the message for us today, we must first understand the message to the original audience and then we will be able to understand truly its meaning and application for the modern Christian. The text of Romans 16, and indeed the letter of Romans, clearly calls for divisions over matters unrelated to the core of Paul's gospel to be put aside for the sake of the unity of the entire church. The message is timeless, one much needed in the Western church today as Christians take sides over social issues that threaten to divide. Paul does not tell the Romans to compromise on their faith, rather to show one another grace and to preserve unity at the cost of one's own individuality. Finally, Romans 16 offers a clear picture of women who were active participants in the early Christian movement. Women and men worked together, and both were commended for their dedicated service in the cause of the gospel. Such co-operation serves as a role model for both women and men of the church today.

To call Romans 16 a mere list of greetings is to do it a great injustice, just as considering the entire letter to the Romans outside of its original audience distorts its overall message. Methods that focus on cultural context are needed in the exegeting of biblical texts. It is essential that we bridge the culture and time gap that exists between us and the world from which the text originates. Hopefully this study has prompted us to dig deeper into the ancient world and to think outside of our often Western, Caucasian, male-centered world view. Schüssler Fiorenza encourages the reader to consider that Romans 16 and its mention of women in Christian leadership are not the sum total of all examples of women in the early church, but are in fact only the "tip of an iceberg" (1986, 423). This author would exhort the reader to recognize this growing field of anthropological studies and cultural context is also just the beginning. Going back in time will never be possible, but we might come a little closer to biblical truth if we begin to step outside of our own cultural constraints and immerse ourselves in a culture and time far different from our own.

# Notes

1. See Naomi Steinberg, *Kinship and Marriage in Genesis: A Household Perspective* (Minneapolis: Fortress Press, 1993); Phyllis Bird, "Women's Religion in Ancient Israel," in *Women's Earliest Records: From Ancient Egypt and Western Asia* (ed. Barbara S. Lesko; Atlanta: Scholars Press, 1989); Carolyn Osiek, *What are they Saying About the Social Setting of the New Testament?* rev. ed. (New York: Paulist Press, 1992); Carol Meyers, "Women and the Domestic Economy of Early Israel" in *Women's Earliest Records: From Ancient Egypt and Western Asia* (ed. Barbara S. Lesko; Atlanta: Scholars Press, 1989).

# Bibliography

Abu-Lughod, Lila. 1986. *Veiled Sentiments: Honor and Poetry in A Bedouin Society*. Berkley: University of California Press.

Abu-Zahra, N. 1976. Family and Kinship in a Tunisian Peasant Community. Pages 157-172 in *Mediterranean Family Structures*. Edited by J.G. Peristiany. Cambridge: Cambridge University Press.

Achtemeier, Paul J. 1985. *Romans*. Interpretation: A Bible Commentary for Teaching and Preaching. Atlanta: John Knox Press.

Aeschylus. *Agamemnon*. 1957(1926). Translated by H.W. Smyth. LCL. London: William Heinemann.

Aland, Barbara, Kurt Aland, Johannes Karavidopoulos, Carlo M. Martini and Bruce Metzger, eds. 1993. *The Greek New Testament*, 4th revised edition. New York: United Bible Societies.

Alexander, Patrick H., John F. Kutsko, James D. Ernest, Shirley A. Decker-Lucke, David L. Petersen, eds. 1999. *The SBL Handbook of Style: For Ancient Near Eastern, Biblical, and Early Christian Studies*. Peabody, Mass.: Hendrickson.

Apocrypha. New Revised Standard Version.

Appian. *Roman History: The Civil Wars*, Books 1 & 4. 1990-1991. Translated by H. White. LCL. Cambridge: Harvard University Press.

Archer, Léonie J. 1983. The Role of Jewish Women in the Religion, Ritual and Cult of Graeco-Roman Palestine. Pages 273-287 in *Images of Women in Antiquity*. Edited by Averil Cameron and Amélie Kuhrt. London: Routledge.

——. 1990. *Her Price is Beyond Rubies: The Jewish Woman in Graeco-Roman Palestine*. Sheffield: Sheffield Academic Press.

——. 1994. Notions of Community and the Exclusion of the Female in Jewish History and Historiography. Pages 53-69 in *Women in Ancient Societies: An Illusion of the Night*. Edited by Léonie J. Archer, Susan Fischler and Maria Wyke. London: Macmillan.

Archer, Léonie J., Susan Fischler and Maria Wyke, eds. 1994. *Women in Ancient Societies: An Illusion of the Night*. London: Macmillan.

Aristophanes. *The Clouds*. 1992(1924). Translated by Benjamin Bickley Rogers. LCL. Cambridge: Harvard University Press.

———. *The Ecclesiazusae*. 1991(1924). Translated by Benjamin Bickley Rogers. LCL. Cambridge: Harvard University Press.
———. *The Lysistrata*. 1991(1924). Translated by Benjamin Bickley Rogers. LCL. Cambridge: Harvard University Press.
———. *The Thesmorphoriazusae* 1991(1924). Translated by Benjamin Bickley Rogers. LCL. Cambridge: Harvard University Press.
———. *The Wasps*. 1991(1924). Translated by Benjamin Bickley Rogers. LCL. Cambridge: Harvard University Press.
Aristotle. *Generation of Animals*. 1932. Translated by A.L. Peck. LCL. London: William Heinemann.
———. *The Politics*. 1932. Translated by H. Rackham. LCL. London: William Heinemann.
Asano-Tamanoi, Mariko. 1987. Shame, Family and State in Catalonia and Japan. Pages 104-120 in *Honour and Shame and the Unity of the Mediterranean*. Edited by David D. Gilmore. Washington, D.C.: American Anthropological Association.
Ascough, Richard S. 1998. *What are They Saying About the Formation of Pauline Churches?* New York: Paulist Press.
Atkins, Robert A. 1991. *Egalitarian Community: Ethnography and Exegesis*. London: University of Alabama Press.
Aune, David. 1987. *The New Testament in its Literary Environment*. Vol. 8 of *Library of Early Christianity*. Edited by Wayne A. Meeks. Philadelphia: Westminster Press.
Bach, Alice. 1990. *The Pleasure of Her Text: Feminist Readings of Biblical and Historical Texts*. Philadelphia: Trinity Press International.
Baker, Carolyn D. 1995. Phoebe: Radiant One. *Paraclete* 29/2:10-14.
Balsdon, J.P.V.D. 1962. *Roman Women: Their History and Habits*. London: The Bodley Head.
Baroja, Julio C. 1966. Honour and Shame: A Historical Account of Several Conflicts. Pages 79-138 in *Honour and Shame: The Values of Mediterranean Society*. Edited by J.G. Peristiany. London: Weidenfeld & Nicolson.
Barrett, C.K. 1963. *Reading Through Romans*. London: Epworth Press.
———. 1991. *A Commentary on the Epistle to the Romans*, 2nd ed. Black's New Testament Commentaries. London: A&C Black.
Baskin, Judith R., ed. 1998. *Jewish Women in Historical Perspective*, 2nd ed. Detroit: Wayne State University Press.
Bauckham, Richard. 1983. The *Liber Antiquitatum Biblicarum* of Pseudo-Philo and the Gospels as 'Midrash'. Pages 33-76 in *Gospel Perspectives: Studies in Midrash and Historiography*, vol. 3. Edited by RT. France and David Wenham. Sheffield: JSOT Press.
———. 2002. *Gospel Women: Studies of the Named Women in the Gospels*. Grand Rapids, Mich.: Eerdmans.
Bauman, Richard A. 1992. *Women and Politics in Ancient Rome*. London: Routledge.

Beard, Mary. 1995. Re-reading (Vestal) Virginity. Pages 166-177 in *Women in Antiquity: New Assessments*. Edited by Richard Hawley and Barbara Levick. London: Routledge.
Benedict, Peter. 1976. Aspects of the Domestic Cycle in a Turkish Provincial Town. Pages 219-242 in *Mediterranean Family Structures*. Edited by J.G Peristiany. Cambridge: Cambridge University Press.
Biale, Rachel. 1984. *Women and Jewish Law: An Exploration of Women's Issues in Halakhic Sources*. New York: Shocken Books.
*Bible Windows 4.0* (CD ROM). 1995. Cedar Hill, Tex.: Silver Mountain Software.
Billigmeier, Jon-Christian and Judy A. Turner. 1981. The Socio-Economic Roles of Women in Mycenaean Greece: A Brief Survey from Evidence of the Linear Tablets. Pages 1-18 in *Reflections of Women in Antiquity*. Edited by Helene P. Foley. New York: Gordon & Breach Science Publishers.
Bird, Phyllis. 1989. Women's Religion in Ancient Israel. Pages 283-298 in *Women's Earliest Records: From Ancient Egypt and Western Asia*. Edited by Barbara S. Lesko. Atlanta: Scholars Press.
Black, Matthew. 1973. Romans 16: Personal Greetings. Pages 178-186 in *New Century Bible*. Edited by Ronald E. Clements and Matthew Black. London: Oliphants.
Blok, Anton. 1981. Rams and Billy-goats: A Key to the Mediterranean Code of Honour. *Man* 16(3): 427-440.
Blundell, Sue. 1995. *Women in Ancient Greece*. London: British Museum Press.
———. 1998. *Women in Classical Athens*. London: Bristol Classical Press.
Bourdieu, Pierre. 1966. The Sentiment of Honour in Kabyle Society. Pages 191-242 in *Honour and Shame: The Values of Mediterranean Society*. Edited by J.G. Peristiany. London: Weidenfeld & Nicolson.
Bow, Beverly and George W.E. Nickelsburg. 1991. Patriarchy with a Twist: Men and Women in Tobit. Pages 127-143 in *"Women Like This": New Perspectives on Jewish Women in the Greco-Roman World*. Edited by Amy-Jill Levine. Atlanta: Scholars Press.
Bowie, A.M. 1993. *Aristophanes: Myth, Ritual and Comedy*. Cambridge: Cambridge University Press.
Bradley, Keith R. 1991. *Discovering the Roman Family: Studies in Roman Social History*. New York: Oxford University Press.
Brandes, Stanley. 1987. Reflections on Honour and Shame in the Mediterranean. Pages 121-134 in *Honour and Shame and the Unity of the Mediterranean*. Edited by David D. Gilmore. Washington, D.C.: American Anthropological Association.
Brändle, Rudolf and Ekkehard W. Stegemann. 1998. The formation of the First "Christians Congregations" in Rome in the Context of the Jewish Congregation. Pages 117-127 in *Judaism and Christianity in First-Century Rome*. Edited by Karl P. Donfried and Peter Richardson. Grand Rapids, Mich.: Eerdmans.
Bray, Gerald, ed. 1998. Romans. Vol. 6 of *Ancient Christian Commentary on Scripture*. Edited by Thomas C. Oden. Downers Grove: Ill.: InterVarsity Press.

Brooke, George J. 1992. Susanna and Paradise Regained. Pages 92-111 in *Women in the Biblical Tradition*. Edited by George J. Brooke. Lewiston, N.Y.: Edwin Mellen Press.

——, ed. 1992. *Women in the Biblical Tradition*. Lewiston, N.Y.: Edwin Mellen Press.

Brooten, Bernadette. 1977. Junia...Outstanding among the Apostles. Pages 141-144 in *Women Priests, A Catholic Commentary on the Vatican Declaration*. Edited by L. Swidler. New York: Paulist Press.

——. 1982. *Women Leaders in the Ancient Synagogue: Inscriptional Evidence and Background Issues*. Chico, Calif.: Scholars Press.

Brown, Cheryl Anne. 1992. *No Longer Be Silent: First Century Jewish Portraits of Biblical Women*. Louisville: Westminster/John Knox Press.

Brown, Raymond E. and John P. Meier. 1983. *Antioch and Rome: New Testament Cradles of Catholic Christianity*. New York: Paulist Press.

Bruce, F.F. 1974. *Romans: An Introduction and Commentary by F.F. Bruce*. London: InterVarsity Press.

——. 1991. The Romans Debate—Continued. Pages 175-194 in *The Romans Debate*, rev. ed. Edited by Karl P. Donfried. Peabody, Mass.: Hendrickson.

Buttrick, George Arthur. 1954. Romans: Test, Exegesis and Exposition. In *The Interpreter's Bible*, vol. 9. New York: Abingdon Press.

Byrne, Brenden. 1988. *Paul and the Christian Woman*. Collegeville, Minn.: The Liturgical Press.

Cabrol, F. and H. Leclerc. 1948. *Dictionaire d'Archéologie et de Liturgie*, vol. 14-2. Paris. col. 1799-1874.

Cameron, Averil, and Amélie Kuhrt, eds. 1993. *Images of Women in Antiquity*, rev. ed. London: Routledge.

Camp, Claudia V. 1991. Understanding a Patriarchy: Women in Second Century Jerusalem Through the Eyes of Ben Sira. Pages 1-39 in *"Women Like This": New Perspectives on Jewish Women in the Greco-Roman World*. Edited by Amy-Jill Levine. Atlanta: Scholars Press.

Campbell, J.K. 1964. *Honour, Family, and Patronage: A Study of Institutions and Moral Values in a Greek Mountain Community*. Oxford: Oxford University Press.

——. 1966. Honour and the Devil. Pages 139-170 in *Honour and Shame: The Values of Mediterranean Society*. Edited by J.G. Peristiany. London: Weidenfeld & Nicolson.

Campbell, William S. 1992. *Paul's Gospel in an Intercultural Context: Jew and Gentile in the Letter to the Romans*. New York: Peter Lang.

Cantarella, Eve. 1987. *Pandora's Daughters: The Role and Status of Women in Greek and Roman Antiquity*. Maureen B. Fant, trans. Baltimore: The Johns Hopkins University Press.

Caplan, Pat, ed. 1987. *The Cultural Construction of Sexuality*. London: Routledge.

Caraveli, Anna. 1986. The Bitter Wounding: The Lament as Social Protest. Pages 169-194 in *Gender and Power in Rural Greece*. Edited by Jill Dubisch. Princeton: Princeton University Press.

Carletti, Sandro. 1982. *Guide to the Catacombs of Priscilla*. Translated by Alice Mulhern. Vatican City: Pontifical Commission for Sacred Archaeology.

Carney, T. F. 1975. *The Shape of the Past: Models and Antiquity*. Lawrence, Kans.: Coronado.

Cartledge, Paul. 1998. The Glory that was Greece in *The Cambridge Illustrated History of Ancient Greece*. Edited by Paul Cartledge. Cambridge: Cambridge University Press.

Castelli, Elizabeth A. 1994. Romans. Pages 272-300 in *Searching the Scriptures: Volume Two: A Feminist Commentary*. Edited by Elisabeth Schüssler Fiorenza. New York: Crossroad.

Catullus, Gaius Valerius. *Poems*. 1988. Translated by Francis Warre Cornish. LCL. Cambridge: Harvard University Press.

Cesara, M. 1982. *Reflections of a Woman Anthropologist: No Hiding Place*. London: Academic Press.

Chariton. *Callirhoe*. 1995. Translated by G.P. Goold. LCL. London: Harvard University Press.

Charlesworth, James H., ed. 1983. *The Old Testament Pseudepigrapha*, vol. 1. New York: Doubleday.

———, ed. 1985. *The Old Testament Pseudepigrapha*, vol. 2. New York: Doubleday.

Chrysostom, John. *Ad Homilias in Epistolam ad Romanos*, 30 & 31. *Patrologiae Cursus Completus, Latinae, Patrologiae Graecae Tomus*, vol. 60. 1862. Edited by Jacques Paul Migne. Paris.

———. 1889. *Homilies on the Epistle to the Romans*. Edited by Philip Schaff. New York: The Christian Literature Company.

Cicero. *Brutus*. 1939. Translated by G.L. Hendrickson. LCL. Cambridge: Harvard University Press.

———. *De divinatione*. 1927. Translated by William Armistead Falconer. LCL. New York: G.P. Putnam's Sons.

———. *De Finibus Bonorum et Malorum*. 1914. Translated by H. Rackham. LCL. New York: The MacMillan Co.

———. *De Officiis*. 1921. Translated by Walter Miller. LCL. New York: The MacMillan Co.

———. *De republica* and *De legibus*. 1928. Translated by Clinton Walker Keyes. LCL. New York: Putnam's Sons.

———. *In Catilinam I-IV*; *Pro Murena*; *Pro Sulla*; *Pro Flacco*. 1976. Translated by C. MacDonald. LCL. Cambridge: Harvard University Press.

———. *Letters to Atticus*. 1999. Translated by D.R. Shackleton Bailey. 4 vols. LCL. Cambridge: Harvard University Press.

———. *Letters to Atticus*, Book 9. 1984. Translated by E.O. Winstedt. LCL. Cambridge: Harvard University Press.

———. *Letters to Brutus*. 1953. Translated by M. Cary. LCL. Cambridge: Harvard University Press.

———. *Letters to His Brother Quintus*. 1953. Translated by W. Glynne Williams. LCL. Cambridge: Harvard University Press.

———. *Letters to His Friends*. 1958-1960. Translated W. Glynne Williams. 3 vols. LCL. Cambridge: Harvard University Press.

——. *Letter to Octavian*. 1953. Translated by Mary Henderson. LCL. Cambridge: Harvard University Press.
——. *Paradoxa Stoicorum*. 1942. Translated by H. Rackham. LCL. Cambridge: Harvard University Press.
——. *Philippics*. 1926. Translated by Walter C.A. Ker. LCL. New York: G.P. Putnam's Sons.
——. *Orator*. 1939. Translated by G.L. Hendrickson. LCL. Cambridge: Harvard University Press.
——. *The Speeches*. 1958. Translated by R. Gardener. LCL. Cambridge: Harvard University Press.
——. *The Speeches: Pro Archia Poeta; Post Reditum in Senatu; Post Reditum ad Quirites; De Domo Sua; De Haruspicum Responsis; Pro Plancio*. 1928. Translated by N.H. Watts. LCL. New York: G.P. Putnam's Sons.
——. *The Speeches: Pro Lege Manila; Pro Caecina; Pro Cluentio; Pro Rabirio; Perduellionis*. 1927. Translated by H. Grose Hodge. LCL. New York: G.P. Putnam's Sons.
——. *The Speeches: Pro Publio Quinctio* and *Pro Sexto Roscio Amerino*. 1930. Translated by John Henry Freese. LCL. New York: G.P. Putnam's Sons.
——. *Tusculan Disputations*. 1945. Translated by J.E. King. LCL. Cambridge: Harvard University Press.
——. *The Verrine Orations*. 1928-1935. Translated by L.H.G Greenwood. vols. 1 & 2. LCL. New York: G.P. Putnam's Sons.
Clark, Gillian. 1989. *Women in the Ancient World*. Oxford: Oxford University Press.
Cohen, David. 1996. Seclusion, Separation, and the Status of Women in Classical Athens. Pages 134-145 in *Women in Antiquity*. Edited by Ian McAuslan and Peter Walcott. Oxford: Oxford University Press.
Cohen, Shaye J.D., ed. 1993. *The Jewish Family in Antiquity*. Atlanta: Scholars Press.
Collins, Adela Yarbro, ed. 1985. *Feminist Perspectives on Biblical Scholarship*. Chico, Calif.: Scholars Press.
Corley, Kathleen E. 1993. *Private Women, Public Meals: Social Conflict in the Synoptic Tradition*. Peabody, Mass.: Hendrickson Publishers.
Cornwall, Andrea and Nancy Lindisfarne, eds. 1994. *Dislocating Masculinity: Comparative Ethnographies*. London: Routledge.
Cotton, Hannah M. 1984. Greek and Latin Epistolary Formulae: Some Light on Cicero's Letter Writing. *American Journal of Philology* 105:409-425.
——. 1997. The Archive of Salome Komaïs Daughter of Levi: Another Archive from the 'Cave of Letters'. In *Discoveries in the Judean Desert 27: Aramaic, Hebrew and Greek Documentary Texts from Nahal Hever*. Edited by Hannah M. Cotton and Ada Yardeni. Oxford: Clarendon Press.
Cotton, Hannah M. and Ada Yardeni. 1997. *Discoveries in the Judean Desert 27: Aramaic, Hebrew and Greek Documentary Texts from Nahal Hever*. Oxford: Clarendon Press.
Cowan, Jane K. 1991. Going Out For Coffee? Contesting the Grounds of Gendered Pleasures in Everyday Sociability. Pages 180-202 in *Contested Identities:*

*Gender and Sexuality in Modern Greece*. Edited by Peter Loizos and Evthymios Papataxiarchis. Princeton: Princeton University Press.

Cranfield, C.E.B., ed. 1979. Commentary on Romans. In *The International Critical Commentary*, vol. 2. Edinburgh: T&T Clark.

Danforth, Loring M. 1991. The Resolution of Conflict through Song in Greek Ritual Therapy. Pages 98-113 in *Contested Identities: Gender and Sexuality in Modern Greece*. Edited by Peter Loizos and Evthymios Papataxiarchis. Princeton: Princeton University Press.

Davila, James. 2000. *Liturgical Works: Eerdmans Commentaries on the Dead Sea Scrolls*. Grand Rapids, Mich.: Eerdmans.

Davis, John. 1987 Family and State in the Mediterranean. Pages 22-34 in *Honour and Shame and the Unity of the Mediterranean*. Edited by David D. Gilmore. Washington, D.C.: American Anthropological Association.

DeForest, Mary, ed. 1993. *Woman's Power, Man's Game: Essays on Classical Antiquity in Honor of Joy K. King*. Wauconda, Ill.: Bolchazy-Carducci Publishers.

Delaney, Carol. 1987. Seeds of Honor, Fields of Shame. Pages 34-48 in *Honour and Shame and the Unity of the Mediterranean*. Edited by David D. Gilmore. Washington, D.C.: American Anthropological Association.

Demers, Patricia. 1992. *Women as Interpreters of the Bible*. New York: Paulist Press.

Demosthenes. 1986 (1949). Translated by Norman W. DeWitt and Norman J. DeWitt, LCL. Cambridge, Mass: Harvard University Press.

———. 1990 (1939). *Private Orations*. Translated by A. Murray. LCL. Cambridge, Mass: Harvard University Press.

———. *De Falsa Legatione*. 1926. Translated by C.A. Vince and J.H. Vince. London: William Heinemann.

Dewald, Carolyn. 1981. Women and Culture in Herodotus' *Histories*. Pages 91-126 in *Reflections of Women in Antiquity*. Edited by Helene P. Foley. New York: Gordon & Breach Science Publishers.

Didorus of Sicily. 1962. Translated by C.H. Oldfather. LCL. London: William Heinemann.

Dimen, Murial. 1986. Servants and Sentries: Women, Power and Social Reproduction in Kriovrisi. Pages 53-67 in *Gender and Power in Rural Greece*. Edited by Jill Dubisch. Princeton: Princeton University Press.

Dio. *Roman History*, Books 51-60. 1980-1994. Translated by E. Cary. LCL. London: William Heinemann.

Dio Chrysostom. 1932. Translated by J.W. Cohoon. LCL. London: William Heinemann.

Dion, Paul E. 1992. 'Letters (Aramaic).' Pages in 285-290 in vol. 3 of *The Anchor Bible Dictionary*. Edited by David Noel Freedman. New York: Doubleday.

Dionysius of Halicarnassus. *The Roman Antiquities*. 1945. Translated by Earnest Cary. LCL. London: William Heinemann.

Dixon, Suzanne. 1988. *The Roman Mother*. London: Croom Helm.

Dodd, C.H. 1932. *The Epistle of Paul to the Romans*. The Moffatt New Testament Commentary. New York: Harper & Brothers.

Donaldson, James. 1907. *Woman; Her Position and Influence in Ancient Greece and Rome, and Among the Early Christians*. London: Longmans, Green and Co.

Donfried, Karl P., ed. 1991. *The Romans Debate*, rev. ed. Peabody, Mass.: Hendrickson.

Donfried, Karl P. and Peter Richardson. 1998. *Judaism and Christianity in First-Century Rome*. Grand Rapids, Mich.: Eerdmans.

Doty, William G. 1973. *Letters in Primitive Christianity*. Philadelphia: Fortress Press.

Douglas, Mary. 1966. *Purity and Danger: An Analysis of Concepts of Pollution and Taboo*. London: Routledge & Kegan Paul.

Dover, Kenneth James. 1974. *Greek Popular Morality in the Time of Plato and Aristotle*. Oxford: Blackwell.

———. 1984. Classical Greek Attitudes to Sexual Behaviour. Pages 143-158 in *Women in the Ancient World: The Arethusa Papers*. Edited by John Peradotto and J.P. Sullivan. Albany, N.Y.: State University of New York Press.

Dubisch, Jill. 1986. Culture Enters Through the Kitchen: Women, Food, and Social Boundaries in Rural Greece. Pages 195-214 in *Gender and Power in Rural Greece*. Edited by Jill Dubisch. Princeton: Princeton University Press.

———. 1991. Gender, Kinship and Religion: "Reconstructing" the Anthropology of Greece. Pages 29-46 in *Contested Identities: Gender and Sexuality in Modern Greece*. Edited by Peter Loizos and Evthymios Papataxiarchis. Princeton: Princeton University Press.

———. 1995. *In a Different Place: Pilgrimage, Gender, and Politics at a Greek Island Shrine*. Princeton: Princeton University Press.

———, ed. 1986. *Gender and Power in Rural Greece*. Princeton: Princeton University Press.

DuBoulay, Juliet. 1976. Lies, Mockery and Family Integrity. Pages 389-406 in *Mediterranean Family Structures*. Edited by J.G Peristiany. Cambridge: Cambridge University Press.

———. 1986. Women: Images of Their Nature and Destiny in Rural Greece. Pages 139-168 in *Gender and Power in Rural Greece*. Edited by Jill Dubisch. Princeton: Princeton University Press.

———. 1991. Cosmos and Gender in Village Greece. Pages 47-78 in *Contested Identities: Gender and Sexuality in Modern Greece*. Edited by Peter Loizos and Evthymios Papataxiarchis. Princeton: Princeton University Press.

Dunn, James D.G. 1988. *Romans* (*Word Biblical Commentary*, vols. 38a,b). Dallas: Word Books.

Edersheim, Alfred. 1993 (1876). *Sketches of Jewish Social Life in the Days of Christ*. Grand Rapids, Mich.: Eerdmans.

Elder, Linda Bennett. 1994. The Women Question and Female Ascetics Among Essenes. *Biblical Archaeologist* 57:220-234.

Elliott, John H. 1993. *What is Social-Scientific Criticism?* Minneapolis: Fortress Press.

Engberg-Pedersen, Troels, ed. 1995. *Paul in His Hellenistic Context*. Minneapolis: Fortress Press.

Epictetus. 1946. *The Discourses as reported by Arrian, the Manual, and fragments*. W.A. Oldfather, trans. LCL. London: William Heinemann.

Esler, Philip F. 1994. *The First Christians in their Social Worlds: Social-scientific Approaches to New Testament Interpretation*. London: Routledge.

——, ed. 1995. *Modeling Early Christianity: Social-scientific Studies of the New Testament in its Context*. London: Routledge.

Euripides. *Andromache*. 1988 (1912). Translated by Arthur S. Way. LCL. Cambridge, Mass.: Harvard University Press.

——. *Medea*. 1994. Translated by David Kovacs. LCL. Cambridge: Harvard University Press.

Evans, John K. 1991. *War, Women and Children in Ancient Rome*. London: Routledge.

Fallers, Lloyd A. and Margaret C. Fallers. 1976. Sex Roles in Edremit. Pages 243-260 in *Mediterranean Family Structures*. Edited by J.G Peristiany. Cambridge: Cambridge University Press.

Fantham, Elaine, Helene P. Foley, Natalie Boymel Kampen, Sarah B. Pomeroy and H.A. Shapiro. 1994. *Women in the Classical World: Image and Text*. Oxford: Oxford University Press.

Fasola, Umberto M. 1986. *Domitilla's Catacomb and the Basilica of the Martyrs Nereus and Achilleus*. Edited by Philippe Pergola. Translated by Frances Pinnock, trans. Vatican City: Papal Commission for Sacred Archaeology.

Fernea, E. Warnock. 1989 (1969). *Guests of the Sheik: An Ethnography of an Iraqi Village*. New York: Anchor Books.

Finger, Reta Halteman. 1988. Phoebe: Role Model for Leaders. *Daughters of Sarah* 14/2:5-7.

Fiorenza, Elisabeth Schüssler. 1983. *In Memory of Her: A Feminist Theological Reconstruction of Christian Origins*. New York: Crossroad.

——. 1986. Missionaries, Apostles, Coworkers: Romans 16 and the Reconstruction of Women's Early Christian History. *Word and World* 6:420-433.

——. 1992. *But She Said: Feminist Practices of Biblical Interpretation*. Boston: Beacon Press.

——, ed. 1993. *Searching the Scriptures, Vol. 1: A Feminist Introduction*. New York: Crossroad.

——, ed. 1994. *Searching the Scriptures, Vol. 2: A Feminist Commentary*. New York: Crossroad.

Fitzmyer, Joseph A. 1993. *Romans: A New Translation with Introduction and Commentary*. The Anchor Bible. New York: Doubleday.

Flint, Peter W. and James C. VanderKam, eds. 1999. *The Dead Sea Scrolls After Fifty Years: A Comprehensive Assessment*. Boston: Brill.

Flory, M.B. 1984. Where Women Preceded Men, Factors Influencing the Order of Names in Roman Epitaphs. *CJ* 79: 216-224.

Foley, Helene P. 1981. The Concept of Women in Athenian Drama. Pages 127-168 in *Reflections of Women in Antiquity*. Edited by Helene P. Foley. New York: Gordon & Breach Science Publishers.

——, ed. 1981. *Reflections of Women in Antiquity*. New York: Gordon and Breach Science Publishers.

Foxhall, Lin. 1995. Women's Ritual and Men's Work in Ancient Athens. Pages 97-110 in *Women in Antiquity: New Assessments*. Edited by Richard Hawley & Barbara Levick. London: Routledge.

France, RT. and David Wenham, eds. 1983. *Gospel Perspectives: Studies in Midrash and Historiography*, vol. 3. Sheffield: JSOT Press.

Freedman, David Noel, ed. 1992. *The Anchor Bible Dictionary*, vol. 5. New York: Doubleday.

Frerichs, Ernest S. 1989. Introduction to Ancient Israel in Pages 261-264 in *Women's Earliest Records: From Ancient Egypt and Western Asia*. Edited by Barbara S. Lesko. Atlanta: Scholars Press.

Friedl, Ernestine. 1986. The Position of Women: Appearance and Reality. Pages 42-52 in *Gender and Power in Rural Greece*. Edited by Jill Dubisch. Princeton: Princeton University Press.

Gamble, Harry, Jr. 1977. *The Textual History of the Letter to the Romans: A Study in Textual and Literary Criticism*. Grand Rapids, Mich.: Eerdmans.

Gardner, Jane F. 1986. *Women in Roman Law and Society*. London: Croom Helm.

Garlick, Barbara, Suzanne Dixon and Pauline Allen, eds. 1992. *Stereotypes of Women in Power: Historical Perspectives and Revisionist Views*. New York: Greenwood Press.

Gillman, Florence M. 1992a. *Women Who Knew Paul*. Collegeville, Minn.: The Liturgical Press.

——. 1992b. 'Phoebe.' In *The Anchor Bible Dictionary*, vol. 5. New York: Doubleday.

Gilmore, David D. 1987. Honor, Honesty, Shame: Male Status in Contemporary Andalusia. Pages 90-103 in *Honour and Shame and the Unity of the Mediterranean*. Edited by David D. Gilmore. Washington, D.C.: American Anthropological Association.

——, ed. 1987. *Honour and Shame and the Unity of the Mediterranean*. Washington, D.C.: American Anthropological Association.

Giovaninni, Maureen J. 1981. Woman: Dominant Symbol within the Cultural System of a Sicilian Town. *Man* 16(3): 406-426.

——. 1987. Female Chastity Codes in the Circum-Mediterranean: Comparative Perspectives. Pages 61-74 in *Honour and Shame and the Unity of the Mediterranean*. Edited by David D. Gilmore. Washington, D.C.: American Anthropological Association.

Goddard, Victoria. 1987. Honour and Shame: The Control of Women's Sexuality and Group Identity in Naples. Pages 166-192 in *The Cultural Construction of Sexuality*. Edited by Pat Caplan. London: Routledge.

Gold, Barbara K. 1993. The Master Mistress of My Passion: The Lady as Patron in Ancient and Renaissance Letters. Pages 279-304 in *Woman's Power, Man's Game*. Edited by Mary DeForest. Wauconda, Ill.: Bolchazy-Carducci Publishers.

Goodspeed, Edgar J. 1951. Phoebe's Letter of Introduction. *Harvard Theological Review* 44:55-57.

Goodwater, Leanna. 1975. *Women in Antiquity: Annotated Bibliography*. Metuchen: N.J.: The Scarecrow Press.

Guerra, Anthony J. 1995. *Romans and the Apologetic Tradition: The Purpose, Genre and Audience of Paul's Letter.* Cambridge: Cambridge University Press.

Hallett, Judith P. 1984a. *Fathers and Daughters in Roman Society: Women and the Elite Family.* Princeton: Princeton University Press.

——. 1984b. The Role of Women in Roman Elegy: Counter-Cultural Feminism. Pages 241-262 in *Women in the Ancient World: The Arethusa Papers.* Edited by John Peradotto and J.P. Sullivan. Albany, N.Y.: State University of New York Press.

Halpern-Amaru, Betsy. 1991. Portraits of Women in Pseudo-Philo's *Biblical Antiquities.* Pages 83-106 in *"Women Like This": New Perspectives on Jewish Women in the Greco-Roman World.* Edited by Amy-Jill Levine. Atlanta: Scholars Press.

Hanson, K.C. 1996. Kinship. Pages 62-79 in *The Social Sciences and New Testament Interpretation.* Edited by Richard L. Rohrbaugh. Peabody, Mass.: Hendrickson.

Hanson, K.C. and Douglas E. Oakman. 1998. *Palestine in the Time of Jesus: Social Structures and Social Conflicts.* Minneapolis: Fortress Press.

Harding, Susan. 1975. Women and Words in a Spanish Village. Pages 281-308 in *Toward an Anthropology of Women.* Edited by Rayna Reiter. New York: Monthly Review Press.

Harrison, Everett F. 1995. *Romans.* The Expositor's Bible Commentary. Grand Rapids, Mich.: Zondervan.

Hauke, Manfred. 1988. *Women in the Priesthood?: A Systematic Analysis in the Light of the Order of Creation and Redemption.* Translated by David Kipp. San Francisco: Ignatius Press.

Hawley, Richard and Barbara Levick, eds. 1995. *Women in Antiquity: New Assessments.* London: Routledge.

Herzfeld, Michael. 1986. Within and Without: The Category of 'Female' in the Ethnography of Modern Greece. Pages 213-233 in *Gender and Power in Rural Greece.* Edited by Jill Dubisch. Princeton: Princeton University Press.

——. 1987. As in Your Own House: Hospitality, Ethnography, and the Stereotype of Mediterranean Society. Pages 75-89 in *Honour and Shame and the Unity of the Mediterranean.* Edited by David D. Gilmore. Washington, D.C.: American Anthropological Association.

——. 1991. Silence, Submission, and Subversion: Toward a Poetics of Womanhood. Pages 79-97 in *Contested Identities: Gender and Sexuality in Modern Greece.* Edited by Peter Loizos and Evthymios Papataxiarchis. Princeton: Princeton University Press.

Hickey, Anne Ewing. 1987. *Women of the Roman Aristocracy as Christian Monastics.* Anne Arbor, Mich.: UMI Research Press.

Hills, Julian V., ed. 1998. *Common Life in the Early Church.* Harrisburg, Pa.: Trinity Press International.

Hock, Ronald F. 1998. Why New Testament Scholars Should Read Ancient Novels. Pages 121-138 in *Ancient Fiction and Early Christian Narrative.* Edited by R.F. Hock, J.B. Chance and J. Perkins. Atlanta: Scholars Press.

Hoffsten, Ruth Bertha. 1939. *Roman Women of Rank of the Early Empire in Public Life as Portrayed by Dio, Paterculus, Suetonius, and Tacitus: A dissertation presented to the faculty of the graduate school of the University of Pennsylvania in partial fulfilment of the requirements for the degree of doctor of philosophy.* Philadelphia.

Holmberg, Bengt. 1990. *Sociology in the New Testament: An Appraisal.* Minneapolis: Fortress.

*Holy Bible.* New Revised Standard Version, New International Version.

Homer. *The Iliad.* 1924. Translated by A.T. Murray. LCL. London: William-Heinemann.

Horace. *The Odes and Epodes.* 1934. Translated by C.E. Bennett. LCL. Cambridge: Harvard University Press.

——. *Satires.* 1978. Translated by H. Rushton Fairclough. LCL. Cambridge: Harvard University Press.

Horrell, David G., ed. 1999. *Social-Scientific Approaches to New Testament Interpretation.* Edinburgh: T&T Clark.

Hunt, A.S. and C.C. Edgar, eds. 1932. *Select Papyri*, vol. 1. LCL. London: William Heinemann.

Ide, Arthur Frederick. 1980. *Women in Ancient Greece.* Mesquite, Tex.: Ide House.

Ilan, Tal. 1992. Julia Crispina, Daughter of Berenicianus, A Herodian Princess in the Babatha Archive: A Case Study in Historical Identification. *Jewish Quarterly Review* 82:361-381.

——. 1993. Premarital Cohabitation in Ancient Judea: The Evidence of the Babatha Archive and the Mishnah (*Ketubbot* 1.4). *Harvard Theological Review* 86:247-264.

——. 1995. *Jewish Women in Greco-Roman Palestine: An Inquiry into Image and Status.* Tübingen, Germany: J.C.B. Mohr.

——. 1997. *Mine and Yours are Hers: Retrieving Women's History from Rabbinic Literature.* Leiden: Brill.

——. 1999. *Integrating Women into Second Temple History.* Peabody, Mass.: Hendrickson.

Iossifides, A. Marina. 1991. Sisters in Christ: Metaphors of Kinship Among Greek Nuns. Pages 135-155 in *Contested Identities: Gender and Sexuality in Modern Greece.* Edited by Peter Loizos and Evthymios Papataxiarchis. Princeton: Princeton University Press.

Irby-Massie, Georgia L. 1993. Women in Ancient Science. Pages 354-372 in *Woman's Power, Man's Game.* Edited by Mary DeForest. Wauconda, Ill.: Bolchazy-Carducci Publishers.

Irvin, Dorothy. 1980. The Ministry of Women in the Early Church: The Archaeological Evidence. *The Duke Divinity School Review*, vol. 45/2:76-86.

Isaeus. 1983 (1927). Translated by Edward Seymour Forster. LCL. Cambridge, Mass: Harvard University Press.

Jeffers, James. 1998. Jewish and Christian Families in First-Century Rome. Pages 128-150 in *Judaism and Christianity in First-Century Rome.* Edited by Karl P. Donfried and Peter Richardson. Grand Rapids, Mich.: Eerdmans.

Jervis, L. Ann. 1991. *The Purpose of Romans: A Comparative Letter Structure Investigation*. Sheffield: JSOT Press.
Jewett, Robert. 1982. Romans as an Ambassadorial Letter. *Interpretation* 36:5-20.
———. 1988. Paul, Phoebe and the Spanish Mission. Pages 142-161 in *The Social World of Formative Christianity and Judaism*. Edited by Jacob Neusner, Peder Borgen, Ernest S. Frerichs and Richard Horsley. Philadelphia: Fortress Press.
———. 1996. Approaching the Cultural Diversity of Roman Churches: A Proposed New Identity as "Beloved of God". TS.
Josephus. Translated by H. St. J. Thackeray et al. 10 vols. LCL. Cambridge: Harvard University Press, 1926-1965.
Judge, E.A. 1994. Judaism and the Rise of Christianity: A Roman Perspective. *Tyndale Bulletin*, vol. 45: 355-368.
Just, Roger. 1989. *Women in Athenian Law and Life*. London: Routledge.
———. 1991. The Limits of Kinship. Pages 114-134 in *Contested Identities: Gender and Sexuality in Modern Greece*. Edited by Peter Loizos and Evthymios Papataxiarchis. Princeton: Princeton University Press.
Kampen, Natelie Boymel. 1991. Between Public and Private: Women as Historical Subjects in Roman Art. Pages 218-248 in *Women's History and Ancient History*. Edited by Sarah B. Pomeroy. Chapel Hill: University of North Carolina Press.
Käsemann, Ernst. 1980. *Commentary on Romans*. Translated by Geoffrey W. Bromiley. Grand Rapids, Mich.: Eerdmans.
Katzoff, Ranon. 1995. Polygamy in *P. Yadin*? Pages 128-132 in *Zeitschrift feur Papyrologie und Epigraphik*. Bonn: Habelt.
Kearsley, R.A. 1999. Women in Public Life in the Roman East: Iunia Theodora, Claudia Metrodora and Phoebe, Benefactress of Paul. *Tyndale Bulletin*, vol. 50: 189-211.
Keener, Craig S. 1992. *Paul, Women and Wives: Marriage and Women's Ministry in the Letters of Paul*. Peabody, Mass.: Hendrickson.
———. 1993. *The IVP Background Commentary*. Downers Grove, Ill.: InterVarsity Press.
Kenna, Margaret. 1976. The Idiom of Family. Pages 347-362 in *Mediterranean Family Structures*. Edited by J.G Peristiany. Cambridge: Cambridge University Press.
Kennedy, Robinette. 1986. Women's Friendships on Crete. Pages 121-138 in *Gender and Power in Rural Greece*. Edited by Jill Dubisch. Princeton: Princeton University Press.
Khuri, Fuad I. 1976. A Profile of Family Associations in Two Suburbs of Beirut. Pages 81-100 in *Mediterranean Family Structures*. Edited by J.G Peristiany. Cambridge: Cambridge University Press.
Kim, Chan-Hie. 1972. *Form and Structure of the Familiar Greek Letter of Recommendation*. SBL Dissertation Series 4. Missola Montana: Scholars Press.
Kiray, Mübeccel. 1976. The Role of Mothers: Changing Intra-familial Relationships in a Small Town in Turkey. Pages 261-272 in *Mediterranean Family*

*Structures*. Edited by J.G Peristiany. Cambridge: Cambridge University Press.

Kleiner, Diana E.E. and Susan B. Matheson, eds. 1996. *I Clavdia: Women in Ancient Rome*. New Haven, Conn: Yale University Art Gallery.

Kraemer, Ross, ed. 1988. *Maenads, Martyrs, Matrons, Monastics: A Sourcebook on Women's Religions in the Greco-Roman World*. Philadelphia: Fortress Press.

——. 1992. *Her Share of the Blessings: Women's Religions Among Pagans, Jews, and Christians in the Greco-Roman World*. New York: Oxford University Press.

——. 1993. Jewish Mothers and Daughters in the Greco-Roman World. Pages 89-112 in *The Jewish Family in Antiquity*. Edited by Shaye J.D. Cohen. Atlanta: Scholars Press.

——. 1998. 'Jewish Women in the Diaspora World of Late Antiquity' in *Jewish Women in Historical Perspective*, 2nd ed. Edited by J. R. Baskin. Detroit: Wayne State University Press.

Kraemer, Ross and Mary Rose D'Angelo, eds. 1999. *Women and Christian Origins*. New York: Oxford University Press.

LaCocque, André. 1990. *The Feminine Unconventional: Four Subversive Figures in Israel's Tradition*. Minneapolis: Fortress Press.

Lampe, Peter. 1987. *Die stradtrömischen Christen in den ersten beiden Jahrhunderten: Studien zur Sozialgeschichte*. Tübingen: Mohr-Siebeck.

——. 1991. The Roman Christians of Romans 16. Pages 216-230 in *The Romans Debate*, rev. ed. Edited by Karl P. Donfried. Peabody, Mass.: Hendrickson.

——. 1992a. 'Junias.' In *The Anchor Bible Dictionary*, vol. 3. New York: Doubleday.

——. 1992b. 'Prisca.' In *The Anchor Bible Dictionary*, vol. 5. New York: Doubleday.

Lane, William L. 1998. Social Perspectives on Roman Christianity during the Formative Years from Nero to Nerva: Romans, Hebrews, 1 Clement. Pages 196-225 in *Judaism and Christianity in First-Century Rome*. Edited by Karl P. Donfried and Peter Richardson. Grand Rapids, Mich.: Eerdmans.

LaPiana, George. 1927. Foreign Groups in Rome During the First Centuries of the Empire. *Harvard Theological Review* 20/4.

Launspach, Charles W.L. 1908. *State and Family in Early Rome*. London: George Bell & Sons.

Lefkowitz, Mary R. 1986. *Women in Greek Myth*. Baltimore: Johns Hopkins University Press.

——. 1996. Wives and Husbands. Pages 67-82 in *Women in Antiquity*. Edited by Ian McAuslan and Peter Walcott. Oxford: Oxford University Press.

Lefkowitz, Mary R. and Maureen B. Fant. 1982. *Women's Life in Greece and Rome: A Sourcebook in Translation*. London: Duckworth.

Leon, Harry J. 1960. *The Jews of Ancient Rome*. Philadelphia: Jewish Publication Society of America.

Lesko, Barbara S., ed. 1989. *Women's Earliest Records: From Ancient Egypt and Western Asia*. Atlanta: Scholars Press.

Levine, Amy-Jill, ed. 1991. *"Women Like This": New Perspectives on Jewish Women in the Greco-Roman World.* Atlanta: Scholars Press.
——. 1992. Sacrifice and Salvation: Otherness and Domestication in the Book of Judith. Pages 17-30 in *"No One Spoke Ill of Her": Essays on Judith.* Edited by James C. VanderKam. Atlanta: Scholars Press.
Levine, Lee I. 1982. *Ancient Synagogues Revealed.* Jerusalem: Israel Exploration Society.
Lewis, Naphtali, ed. 1989. *The Documents from the Bar Kokhba Period in the Cave of Letters: Greek Papyri.* JDS 2. Jerusalem: Israel Exploration Society, the Hebrew University of Jerusalem, and the Shrine of the Book.
Lindisfarne, Nancy. 1994. Variant Masculinities, Variant Virginities: Rethinking 'honour and shame'. Pages 82-96 in *Dislocating Masculinity: Comparative Ethnographies.* Andrea Cornwall and Nancy Lindisfarne, eds. London: Routledge.
Lisón-Tolosana, Carmelo. 1976. The Ethics of Inheritance. Pages 305-316 in *Mediterranean Family Structures.* Edited by J.G Peristiany. Cambridge: Cambridge University Press.
Livy. 1919-1970. Translated by B.O. Foster, F.G. Moore, and E.T. Sage. LCL. Books 1-42. Cambridge: Harvard University Press.
Loizos, Peter. 1991. Gender, Sexuality, and the Person in Greek Culture. Pages 221-234 in *Contested Identities: Gender and Sexuality in Modern Greece.* Edited by Peter Loizos and Evthymios Papataxiarchis. Princeton: Princeton University Press.
Loizos, Peter and Evthymios Papataxiarchis, eds. 1991. *Contested Identities: Gender and Sexuality in Modern Greece.* Princeton: Princeton University Press.
Loraux, Nicole. 1993. *The Children of Athena: Athenian Ideas About Citizenship and the Division Between the Sexes.* Translated by Caroline Levine. Princeton: Princeton University Press.
Lucan. *Pharsalia.* 1928. Translated by J.D. Duff. LCL. New York: G.P. Putnam's Sons.
Lucretius. *de Rerum Natura.* 1924. Translated by W.H.D. Rouse. LCL. Cambridge: Harvard University Press.
Lukes, Steven, ed. 1986. *Power.* Washington Square, N.Y.: New York University Press.
MacHaffie, Barbara J. 1986. *Her Story: Women in Christian Tradition.* Philadelphia: Fortress Press.
MacMullen, Ramsay. 1980. Women in Public in the Roman Empire. *Historia* 29: 210.
Malina, Bruce J., 1993. *The New Testament World: Insights from Cultural Anthropology*, rev. ed. Louisville, Ky.: Westminster/John Knox.
——. 1996. *The Social World of Jesus and the Gospels*, rev. ed. London: Routledge.
Manson, T. W. 1991. St. Paul's Letter to the Romans—and Others. Pages 3-15 in *The Romans Debate*, rev. ed. Edited by Karl P. Donfried. Peabody, Mass.: Hendrickson.

Marcus, Michael A. 1987. 'Horsemen are the Fence of the Land': Honor and History Among the Ghiyata of Eastern Morocco. Pages 49-60 in *Honour and Shame and the Unity of the Mediterranean*. Edited by David D. Gilmore. Washington, D.C.: American Anthropological Association.

Martial. *Epigrams*. Translated by Walter C.A. Ker. LCL. New York: G.P. Putnam's Sons.

Martínez, Florentino García and Eibert J.C. Tigchelaar, eds. 1997-1998. *The Dead Sea Scrolls Study Edition*, 2 vols. Leiden: Brill.

Mason, J.P. 1975. Sex and Symbol in the Treatment of Women: The Wedding Rite in a Libyan Oasis Community. *American Ethnologist* 2(4): 649-661.

Massey, Lesly F. 1989. *Women and the New Testament: An Analysis of Scripture in Light of New Testament Era Culture*. London: McFarland & Company.

McAuslan, Ian and Peter Walcott, eds. 1996. *Women in Antiquity*. Oxford: Oxford University Press.

McDonald, J. I .H. 1970. Was Romans XVI a Separate Letter? *New Testament Studies* 16:369-372.

McVann, Mark. 1998. Family-Centredness. Pages 75-79 in *Handbook of Biblical Social Values*. Edited by John J. Pilch and Bruce J. Malina. Peabody, Mass.: Hendrickson.

Meeks, Wayne A. 1983. *The First Urban Christians: The Social World of the Apostle Paul*. New Haven: Yale University Press.

Meiselman, Moshe. 1978. *Jewish Women in Jewish Law*. New York: Ktav Publishing House.

Metzger, Bruce M. 1994. *A Textual Commentary on the Greek New Testament*. 2nd edition. New York: United Bible Societies.

Meyers, Carol. 1988. *Discovering Eve: Ancient Israelite Women in Context*. New York: Oxford University Press.

——. 1989. Women and the Domestic Economy of Early Israel. Pages 265-278 in *Women's Earliest Records: From Ancient Egypt and Western Asia*. Edited by Barbara S. Lesko. Atlanta: Scholars Press.

Moo, Douglas J. 1996. *The Epistle to the Romans*. The New International Commentary on the New Testament. Grand Rapids, Mich.: Eerdmans.

Moore, Henrietta. 1988. *Feminism and Anthropology*. Oxford: Polity Press.

Morris, Leon. 1988. *The Epistle to the Romans*. Grand Rapids, Mich.: Eerdmans.

Mounce, Robert H. 1995. *Romans*. The New American Commentary. Broadman & Holman Publishers.

Moxnes, Halvor. 1996. Honor and Shame. Pages 19-40 in *The Social Sciences and New Testament Interpretation*. Edited by Richard L. Rohrbaugh. Peabody, Mass.: Hendrickson.

——, ed. 1997. *Constructing Early Christian Families: Family as Social Reality and Metaphor*. London: Routledge.

Mullins, Terrence Y. 1968. Greeting as a New Testament Form. *Journal of Biblical Literature* 87:418-426.

Murphy, Cullen. 1998. *The Word According the Eve: Women and the Bible in Ancient Times and Our Own*. Boston: Houghton Mifflin.

Murray, John. 1965. *The Epistle to the Romans*, vol. 2. Grand Rapids, Mich.: Eerdmans.
Myerscough, Richard. 1996. Exegesis 21: Was Phoebe really a deacon? *Foundations* 36:24-26.
Nepos, Cornelius. *On the Great Generals of Foreign Nations*. 1994. Translated by John C. Rolfe. LCL. Cambridge: Harvard University Press.
Neusner, Jacob, Peder Borgen, Ernest S. Frerichs and Richard Horsley, eds. 1988. *The Social World of Formative Christianity and Judaism*. Philadelphia: Fortress Press.
Newson, Carol A. and Sharon H. Ringe, eds. 1992. *The Women's Bible Commentary*. Louisville, Ky.: Westminster/John Knox Press.
Neyrey, Jerome H. 1990. *Paul, in Other Words: A Cultural Reading of His Letters*. Louisville, Ky.: Westminster/John Knox.
Niditch, Susan. 1998. Portrayals of Women in the Hebrew Bible. Pages 25-45 in *Jewish Women in Historical Perspective*, 2nd ed. Edited by J. R. Baskin. Detroit: Wayne State University Press.
Nixon, Lucia. 1995. The Cults of Demeter and Kore. Pages 75-96 in *Women in Antiquity: New Assessments*. Edited by Richard Hawley and Barbara Levick. London: Routledge.
Oates, Whitney Jennings and Charles Theophilus Murphy. 1949. *Greek Literature in Translation*. New York: Longmans, Green & Co.
O'Faolain, Julia and Lauro Martines, eds. 1973. *Not in God's Image: Women in History from the Greeks to the Victorians*. New York: Harper.
Osiek, Carolyn. 1992. *What are they Saying About the Social Setting of the New Testament?*, rev. ed. New York: Paulist Press.
——. 1998. Relatedness. Pages 176-178 in *Handbook of Biblical Social Values*. Edited by John J. Pilch and Bruce J. Malina. Peabody, Mass.:   Hendrickson.
Osiek, Carolyn and David L. Balch. 1997. *Families in the New Testament World: Households and House Churches*. Louisville, Ky.: Westminster/John Knox.
Ovid. *The Art of Love, and Other Poems*. 1979. Translated by J.H. Mozley. LCL. Cambridge: Harvard University Press.
——. *Fasti*. 1931. Translated by James George Frazer. LCL. New York: G. Putnam's Sons.
——. *The Heroides; The Amores*. 1914. Translated by Grant Showerman. LCL. New York: The MacMillan Co.
——. *Metamorphoses*. 1926. Translated by Frank Justus Miller. LCL. New York: G. Putnam's Sons.
——. *Tristia; Ex Ponto*. 1988. Translated by Arthur Leslie Wheeler. Cambridge: Harvard University Press.
Pantel, Pauline Schmitt. 1992. *A History of Women in the West: I. From Ancient Goddesses to Christian Saints*. Translated by Arthur Goldhammer. George Duby and Michelle Perrot, gen. eds. Cambridge: The Belknap Press of Harvard University Press.
Papataxiarchis, Evthymios. 1991. Friends of the Heart: Male Commensal Solidarity, Gender, and Kinship in Aegean Greece. Pages 156-179 in *Contested*

*Identities: Gender and Sexuality in Modern Greece.* Edited by Peter Loizos and Evthymios Papataxiarchis. Princeton: Princeton University Press.

Pardee, D. 1992. 'Letters (Hebrew).' Pages 282-285 in *The Anchor Bible Dictionary*, vol. 3. New York: Doubleday.

Parsons, Mikeal C. 1992. Appendices in the New Testament. *Themélios* 17/2:11-13.

Pavilides, Eleftherios and Jana Hesser. 1986. Women's Roles and House Form and Decoration in Eressos, Greece. Pages 68-96 in *Gender and Power in Rural Greece.* Edited by Jill Dubisch. Princeton: Princeton University Press.

Peradotto, John and J.P. Sullivan, eds. 1984. *Women in the Ancient World: The Arethusa Papers.* Albany, N.Y.: State University of New York Press.

Peristiany, J.G. 1966. Honour and Shame in a Cypriot Highland Village. Pages 171-190 in *Honour and Shame: The Values of Mediterranean Society.* Edited by J.G Peristiany. London: Weidenfeld & Nicolson.

——, ed. 1966. *Honour and Shame: The Values of Mediterranean Society.* London: Weidenfeld & Nicolson.

——, ed. 1976. *Mediterranean Family Structures.* Cambridge: Cambridge University Press.

Peristiany, J.G. and Julian Pitt-Rivers. 1992. *Honor and Grace in Anthropology.* Cambridge: Cambridge University Press.

Pervo, Richard I. 1991. Aseneth and Her Sisters: Women in Jewish Narrative and in the Greek Novels. Pages 145-160 in *"Women Like This": New Perspectives on Jewish Women in the Greco-Roman World.* Edited by Amy-Jill Levine. Atlanta: Scholars Press.

Peskowitz, Miriam. 1993. 'Family/ies' in Antiquity: Evidence from Tannaitic Literature and Roman Galilean Architecture. Pages 9-36 in *The Jewish Family in Antiquity.* Edited by Shaye J.D. Cohen. Atlanta: Scholars Press.

Peters, Emrys Lloyd. 1976. Aspects of Affinity in A Lebanese Maronite Village. Pages 27-80 in *Mediterranean Family Structures.* Edited by J.G Peristiany. Cambridge: Cambridge University Press.

Petronius. 1913. *Poems.* Translated by Michael Hesteltine. LCL. London: William Heinemann.

——. 1913. *Satyricon.* Translated by Michael Hesteltine. LCL. London: William Heinemann.

Philo. 1929-1941. Translated by F. H. Colson, G.H. Whitaker, and Ralph Marcus et al. LCL. London: William Heinemann.

Pilch, John J. and Bruce Malina, eds. 1998. *Handbook of Biblical Social Values.* Peabody, Mass.: Hendrickson.

Pitt-Rivers, Julian. 1961. *The People of the Sierra,* 2nd ed. Chicago: Phoenix Books, University of Chicago Press.

——. 1966. Honour and Social Status. Pages 19-78 in *Honour and Shame: The Values of Mediterranean Society.* Edited by J.G Peristiany. London: Weidenfeld & Nicolson.

——. 1976. Ritual Kinship in the Mediterranean: Spain and the Balkans. Pages 317-334 in *Mediterranean Family Structures.* Edited by J.G Peristiany. Cambridge: Cambridge University Press.

Pizzuto-Pomaco, Julia. 2000. Unity in the Midst of Diversity: The Early Church at Rome as Reflected in Romans 16. Pages 88-103 in *Who Killed Goliath?: Reading the Bible with Heart and Mind*. Edited by Robert F. Shedinger and Deborah J. Spink. Valley Forge, PA: Judson Press.

Plato. *Laws*, Book 4. 1926. Translated by R.G. Bury. LCL. London: William Heinemann.

——. *Protagorus*. 1924. Translated by W.R.M. Lamb. LCL. London: William Heinemann.

——. *The Republic*, Book 5. 1993. Translated by S. Halliwell. Warminster, England: Aris & Phillips.

Pliny. *Letters*. 1915. Translated by W. Melmoth. LCL. London: William Heinemann.

——. *Letters*. 1969. Translated by B. Radice. LCL. Cambridge: Harvard University Press.

——. *Panegyricus*. 1969. Translated by B. Radice. LCL. Cambridge: Harvard University Press.

Plutarch. *Advice to the Bride and Groom*; *Sayings of Spartan Women*; *Bravery of Women* from *Moralia*, vol. 3. 1931. Translated by Frank Cole Babbitt. LCL. London: William Heinemann.

——. *Agis and Cleomenes* from *Plutarch's Lives*, vol. 10. 1921. Translated by Bernadotte Perrin. LCL. London: William Heinemann.

——. *Caesar* from *Plutarch's Lives*. 1986. Translated by B. Perrin. LCL. Cambridge: Harvard University Press.

——. *Consolation to His Wife* from *Moralia*, vol. 7. 1919. Translated by Phillip H. DeLacy and Benedict Einarson. LCL. London: William Heinemann.

——. *Crassus* from *Plutarch's Lives*. 1984. Translated by B. Perrin. LCL. Cambridge: Harvard University Press.

——. *Demetrius and Antony* from *Plutarch's Lives*, vol. 9. 1920. Translated by Bernadotte Perrin. LCL. London: William Heinemann.

——. *How to Profit by One's Enemies* from *Moralia*. 1928. Translated by F.C. Babbitt. LCL. London: William Heinemann.

——. *Love Stories* from *Moralia*, vol. 10. 1936. Translated by Harold North Fowler. LCL. London: William Heinemann.

——. *Numa* from *Plutarch's Lives*. 1914. Translated by B. . LCL. London: William Heinemann.

——. *Pericles and Fabius* from *Plutarch's Lives*, vol. 3. 1984 (1916). Translated by Bernadotte Perrin. LCL. Cambridge: Harvard University Press.

——. *Pompey* from *Plutarch's Lives*. 1990. Translated by B. Perrin. LCL. Cambridge: Harvard University Press.

——. *Roman Questions* from *Moralia*. 1936. Translated by F.C. Babbitt. LCL. London: William Heinemann.

——. *Solon and Publicola*; *Lycurgus and Numa* from *Plutarch's Lives*, vol. 1. 1914. Translated by Bernadotte Perrin. LCL. London: William Heinemann.

——. *Sulla* from *Plutarch's Lives*. 1914. Translated by B. Perrin. LCL. London: William Heinemann.

———. *Tiberius and Caius Gracchus* from *Plutarch's Lives*. 1921. Translated by B. Perrin. LCL. London: William Heinemann.
Pomeroy, Sarah B. 1975. *Goddesses, Whores, Wives, and Slaves: Women in Classical Antiquity*. New York: Shocken Books.
———. 1984. *Women in Hellenistic Egypt: From Alexander to Cleopatra*. New York: Shocken Books.
———, ed. 1991. *Women's History and Ancient History*. Chapel Hill: University of North Carolina Press.
———. 1995. Women's Identity and the Family in the Classical *Polis*. Pages 111-121 in *Women in Antiquity: New Assessments*. Edited by Richard Hawley and Barbara Levick. London: Routledge.
Porten, Bezalel with J.J. Farber, C.J. Martin, G. Vittmann, Leslie S.B. MacCoull and Sarah Clarkson, eds., S. Hopkins and R. Katzoff, contributors. 1996. *The Elephantine Papyri in English: Three Millennia of Cross Cultural Continuity and Change*. Leiden: Brill.
Porten, Bezalel and Ada Yardeni, eds. 1986. *Textbook of Aramaic Documents from Ancient Egypt Letters*. Winona Lake, Ind.: Eisenbrauns.
Raynor, Diane, ed. 1991. *Sappho's Lyre: Archaic Lyric and Women Poets of Ancient Greece*. Berkeley: University of California Press.
Reiter, Rayna. 1975. Men and Women in the South of France: Public and Private Domains. Pages 252-282 in *Toward and Anthropology of Women*. Edited by Rayna Reiter. New York: Monthly Review Press.
———, ed. 1975. *Toward and Anthropology of Women*. New York: Monthly Review Press.
Richardson, Peter. 1979. *Paul's Ethic of Freedom*. Philadelphia: Westminster Press.
———. 1980. From Apostles to Virgins: Romans 16 and the Roles of Women in the Early Church. *Toronto Journal of Theology* 2:232-261.
Rogers, Susan Carol. 1975. Female Forms of Power and the Myth of Male Dominance: A Model of Female/Male Interaction in Peasant Society. *American Ethnologist* 2(4): 727-756.
Rohrbaugh, Richard L., ed. 1996. *The Social Sciences and New Testament Interpretation*. Peabody, Mass.: Hendrickson.
Russell, Bertrand. 1986. The Forms of Power. Pages 19-27 in *Power*. Edited by Steven Lukes. Washington Square, N.Y.: New York University Press.
Russell, Letty M., ed. 1985. *Feminist Interpretation of the Bible*. Oxford: Basil Blackwell.
Rutgers, Leonard Victor. 1995. *The Jews in Late Ancient Rome: Evidence of Cultural Interaction in the Roman Diaspora*. Leiden: E.J. Brill.
———. 1998. Roman Policy toward the Jews: Expulsions from the City of Rome during the First Century C.E. Pages 93-116 in *Judaism and Christianity in First-Century Rome*. Edited by Karl P. Donfried and Peter Richardson. Grand Rapids, Mich.: Eerdmans.
Salamone, S.D. and J.B. Stanton. 1986. Introducing the Nikokyra: Ideality and Reality in Social Process. Pages 97-120 in *Gender and Power in Rural Greece*. Edited by Jill Dubisch. Princeton: Princeton University Press.

Sanday, William and Arthur C. Headlam. 1902. *A Critical and Exegetical Commentary on the Epistle to the Romans.* The International Critical Commentary. Edinburgh: T&T Clark.

Sanders, E.P. 1977. *Paul and Palestinian Judaism.* London: SCM Press, Ltd.

———. 1990. *Jewish Law from Jesus to the Mishna: Five Studies.* London: SCM Press.

———. 1992. *Judaism: Practice and Belief, 63 BCE-66CE.* London: SCM Press.

Satlow, Michael. 1993. Reconsidering the Rabbinic *ketubah* Payment. Pages 133-154 in *The Jewish Family in Antiquity.* Edited by Shaye J.D. Cohen. Atlanta: Scholars Press.

Schaps, David M. 1979. *Economic Rights of Women in Ancient Greece.* Edinburgh: Edinburgh University Press.

Scheid, John. 1992. The Religious Roles of Roman Women. Pages 377-408 in *A History of Women in the West: I. From Ancient Goddesses to Christian Saints.* Edited by Pauline Schmidt Pantel. Translated by Arthur Goldhammer. Cambridge: The Belknap Press of Harvard University Press.

Scholer, David M. 1980. Paul's Women Co-workers in the Ministry of the Church. *Daughters of Sarah* 20/14: 3-6.

Schottroff, Luise. 1991. *Let the Oppressed Go Free: Feminist Perspectives on the New Testament.* Kidder, Annemarie S., trans. Louiseville, Ky.: Westminster/John Knox Press.

Schreiber, Stefan. 2000. Arbeit mit der Gemeinde (Röm 16.6, 12). *New Testament Studies,* vol. 46/2:204-226.

Schuller, Eileen M. 1994. Women in the Dead Sea Scrolls. Pages 115-131 in *Methods of Investigation of the Dead Sea Scrolls and the Khirbet Qumran Site: Present Battle and Future Prospects.* Edited by Michael Wise, Norman Golb, John J. Collins and Dennis G. Pardee. New York: The New York Academy of Sciences.

Schulz, Ray R. 1987. Romans 16:7: Junia or Junias? *The Expository Times* 98: 108-110.

Sealy, Raphael. 1990. *Women and Law in Classical Greece.* Chapel Hill, N.C.: University of North Carolina Press.

Seddon, David. 1976. Aspects of Kinship and Family Structure Among the Ulad Stut of Zaio Rural Commune, Nador Province, Morocco. Pages 173-194 in *Mediterranean Family Structures.* Edited by J.G Peristiany. Cambridge: Cambridge University Press.

Seltman, Charles. 1956. *Women in Antiquity.* London: Thames & Hudson.

Semonides of Amorgus. *On Women.* 1944. Pages 925-926 in *Greek Literature in Translation.* Edited by Whitney Jennings Oates and Charles Theophilus Murphy. New York: Longmans, Green & Co.

Seneca. *Ad Lucilium Epistulae Morales.* 1953. Translated by Richard M. Gummere. LCL. London: William Heinemann.

Seneca (The Elder). *Controversiae,* Book 9. 1974. Translated by M. Winterbottom. LCL. London: William Heinemann.

Sered, Susan Starr. 1992. *Women as Ritual Experts: The Religious Lives of Elderly Jewish Women in Jerusalem.* New York: Oxford University Press.

Shedinger, Robert F. and Deborah J. Spink, eds. 2000. *Who Killed Goliath?: Reading the Bible with Heart and Mind*. Valley Forge, PA: Judson Press.
Silius Italicus. *Punica*. 1934. Translated by J.D. Duff. LCL. New York: G. Putnam's Sons.
Silverman, Sydel F. 1967. Life Crisis as a Clue to Social Function: The Case of Italy. Pages 309-321 in *Toward and Anthropology of Women*. Edited by Rayna Reiter. New York: Monthly Review Press.
Skinner, Marilyn, ed. 1987. *Rescuing Creusa: New Methodological Approaches to Women in Antiquity*. Lubbock, Tex.: Texas Tech University Press.
Soderlund, Sven K. and N.T. Wright. 1999. *Romans and the People of God: Essays in Honor of Gordon D. Fee on the Occasion of His 65th Birthday*. Grand Rapids, Mich.: Eerdmans.
Sophocles. *Antigone*. 1994. Translated by Hugh Lloyd-Jones. LCL. Cambridge: Harvard University Press.
——. *Electra*. 1913. Translated by F. Storr. LCL. London: William Heinemann.
Spence-Jones, H.D.M. 1911. *The Early Christians in Rome*. New York: John Lane Company.
Stagg, Evelyn and Frank Stagg. 1978. *Woman in the World of Jesus*. Philadelphia: Westminster Press.
Stanton, Elizabeth Cady. 1993. *The Woman's Bible*. Boston: Northeastern University Press.
Staples, Ariadne. 1998. *From Good Goddess to Vestal Virgins: Sex and Category in Roman religion*. London: Routledge.
Statius. *Silvae*. 1928. Translated by J.H. Mozley. LCL. New York: G.P. Putnam's Sons.
Steinberg, Naomi. 1993. *Kinship and Marriage in Genesis: A Household Perspective*. Minneapolis: Fortress Press.
Stevenson, J. 1978. *The Catacombs: Rediscovered Monuments of Early Christianity*. London: Thames & Hudson.
Stone, Michael E., ed. 1984. *Jewish Writings of the Second Temple Period*, Philadelphia: Fortress Press.
Stowers, Stanley K. 1986. *Letter Writing in Greco-Roman Antiquity*. Philadelphia: Westminster Press.
——. 1992. 'Letters (Greek and Latin).' Pages 290-293 in *The Anchor Bible Dictionary*, vol. 3. New York: Doubleday.
——. 1994. *A Rereading of Romans: Justice, Jews, and Gentiles*. New Haven, Conn.: Yale University Press.
Strabo. *The Geography*. 1924. Translated by Horace Leonard Jones. LCL. London: William Heinemann.
Stuhlmacher, Peter. 1994. *Paul's Letter to the Romans: A Commentary*. Translated by Scott J. Hafemann. Eugene, Ore.: Wipf & Stock Publishers.
Suetonius. 1914. *The Lives of the Caesars*. Translated by J.C. Rolfe. LCL. London: William Heinemann.
Swartley, Willard M. 1983. *Slavery, Sabbath, War, and Women: Case Issues in Biblical Interpretation*. Scottdale, Pa.: Herald Press.

Swidler, Leonard. 1976. *Women in Judaism: The Status of Women in Formative Judaism*. Metuchen, N.J.: Scarecrow Press.

Tacitus, Cornelius. *The Histories and The Annals*. Translated by C.H. Moore and J. Jackson. 4 vols. LCL. Cambridge: Harvard University Press, 1937.

Tentori, Tullio. 1976. Social Classes and Family in A Southern Italian Town: Matera. Pages 273-286 in *Mediterranean Family Structures*. Edited by J.G Peristiany. Cambridge: Cambridge University Press.

Terence. *The Lady of Andros*; *The Self-tormentor* and *The Eunuch*. 1912. Translated by John Sargeaunt. LCL. New York: The MacMillan Co.

———. *Phormio*; *The Mother-in-law* and *The Brothers*. 1995. Translated by John Sargeaunt. LCL. Cambridge: Harvard University Press.

Theocritus. 1949. *The Syracusan Women*. Pages 942-946 in *Greek Literature in Translation*. Edited by Whitney Jennings Oates and Charles Theophilus Murphy. New York: Longmans, Green & Co.

Thorley, John. 1996. Junia, A Woman Apostle. *Novum Testamentum* 38:18-29.

Thucydides. *History of the Peloponnesian War*. 1919-1935. Translated by C. Foster Smith. 4 vols. LCL. London: William Heinemann.

Tibullus. *Poems*. 1988. Translated by J.P. Postgate. LCL. Cambridge: Harvard University Press.

Tomes, Roger. 1992. A Father's Anxieties. Pages 71-91 in *Women in the Biblical Tradition*. Edited by George J. Brooke. Lewiston, N.Y.: Edwin Mellen Press.

Torjesen, Karen J. 1992. In Praise of Nobel Women: Gender and Honor in Ascetic Texts. Pages 41-64 in *Discursive Formations, Ascetic Piety and the Interpretation of Early Christian Literature, Part I*, Semeia 57. Edited by Vincent L. Wimbush. Atlanta: Scholars Press.

———. 1993. *When Women Were Priests: Women's Leadership in the Early Church and the Scandal of their Subordination in the Rise of Christianity*. San Francisco: Harper.

Trebilco, Paul R. 1991. *Jewish Communities in Asia Minor*. Cambridge: Cambridge University Press.

Treggiari, Susan. 1991. *Roman Marriage: Iusti Coniuges from the Time of Cicero to the Time of Ulpian*. Oxford: Clarendon Press.

Trenchard, Warren C. 1982. *Ben Sira's View of Women: A Literary Analysis*. Chico, Calif.: Scholars Press.

Trible, Phyllis. 1984. *Texts of Terror: Literary-Feminist Readings of Biblical Narratives*. Philadelphia: Fortress Press.

Trobisch, David. 1994. *Paul's Letter Collection: Tracing the Origins*. Minneapolis: Fortress Press.

Tucker, Ruth A. and Walter Liefeld. 1987. *Daughters of the Church: Women and Ministry from New Testament Times to the Present*. Grand Rapids, Mich.: Academie Books.

VanderKam, James C., ed. 1992. *"No One Spoke Ill of Her": Essays on Judith*. Atlanta: Scholars Press.

Versnel, H.S. 1996. The Festival for Bona Dea and the Thesmophoria. Pages 182-204 in *Women in Antiquity*. Edited by Ian McAuslan and Peter Walcott. Oxford: Oxford University Press.

Virgil. *The Aeneid; The Minor Poems*. 1930. Translated by H. Rushton Fairclough. LCL. New York: G. Putnam's Sons.
Vivante, Bella, ed. 1999. *Women's Roles in Ancient Civilizations: A Reference Guide*. London: Greenwood Press.
Walters, James C. 1993. *Ethnic Issues in Paul's Letter to the Romans: Changing Self-Definitions in Earliest Roman Christianity*. Valley Forge, PA: Trinity Press International.
Walters, K.R. 1993. Women and Power in Classical Athens. Pages 194-214 in *Woman's Power, Man's Game*. Edited by Mary DeForest. Wauconda, Ill.: Bolchazy-Carducci Publishers.
Warmington, E.H., ed. 1940. *Remains of Old Latin* (including *Tituli Sepulcrales* and *Tituli Sacri*). LCL. Cambridge: Harvard University Press.
Wegner, Judith. 1998. The Image and Status of Women in Classical Rabbinic Judaism. Pages 73-93 in *Jewish Women in Historical Perspective*, 2nd ed. Edited by J. R. Baskin. Detroit: Wayne State University Press.
Weima, Jeffrey A.D. 1994. *Neglected Endings: The Significance of the Pauline Letter Closings*. Sheffield: JSOT Press.
Whelan, Caroline F. 1993. Amica Pauli: The Role of Phoebe in the Early Church. *Journal for the Study of the New Testament* 49:67-85.
Whitaker, Ian. 1976. Familial Roles in the Extended Patrilineal Kin-Group in Northern Albania. Pages 195-204 in *Mediterranean Family Structures*. Edited by J.G Peristiany. Cambridge: Cambridge University Press.
White, John Lee. 1972. The Form and Structure of the Official Petition: A Study in Greek Epistolography. Published by the Society of Biblical Literature for the Seminar on Paul.
———. 1986. *Light from Ancient Letters*. Philadelphia: Fortress Press.
Whitehead, Tony L. and Mary Ellen Conaway, eds. 1986. *Self, Sex and Gender in Cross-Cultural Fieldwork*. Urbana: University of Illinois Press.
Wiedemann, Thomas. 1989. *Adults and Children in the Roman Empire*. London: Routledge.
Wiefel, Von Wolfgang. 1970. *Die Jüdisch Gemeinschaft im Antiken Rom und die Anfänge des Römischen Christentums*. Zurich: Zwingli.
Wikan, Unni. 1982. *Behind the Veil in Arabia*. Chicago: University of Chicago Press.
Willetts, Ronald F., ed. & trans. 1967. *The Law Code of Gortyn*. Berlin: Walter de Gruyter & Co.
Williams, Margaret H., ed. *The Jews Among the Greeks and Romans: A Diasporan Sourcebook*. 1998. Baltimore: The Johns Hopkins University Press.
Wilpert, Guiseppe. 1903. *Roma Sotterranea Le Pitture Delle Catacome Romane Illustrate Da*. Descle Lefebure.
Winkler, John J. 1990. *The Constraint of Desire: The Anthropology of Sex and Gender in Ancient Greece*. London: Routledge.
Wise, Michael, Martin Abegg, Jr. and Edward Cook, eds. 1996. *The Dead Sea Scrolls: A New Translation*. San Francisco: Harper Collins.
Wise, Michael, Norman Golb, John J. Collins and Dennis G. Pardee. 1994. *Methods of Investigation of the Dead Sea Scrolls and the Khirbet QumranSite:*

*Present Battle and Future Prospects*. New York: The New York Academy of Sciences.

Witherington, Ben. 1988. *Women in the Earliest Churches*. Cambridge: Cambridge University Press.

———. 1990. *Women and the Genesis of Christianity*. Cambridge: Cambridge University Press.

Wrong, Dennis H. 1979. *Power: Its Forms, Bases and Uses*. New York: Harper & Row.

Yarbrough, O. Larry. 1985. *Not Like the Gentiles: Marriage Rules in the Letters of Paul*. Atlanta: Scholars Press.

Zeitlin, Froma I. 1981. Travesties of Gender and Genre in Aristophanes' *Thesmophoriazousae*. Pages 169-217 in *Reflections of Women in Antiquity*. Edited by Helene P. Foley. New York: Gordon & Breach Science Publishers. Ziesler, John. 1989. *Paul's Letter to the Romans*. London: SCM Press.

## About the Author

Julia Pizzuto-Pomaco, PhD, currently resides with her family (children Anna, Joshua and John, and husband Joe) in Southern New Jersey, just outside of Philadelphia. She teaches Bible, Religions of the World and Interreligious Dialogue within the Philosophy and Religion Studies Department at Rowan University in Glassboro, N.J. She continues to be a teacher, scholar and pastor.

She was ordained in 1999 by the Presbyterian Church and has served various suburban, urban and rural congregations since then. She is currently involved in leading a small missional group called "Grace Community." Whether she is leading worship at a homeless shelter, group home, nursing home or in a large church building, Pizzuto-Pomaco is at home sharing her insights from the classroom and from her studies. She is happiest when she can combine serving others, helping them get excited about learning and teaching them to look beyond the lens directly in front of them.

At Rowan, Pizzuto-Pomaco teaches incoming freshman about the religions of the world and puts more advanced students through the paces as they study methodology and ancient texts. They first learn that the Bible is not just literature nor a book of fairy stories but that it is rich and diverse in culture and context. She continues to challenge students to identify their own twenty-first-century preconceptions and learn to see the text within its context. She challenges her students to look for women right at the center of the text, on the edges or in what is not said, but implied. She continues to encourage students to listen to the text themselves and ask as many questions as they can muster, while at the same time examining it from every angle.

She can often be heard saying that biblical interpretation is like an onion with many layers: as you peel back one you find another to examine and another. Whenever people use literary, social, historical, cultural or textual tools, they must first examine what they bring to the table so they can attempt to be, in some small way, objective, while always aware that there is still another layer waiting to be pulled back that has yet to be discovered.

www.ingramcontent.com/pod-product-compliance
Lightning Source LLC
Chambersburg PA
CBHW070314240426
43663CB00038BA/2271